D1211682

THE WORLD OF
DOC
HOLLIDAY

THE WORLD OF
DOC HOLLIDAY

History and Historic Images

Victoria Wilcox

TWODOT®

Guilford, Connecticut
Helena, Montana

A · TWODOT® · BOOK

An imprint of Globe Pequot
An imprint and registered trademark of Rowman & Littlefield

Distributed by NATIONAL BOOK NETWORK

Copyright © 2021 Victoria Wilcox

British Library Cataloguing in Publication Information Available

Library of Congress Cataloging-in-Publication Data

ISBN 978-1-4930-4828-1 (cloth : alk. paper)
ISBN 978-1-4930-4829-8 (electronic)

♾™ The paper used in this publication meets the minimum requirements of American National Standard for Information Sciences—Permanence of Paper for Printed Library Materials, ANSI/NISO Z39.48-1992.

CONTENTS

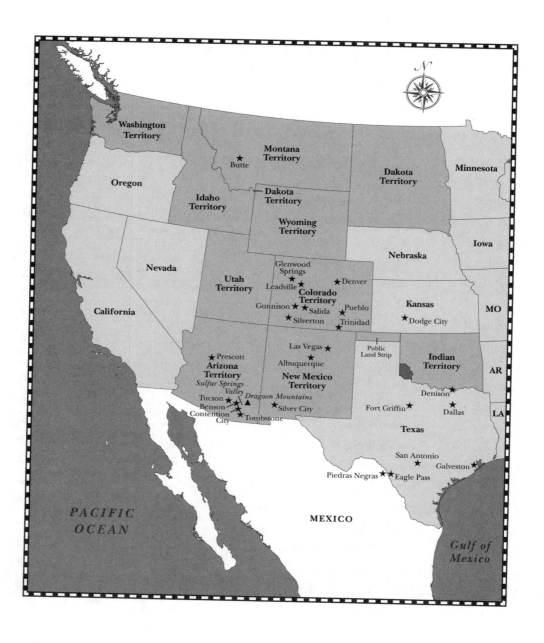

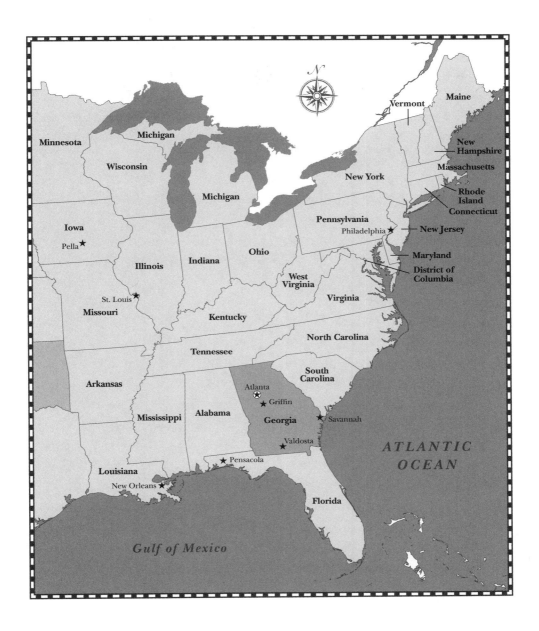

PREFACE

A WORLD OF RAILS

This book began with a ride on the historic Durango & Silverton Narrow Gauge Railroad, the famous scenic train route through the San Juan Mountains of southwestern Colorado. I was on a book tour and headed to the old mining camp of Silverton, high in those mountains, to give a talk about John Henry "Doc" Holliday, who had spent some time gambling there according to a report in an 1885 newspaper. The route was beautiful, the narrow rails clinging to the cliff walls with spectacular views of the Animas River far below—a sight that Doc Holliday had surely also enjoyed on his way to Silverton. And somewhere along the way, I realized that no historian had yet written about Doc's travel routes—and that most of those travels went by rail, as for most of his life he went where the railroads went. He was not a frontiersman, living off the land. He was not a Southern planter living off the labor of slaves who worked the land, although that had been his legacy. He was a modern Victorian man, well-educated and well-trained for a professional career, a man whose life seemed destined to be lived in the cities of nineteenth-century America, cities connected by thousands of miles of rail. If his circumstances hadn't taken a surprising change, sending him West into legend as Doc Holliday, he would likely never have taken part in a posse ride across a Western desert, or taken a stagecoach trip across a precipitous Rocky Mountain pass. But even in the West, Doc made most of his journeys by rail and did most of his sightseeing from the windows of a railcar.

By the time I got back home to Georgia, this book was already coming together in my mind. It would be a different kind of Doc Holliday history: a travelogue of his adventures, filled with images and anecdotes about the people and places that filled his world. The era of rails was also an era of newspapers, so much of the story would come from contemporary newspaper accounts and interviews with Doc himself and the people who knew him. And as the book was inspired by a train ride, the chapter titles are inspired by the names of the railroads Doc traveled—from Georgia to Texas, from Dodge City to Las Vegas, across Arizona, and from New Mexico to Colorado and Montana. For Tombstone, after all, was only a short eighteen months of his adventurous life, and there was so much more to Doc Holliday than a gunfight near the O.K. Corral.

Victoria Wilcox
Peachtree City, Georgia

1

MACON & WESTERN

John Henry Holliday was born on August 14, 1851, in the little city of Griffin, Georgia, in a house near the tracks of the Macon & Western Railroad. Griffin was the cotton-shipping center of the region and could have become the shipping center for the whole state when the rails came, if the north-south and east-west tracks had crossed there as originally planned. But when the city fathers voted against the crossing, the railroad hub went north instead into the piney woods at a place called Terminus that would later be renamed Atlanta. So, Atlanta became the big city and Griffin remained a small city—which may have saved it when Yankee General William T. Sherman marched into Georgia to destroy the rail lines, besieging and burning Atlanta but leaving Griffin as a hospital town further down the railroad.

But the Civil War and Sherman's March to the Sea were still in the unimaginable future when John Henry was a boy, hearing the whistle of the steam engine and seeing the smoke of the locomotive rising up into the blue Georgia sky over his family's two-story home on Tinsley Street. His father, Henry Burroughs Holliday, would walk up from Tinsley and cross the tracks to the City Hall, where he served as clerk of the Spalding County Court. His mother, Alice Jane McKey Holliday, crossed the tracks to visit the shops on Hill Street or Solomon Street. On Sundays, the family would ride in a buggy up Hill Street to the Presbyterian Church just north of the railroad tracks to attend services in the little chapel where John Henry had been christened. It didn't take much room for the Hollidays to fit into their spring-wheeled buggy, as it was just the three of them, John Henry and his parents, his only sibling being a sister who had died as a baby the year before his own birth. But there were plenty of cousins and aunts and uncles to fill his world, and even a foster brother named Francisco Hidalgo, a Mexican orphan whom Henry Holliday had brought back with him after his service in the war with Mexico. And there were often longer drives to visit with the extended family: Alice Jane's parents and younger sisters on their cotton plantation at Indian Creek in Henry County, or Henry's parents and brothers and their families in Jonesboro and Fayetteville.

Griffin was a pretty little city, with an opera house and hotel near the railroad depot, a college, and a library, and the Holliday's life there was pleasant—until Georgia joined with the Confederate States in seceding from the Union and the Civil War began. Young John Henry knew which side his family supported: his McKey grandparents owned dozens of slaves and didn't hold with abolitionist views, and his uncle James Johnson was a lawyer and state senator who had signed the Ordinance of Secession that started the war. His father even donated some farmland outside of Griffin to become Camp Stephens, a training ground for Confederate troops. From the train depot on Hill Street, John Henry watched the railcars load up with new recruits and steam away toward adventure. Then his father and most of his uncles joined the Confederate States Army and left home to fight for States' Rights and the Rebel flag.

A photograph of John Henry made around the time his father left for the war shows a handsome boy with light blue eyes, a high forehead and square chin, and the shadow of what might be a scar on his upper lip. One family story says that he was born with a cleft lip and palate that had to be surgically closed when he was an infant, the procedure performed by his father's brother, Dr. John Stiles Holliday, with anesthesia administered by his mother's cousin, Dr. Crawford Long of Jefferson, Georgia, who was a pioneer in the use of ether. The infant survived the surgery and healed well, except for that thin scar on his lip, and with therapy and teaching by his mother and the ladies of Griffin's Presbyterian Church, John Henry learned to speak with no difficulty.

It was a much less dramatic ailment that caused an early end to his father's military service. Henry Holliday, who had served as a Second Lieutenant in the United States Army during the Mexican War, had enlisted in the Confederate States Army as Captain Quartermaster of the 27th Georgia Infantry, seeing action from Williamsburg to Seven Pines, Cold Harbor to Malvern Hill and being promoted to major on Christmas Day of 1861. But then a long bout of dysentery in the muddy trenches at Richmond bought him a discharge and sent him home to his wife and young son. He arrived in time to bury his own father in the Fayetteville Cemetery, making Henry the new patriarch of the Holliday clan, responsible not just for his own family, but for the wives and children of his brothers and brothers-in-law who were still at the battlefront.

The Griffin that Henry Holliday returned to that second year of the war was much changed from the pleasant place the Hollidays had known before. With Union naval blockades at Savannah and Charleston, supplies had become scarce, and what could get through was sent to the Confederate Army instead of the families at home. By the spring of 1863, flour was selling for $65 a barrel, bread was going for $25 a loaf, and the Confederate dollar was as good as worthless. Then came news of the Battle of Gettysburg and the fall of Vicksburg—there would be no more victories for the South, with the shipping lanes of the Mississippi River cut in two and General Robert E. Lee's army limping back from a devastating defeat in Pennsylvania.

But the war wasn't over yet, and Henry Holliday determined to leave Griffin and move his family away from the battlefront. Far to the south, in the wiregrass wilderness close to the Florida border, the newly born village of Valdosta was filling up with refugees looking for safety before the Yankees arrived to burn their way through Georgia. The Macon & Western Railroad that had been the business heart of Griffin now became the Holliday's escape route, as they loaded their household belongings onto a boxcar at the depot on Hill Street and boarded the train for the long ride to Macon and from there south to Valdosta. The two-hundred-mile journey would take the better part of a week and four railroads to complete: the Macon & Western Railroad from Griffin to Macon; the Central of Georgia from Macon to Savannah; the Savannah, Albany & Gulf from Savannah to Screven; and the Atlantic & Gulf Line from Screven to Valdosta. It may also have taken some negotiating to get tickets for each leg of the journey, as the railroads were crowded with hundreds of refugees headed south and troops and supplies being transported across the state. For eleven-year-old John Henry Holliday, his life on the railroads was just beginning.

RAILROAD STANDARD TIME

Before the era of rail travel, communities set their time based on the local movement of the sun. "High noon" was 12:00, when the sun was directly overhead. Sundials were the standard, and clocks in church towers were set to the sundial so citizens could then set their watches to the church tower clock. Railroad timetables could reliably show the departure and arrival times for stops in nearby towns, but when railroad travel allowed people to move quickly from one distant community to another, the

RAIL-ROAD TIME-TABLES,

PUBLISHED MONTHLY

UNDER THE SUPERVISION OF THE RAIL-ROAD COMPANIES.

MACON & WESTERN ROAD.

Isaac Scott, Pres't, } Macon, Ga.
Alfred L. Tyler, Sup't, } Macon, Ga.

Macon to Atlanta.				◎⟨march 22.⟩◎	Atlanta to Macon.			
Mail.	Fr't.	Fare	Mls.	STATIONS.	Mls.	Fare	Fr't.	Mail.
a. m.	a. m.			Leave Arrive			p. m.	p. m.
9 00	5 30			.........Macon.........	103	5 00	4 00	12 54
9 10				.........Junction.........				12 47
9 35		40	8	.........Howard's.........	95	4 60		12 29
10 00		75	15	..... Crawford's.........	88	4 25		12 05
10 20		1 00	21	.........Smarr's.........	82	4 00		11 45
10 48		1 25	26	.........Forsyth.........	77	3 75		11 23
11 08		1 50	32	.........Collier's.........	71	3 50		11 08
11 27		1 75	37	.........Goggins.........	66	3 25		10 46
11 45		2 00	43	.........Barnesville.........	61	3 00		10 30
12 15		2 40	49	.........Milner.........	54	2 50		10 10
12 35		2 55	54	.........Thornton.........	49	2 35		9 45
1 20		3 20	60	.........Griffin.........	43	2 00		9 25
1 45		3 05	67	.........Fayette.........	36	1 75		8 58
2 15		3 65	74	.........Lovejoy's.........	29	1 35		8 31
2 40		4 00	81	.........Jonesboro.........	22	1 00		8 08
2 58		4 25	86	.........Morrow's.........	17	75		7 30
3 20		4 50	92	.....Rough & Ready..	11	50		7 08
3 38		4 75	97	.........East Point.......	6	25		6 55
4 00	4 10	5 00	103	.........Atlanta.......			6 30	6 30
p. m.	p. m.			Arrive Leave			a. m.	a. m.

CONNECTIONS.—At Macon with Central Georgia [p56], and South-Western (p54), Rail-Roads. At Barnesville with Upson county road [p52], to Thomaston. At Atlanta with Georgia Rail-Road [p8], Western & Atlantic Rail-Road [p41], and Atlanta & West Point Rail-Road [p42].

FORSYTH, capital of Monroe county, Georgia, contains besides the county buildings, several churches, the Monroe Female University, and about 600 inhabitants.

GRIFFIN, a flourishing town on the Macon & Western road, capital of Spalding county. The situation is one of the most pleasant and healthy in the State. Population about 3,000.

JONESBOROUGH, a post-village in Fayette county, on the Macon & Western road, 22 miles from Atlanta, and 21 from Griffin. Population about 900.

Macon & Western Road Time Schedule 1862 from Hill and Swayze's Confederate States Rail-Road and Steam-Boat Guide.

differences in time became a problem. If a passenger left a town at noon and traveled for five hours to the west, it should be 5:00 pm when he arrived at his destination—except when it wasn't, as local time might be only 4:45 pm when he arrived, depending on the position of the sun. Railroad timetables might list dozens of different arrival and departure times for the same train, based on the times in distant time zones.

Speedy travel required a better system for keeping time, so the railroad companies took on the job of creating a new time system, dividing the continent into four time sections. In 1873, a group of railroad managers and supervisors came together at the General Time Convention and passed a vote commending the concept of standard time zones called Railway Time: Eastern Time on the 75th meridian; Valley Time at the 90th meridian (later called Central Time); Mountain Time on the 105th meridian; and Pacific Time on the 120th meridian. It took another ten years for the plan to be adopted, but at noon on November 18, 1883, at the 75th Meridian (Eastern Time), the railroads changed to the new time standards, to be known as Railroad and Telegraph Time. In 1918, the Standard Time Act was enacted by Congress, making the railroad time zones the legal time zones in the United States. But for most of Doc Holliday's travels on the railroads, timekeeping was still a problem. It wasn't until two years after the O.K. Corral gunfight that Railroad and Telegraph Time made his departures and arrivals something more reliable.

THE GREAT LOCOMOTIVE CHASE

The Macon & Western's locomotive *Georgia* was built by the Rogers Locomotive & Machine Works company of Paterson, New Jersey, which also built the *General* for the Western & Atlantic Railroad. The *General* became famous in the "Great Locomotive Chase" during the Civil War when it was commandeered by Yankee raiders at Big Shanty (now Kennesaw), Georgia, and headed toward the Federal lines at Chattanooga, Tennessee. But running low on water and wood, the *General* eventually

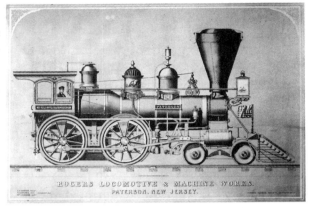

Lithograph: "Rogers Locomotive & Machine Works, Paterson, New Jersey." DeGolyer Library, Southern Methodist University, Railroads, Manuscripts, and Imprints (Ag1982.0212).

lost steam pressure and speed, and slowed to a halt two miles north of the town of Ringgold, Georgia, where the raiders abandoned the locomotive. Confederate forces eventually captured the raiders and executed some as spies, although others escaped. The raiders were later awarded the first Congressional Medals of Honor for their service to the Union. The *General* is now on display in the Southern Museum of Civil War and Locomotive History, Kennesaw, Georgia, near where the chase began.

CLOUD'S TOWER

John Henry's maternal grandmother was Jane Cloud McKey, mistress of a cotton plantation along Indian Creek in Henry County, Georgia, and cousin to Aaron Cloud, who owned one of Georgia's most picturesque tourist sites: Cloud's Tower at the top of the mammoth dome of granite called Stone Mountain. The April 10, 1838, Milledgeville *Southern Recorder* announced its construction: "Mr. Aaron Cloud of

"Cloud's Tower and Georgia Railroad train at Stone Mountain, Georgia" from The Student's History of Georgia *by Lawton B. Evans, 1884.*

McDonough, Ga., is now engaged in erecting a tower or observatory on the top of Stone Mountain in Dekalb County."

Cloud's property was recorded in the county deed book as "one hundred fifty feet square on the most elevated part of Stone Mountain . . . with the privilege of a full and perfect view around the mountain . . . plus a carriage way to the named premises." On his property, Aaron Cloud built a 165-foot tower atop a one-hundred-square-foot structure that was available for parties and other gatherings, along with a restaurant and club at the base of the mountain as a destination for travelers on the new railroad from Augusta. Sightseers could stay at the hotel at the base of the mountain, then walk up the one-mile trail to the top of the mountain, 825 feet above the surrounding pine forest, and for a charge of fifty cents climb three hundred steps to the top of the tower for a panoramic view over the plantations and villages of north Georgia. For over a decade, Cloud's Tower was a popular railroad destination, until it was swept off the top of the mountain in a windstorm in 1851—the year John Henry was born. In 1864, the Union Army tore up the railroad tracks north of Stone Mountain during General Sherman's March to the Sea, ending for a time the tourist days of Stone Mountain.

Martha Eleanora Holliday Memorial, Rest Haven Cemetery, Griffin, Georgia. Author's Collection.

MARTHA ELEANORA

John Henry's only sibling was a sister, Martha Eleanora, born eighteen months before his own birth. Sadly, the little girl didn't live to her first birthday, passing away on June 12, 1850. The cause of her death is lost to history, but her parents made sure to memorialize her short life with a granite gravestone inscribed: "In Memory of Martha Eleanora, Daughter of H.B. and A.J. Holliday who died June 12th 1850 aged 6 Months 9 days." The little grave is on a hill at the top of Rest Haven Cemetery on the outskirts of Griffin and appears to be alone in a grassy field. But according to local historians, the grassy field actually contains dozens of unmarked graves, the final resting place of the black residents of nineteenth-century Griffin, the gravesites still evident in an aerial photograph made in the 1950s. At the end of the Civil War, the city cemetery was given over to the former slaves for their burial ground, and white burials were begun across the road at the new Oak Hill Cemetery, leaving Martha Eleonora as the only Holliday family grave at Rest Haven.

DOC'S MEXICAN HERMANO

Francisco Hidalgo was a twelve-year-old orphan of the Mexican War when Henry Holliday brought him home to Georgia. Although Henry, still a bachelor at the time, never officially adopted the boy, he seems to have treated him as part of the family. When Henry married Alice Jane McKey two years later, Francisco came along to the new household, and was still living with the Hollidays in 1851 when Henry and Alice Jane's son John Henry was born. In 1854, Francisco married and moved into a home of his own, but the families stayed close and it may have been from Francisco that young John Henry learned enough Spanish to get by in his later life in the Texas border towns. When the Civil War began, Francisco volunteered to serve in the Confederate Army. Records show a Francis E'Dalgo (an Americanized spelling of his name) enlisted September

Francisco E'Dalgo, from a charcoal portrait on loan to the Holliday-Dorsey-Fife Museum, Fayetteville, Georgia. Author's Collection.

1861 in the 30th Georgia Regiment Volunteer Infantry. He served for the duration of the war, surrendering on April 26, 1865, at Greensboro, North Carolina. After the war, he returned home to Georgia, working as a barber in Griffin and farming land near the town of Jenkinsburg. The Edalgos (the family spelling of the name) were founding members of Jenkinsburg's County Line Baptist Church, where there stands a lasting memorial to Francisco's love for his adopted country: his gravestone, placed after his early death from consumption, shows his birthdate as July 4, 1835. As an orphan, Francisco wasn't sure of his actual birthdate, so he chose a date that was symbolic of his new life in America. It's likely that John Henry was one of the mourners present at Francisco's funeral at County Line Baptist Church in January 1873, as he visited the courthouse in nearby Griffin on the same day to sign some legal papers. Until Doc Holliday met Wyatt Earp, Francisco Hidalgo was the closest he came to having a brother.

Historic Griffin Presbyterian Church. Courtesy First Presbyterian Church of Griffin.

AMAZING GRACE

Griffin's Presbyterian Church stood at the corner of North Hill and Chapel Streets, and it was here that John Henry Holliday was christened on March 21, 1852. The fact that the christening took place seven months after his birth on August 14, 1851, suggests that he did indeed have some kind of health crisis as an infant—perhaps the cleft palate deformity as told in the family story, with the ladies of the congregation later helping to teach him how to speak. But charitable as the Presbyterian ladies were, the congregation was stern in its standards. The year John Henry was born, two male members of the church were charged with attending a ball and dance. According to church records: "Both the brethren confess guilty and manifest no signs of repentance, or desire to remain members of the church; therefore, resolved that they be suspended until they show suitable signs of repentance. Resolved, that the session of this church disapprove of dancing at balls and dancing parties, and of parents sending their children to dancing schools."

The ban on dancing wasn't limited to the Presbyterians. The Baptists and the Methodists also taught against such wanton behavior, along with drinking, card playing, and (later in the century) roller skating. But it was another point of doctrine that would later separate Alice Jane McKey from the Presbyterians, with whom she had affiliated on her marriage—their Calvinist tradition that only the "elect" were fitted for heaven, with their election proved by their good works in life. The Doctrine of Election made Presbyterians very charitable members of the community, as they tried to do good to prove themselves of the elect who were saved by the grace of God. But the belief left little hope for sinners, as a man who did evil was clearly not one of the elect and was therefore headed to hell—a doctrine with which Alice Jane disagreed. In her Baptist upbringing, sinners might "grieve the Spirit" of God, but still find salvation through faith. Later, she would join with the Methodists, who believed that Christ's death was sufficient to atone for the sins of the whole world, not just an elect few—something that would become especially important to her while worrying over her sometimes rebellious son.

MR. EARP, SLAVETRADER

Like many railroad towns across the South, Griffin had a slave market. Offices were on Broad Street, a short walk from the courthouse where Henry Holliday worked as Clerk of the Spalding County Court, so he could not have missed the spectacle of slave sales. And in 1855, when his son John Henry was just a four-year-old boy, the slave traders were Earp and Tomlinson—the Mr. Earp being Daniel Earp, uncle of Wyatt Earp. A notice in the local paper read:

> Earp & Tomlinson, *DEALERS IN NEGROES, Griffin, Geo.*
> *The undersigned have associated themselves together for the purpose of BUY-ING AND SELLING NEGROES. They expect to keep on hand a good supply of such Negroes as they can recommend to those wishing to purchase. They are also prepared to give liberal prices for Negroes for those wishing to sell. Call and see, and we will give bargains either in buying or selling. Negroes can be taken to sell on commission.*[1]

The Hollidays would not have been shocked to read about the buying and selling of humans, as they and their kin were all slaveowners. Though Henry had only his house servants and a driver, his wife's family, the McKeys, were the largest slaveowners in the area. As noted in the 1850 Slave Owner Census of Henry County, John Henry's grandfather, William Land McKey, owned twenty-eight slaves while his uncle Jonathan McKey kept fifty-six slaves on his plantation.[2]

When the slavery issue brought talk of States' Rights and Secession, the Hollidays and the McKeys stood firmly on the side of the Confederacy. John Henry's uncle James Johnson, his aunt Martha Holliday Johnson's husband, was a state senator and a signer of the Ordinance of Secession that started the Civil War, and all of the men in the family fought for the Cause. John Henry Holliday would have been a very unusual Southern boy to believe differently than all the men in his life—a belief that would influence the first rumored shootings in his later career.

2

ATLANTIC & GULF LINE

Valdosta was a rustic village in a piney-wood wilderness, with one main road that wound past the stump of a recently felled tree and a scattering of wood frame houses facing the tracks of the Atlantic & Gulf Railway. There was no opera house, as there had been in Griffin, no fine hotel near the depot, no cotton warehouse bustling with business, no college, no library. Valdosta had only one small schoolhouse with unglazed windows and one Union Church where the local congregations took turns holding services: Methodist on first and third Sundays, Baptist on second and fourth Sundays. But if Valdosta seemed provincial, it was also far away from the war.

The Hollidays' new home was even more remote, being seven miles north of town on a 2,450-acre farm at Cat Creek in Lowndes County. But for John Henry, rural life offered something city life did not: space for fishing, riding, and hunting. Local legend says that he grew to be such a good shot that he could shoot the eyes out of a rabbit when it stopped to look at him before it started running again. Nor was the Hollidays' farm at Cat Creek a lonely place, as kin arrived to seek shelter from the war. First came his mother's unmarried McKey sisters, then his Aunt Mary Ann Fitzgerald Holliday and six of her eight children, followed a few months later by her two oldest daughters who had left their convent school in Savannah as Sherman made his way to the sea. The only drawback to having relatives come to stay was that all were female, making the Holliday house a womanly place during the war, as were so many other Southern homes. The grown men, the old men, and the young men had all gone off to fight, and John Henry must have felt some disappointment in being denied such masculine adventures. But having womenfolk around also taught him how to behave as a gentleman, a trait that would follow him through the years. As a Valdosta newspaper later described him: "As a schoolboy, 'Doc' was mischievous but not mean; he was full of vim, as brave as a lion, but not overbearing. He was good natured, always sociable and as neat as a pin."[1]

The girl cousin closest in age to John Henry was Aunt Mary Ann's oldest daughter, Mattie, a small, dark-haired girl with wide brown eyes. Many years later Mattie Holliday would become the model for the fictional character of Melanie Hamilton in the Pulitzer Prize–winning novel, *Gone with the Wind*. Author Margaret Mitchell was cousin to Mattie on her Fitzgerald side, and her description of Melanie might have been taken from a Civil War–era photograph made of young Mattie Holliday:

> *She had a cloud of curly dark hair which was so sternly repressed beneath its net that no vagrant tendrils escaped, and this dark mass . . . accentuated the heart shape of her face. Too wide across the cheek bones, too pointed at the chin, it was a sweet, timid face but a plain face, and she had no feminine tricks of allure to make observers forget its plainness. She looked—and was, as simple as earth, as good as bread, as transparent as spring water.*

Though the character of Melanie is overshadowed by the captivating Scarlett O'Hara, Margaret Mitchell considered her the heroine and heart of the story. And it's proof of John Henry's heart-felt affection for his sweet-natured cousin Mattie that the two would remain close through the years, sharing a correspondence that spanned his lifetime in the West and spawned stories of a youthful romance between the cousins.

Aunt Mary Ann's visit also brought the far-away war closer to home as she recounted the family's escape from the Battle of Jonesboro, a story retold in Mattie's later memoirs:

> *General Sherman was battling in Tennessee and making headway. In May [1864] his batteries were throwing shells into Atlanta and raiding parties sent in different directions to destroy railroads and farm products. Finally, Atlanta was captured. On September 1st and 2nd, a big battle was fought in Jonesboro.*
>
> *She [Mary Ann] at the solicitation of her Uncle Phillip Fitzgerald went with her family . . . to his farm, four miles out of Jonesboro, and remained two weeks. Returning, they found only the frame work of their home standing. . . . Then came the refugeeing. Two weeks in a box car with the remnants of household conveniences for makeshift. At night the car stayed on sidetrack. Although the times*

were lawless, God watched over this little family and rewarded the confidence of mother. Times were hard, food very scarce, but He saw they never went hungry.

At the expiration of two weeks, they got to Gordon, 40 miles below Macon. Here, they had to leave the car and wait two weeks for one to take them farther South. In all the stops and waiting, unexpected friends met and helped to make them as comfortable as was in their power. And so, at the end of a long and tiresome journey of several hundred miles, they reached Valdosta, Georgia, and the car stopped. There stood H. B. Holliday, her brother-in-law, hitching his horse to a rack. Her destination was his farm seven miles out of town. He did not know of her coming. She had no means of communication, but God in whom she had trusted arranged for her here as in every other circumstance of that eventful journey. This good brother took the family to his home, gave them a house on his farm and provided for them till his brother returned after the surrender, May 24, 1865.[2]

The Holliday farm at Cat Creek remained a refuge in the months following the war, as the men in the family slowly found their way back from the battlefront. Captain Robert Kennedy Holliday, Mattie's father, had finished the war in a Yankee prison camp and came to collect his wife and daughters. Uncle James McKey, a medical doctor who had served as a surgeon during the war, came tending to Uncle William McKey, who'd been severely wounded in the fighting. And the youngest McKey uncle, Thomas Sylvester, walked 150 miles from Macon where he'd served as an orderly in a military hospital. One family story says that when word arrived that Tom McKey was on his way, John Henry took a pistol and a horse and rode out to find his favorite uncle and carry him back—a brave thing for a boy to do in those troubled times. But the family reunion didn't last for long, as the McKey brothers moved across the Florida line to take up land in Hamilton County at Banner Plantation, and Captain Holliday took his own family back to what remained of their life in Jonesboro.

The postwar years were difficult all over the South, with the railroads broken up, the economy wrecked, and sickness spreading through the malnourished population. In September 1866, John Henry's mother, Alice Jane McKey Holliday, died at the young age of thirty-seven, and was buried in Sunset Hill Cemetery in Valdosta. As her obituary in the local paper reported:

She was confined to her bed for a number of years, and was indeed a great suf-fer. She bore her afflictions with Christian fortitude. It has never fallen to my lot to know a more cheerful Christian. It was a great pleasure to visit her to see the triumph of religion over the ills of life. She was deeply solicitous about the welfare of all she loved. She fully committed them into the hands of a merciful God with the full awareness that God would hear and answer her prayers, and that her instructions and Christian example would still speak. She was deeply anxious about the faith of her only child. She had her faith written so her boy might know what his mother believed. She was for a time a member of the Pres-byterian Church and never subscribing in heart to their article on election she determined to change her Church relation as she was not willing to die and leave on record for her boy, that she subscribed to said faith. She therefore joined the M.E. [Methodist Episcopalian] Church whose doctrines she heartily accepted. I visited her a few days before her death; she was calm, cheerful, joyful. She said to me that there was not a dimming veil between her and her God. She thus passed away from the Church militant to the Church triumphant, leaving her friends to mourn not as those who have no hope, knowing their loved one is not dead but sleepeth.[3]

There is no remaining record of the cause of Alice Jane Holliday's passing, only that she had suffered greatly and had been confined to her bed "for a number of years." This does not sound like consumption, which generally has a much shorter confinement period preceding death, though many writers still assume that illness. Whatever the cause, a proper period of mourning was expected, with the bereaved widower wearing somber colors and declining social engagements for a year. But a shocking three months after his wife's passing, the forty-seven-year-old Henry Hol-liday took a new young wife: Rachel Martin, the twenty-three-year-old daughter of a neighboring farm family. The speed of the marriage was stunning, the age of the bride was surprising (Rachel was closer in age to her new stepson than to her new husband), and the McKey family's response was swift: the dead Alice Jane's brothers sued to retrieve her inheritance so it wouldn't go to Henry and the new Mrs. Holli-day. And caught in the middle of the legal battle was fifteen-year-old John Henry, who was half McKey and half Holliday and surely torn between the two sides of his family as they fought over his inheritance.

Henry Holliday further unsettled the family by moving them from the farm at Cat Creek to a cottage on Savannah Street in Valdosta. While the move gave John Henry an opportunity to advance his education by attending the new Valdosta Institute, it also put him in close contact with the angry young men of the town who were itching for a chance to get back at the Yankees. Reconstruction had brought martial law to Georgia, with Federal troops posted in every town and a black garrison in Valdosta, and tempers were running hot. Though John Henry was known as a good student, rumors linked him with the town boys in a plan to protest the visit of a Yankee politician by blowing up the county courthouse. The plot was discovered before the explosion went off, but the plotters were arrested and sent to Savannah for a military trial. The fact that John Henry's name does not appear on the court documents seems to support a family story that Henry Holliday saved him from arrest by sending him away to Jonesboro for the summer to stay with his Holliday cousins—including his favorite girl cousin, Mattie.

The time away may have helped him to cool his own temper and focus on his future plans. Valdosta had recently gained a dentist, Dr. Lucian Frink, a graduate of the Pennsylvania College of Dental Surgery in Philadelphia. So, on his return from Jonesboro, John Henry began an internship with Dr. Frink, learning the basics of the dental profession in preparation for applying to attend the same school himself after graduating from the Valdosta Institute. To help pay his college expenses he took a job on the Atlantic & Gulf Railway, likely working as a ticket agent at the depot on South Patterson Street. Now the same railroad that had brought him to the piney woods of South Georgia as a young refugee with an uncertain future would take him away again to a future beyond his wildest imaginings.

VAL D'OSTA

The coming of the Atlantic & Gulf Railway to South Georgia had a profound effect on the state. New counties were established, and several county seats were moved to put them along the rail route, including Lowndes County's original county seat of Troupeville, named for Georgia Governor George Troup. When the rails bypassed Troupeville, most of the townspeople abandoned the site and settled a new town four miles away where the railroad crossed the Withlacoochee River. Not wanting to offend Governor Troup, they named their new town in honor of his plantation, called Val d'Osta (after the Valle d'Aosta alpine valley in Italy), coining the new word Valdosta. The first

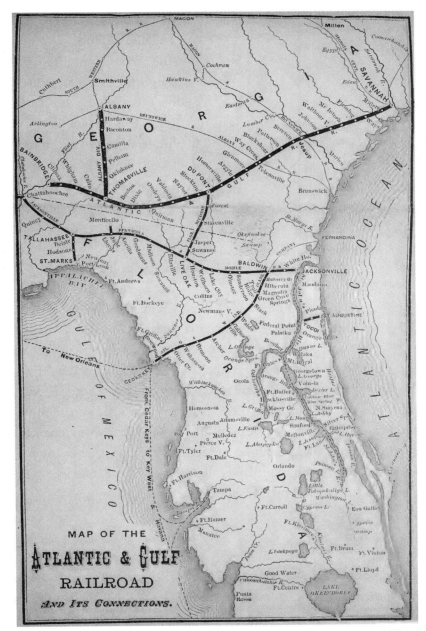

Map of the Atlantic & Gulf Railway from Guide to Southern Georgia and Florida.

train depot in Valdosta was opened in 1860, allowing Civil War refugees to travel from central and coastal Georgia to the new town and helping to populate the previously sparsely settled wiregrass region.

Thomas Edison, President Herbert Hoover, and Henry Ford, Smiths Creek Depot during Lights Golden Jubilee, October 21, 1929. From the Collections of The Henry Ford.

JOHN HENRY, HENRY FORD, AND THOMAS EDISON

The first locomotive to arrive in Valdosta, and the engine that may have pulled the train that carried John Henry Holliday to his new home, was the wood-burning *Satilla No. 3*, built in 1858 by the Rogers Locomotive & Machine Works of Paterson, New Jersey. The engine was named by the Atlantic & Gulf Line for the Satilla River, like many of the railroad company's engines that were named after the original Creek and Cherokee words for the rivers of Georgia: Satilla, Tatnall, Altamaha, Alapaha, Ochlocknee, Okapilco, Aucilla, Ogeechee, Piscola, and Withlacoochee. After decades of service, the *Satilla* was bought and restored by Henry Ford at his River Rouge Complex in Michigan. The locomotive's most famous travels came when it carried Henry Ford, Thomas Edison, and President Herbert Hoover to the 1929 dedication of the Edison Institute, now the Henry Ford Museum. In honor of the occasion, the locomotive was renamed the *President*. In 1940, the old *Satilla* went into service again, carrying actor Mickey Rooney on a promotional tour for the film *Young Tom Edison*. The *Satilla No. 3/President* is now on display at the Henry Ford Museum in Dearborn, Michigan.

TALES OF TARA

The classic Old South house is two stories tall with graceful white columns across a wide front porch, an architectural style called "Greek Revival." While John Henry didn't grow up in such a house, he did make regular visits to two of them: the Fayetteville home of his uncle Dr. John Stiles Holliday, and the Jonesboro home of his aunt Martha Holliday Johnson and her husband, State Senator James Johnson. Both homes were built in the 1850s, prior to the Civil War, and saw Yankee and Confederate troops passing by, and both homes are still standing. The Johnson-Blalock House was used as a Confederate commissary and field hospital during the Battle of Jonesboro in

1864 and is now privately owned. The John Stiles Holliday home is now the Holliday-Dorsey-Fife Museum (named after the three famous Fayette County families who lived there over the years), a site on the National Register of Historic Places. The house is open to the public and contains exhibits about the Civil War in Georgia, Doc Holliday, and his family's interesting connections to *Gone with the Wind*.

Antebellum home of Dr. John Stiles Holliday, Fayetteville, Georgia. Courtesy Holliday–Dorsey–Fife Museum.

SHERMAN'S BOW TIES

Mattie Holliday's memoirs tell a very personal story of the Battle of Jonesboro, when war came to her hometown and her family was forced to flee for safety. The Macon & Western Railroad that ran through Jonesboro was an important Confederate supply line and a target of Federal troops in the 1864 Atlanta Campaign. Union General William T. Sherman tried twice to cut the rail line, with cavalry raids in late July and mid-August. When those attempts failed (with a few miles of torn track quickly repaired), Sherman concluded that only a massive infantry sweep would destroy the Macon & Western Railroad. On August 25, Sherman marched most of his army south and then southeast toward Jonesboro, fifteen miles below Atlanta. On August 31, Union troops reached the railroad in Jonesboro and began tearing up the Macon & Western tracks, heating the rails over bonfires and bending them into "Sherman's Bow Ties" that couldn't be easily repaired and replaced. After the two-day-long Battle of Jonesboro, General Sherman telegraphed a message to Washington, D.C.: "Atlanta is ours and fairly won."

LOGAN'S FORCES TEARING UP THE RAILROAD AT JONESBORO.

"Logan's Forces Tearing Up the Railroad at Jonesboro," from The Biography and Public Services of Hon. James G. Blaine: Giving a Full Account of Twenty Years in the National Capital *by Hugh Craig, 1884, page 510.*

GRAVES IN THE GARDEN

Father Emmeran Bliemel. Courtesy Saint Vincent Archabbey, Latrobe, Pennsylvania.

When Mary Ann Fitzgerald Holliday (Mattie's mother) took her family back home after the Battle of Jonesboro, she found her house in ruins—and two fresh graves in the backyard garden. As described by historian Joseph Henry Hightower Moore:

When the Battle of Jonesboro was fought, August 31–September 1, 1864, an incident occurred which subsequently involved Mrs. Robert K. Holliday and her oldest daughter, Miss Martha Holliday [Mattie]. . . . During the first day of the battle, Colonel William Grace, commander of the 10th Tennessee Regiment, C.S.A., received a mortal wound. His troops moved him to what seemed a relatively safe location behind the lines of the heaviest fighting, and there he was ministered to by the Chaplain of the 10th Tennessee Regiment . . . Father Emmeran Bliemel of the Order of St. Benedict [pictured]. As Father Bliemel was in the process of giving the last rites of the Church to his wounded commander, he was himself struck by a shell and instantly killed. When Colonel Grace died shortly after, both his body and that of Father Bliemel were moved to a grove of trees in Jonesboro, and there, side by side, they received temporary burial . . . in the garden of the Holliday home. Mrs. Holliday and her children saw that the graves were marked for identification and proceeded to care for the grave sites until the remains of the two men were moved to the . . . Memorial Cemetery on the north side of town . . . Mrs. Holliday arranged for Father Thomas O'Reilly of the Shrine of the Immaculate Conception in Atlanta to come to Jonesboro and perform a proper Catholic burial for them. The Hollidays continued to care for the graves, in their new location, until Captain Holliday's death in 1872, when Mrs. Holliday and her family moved to Atlanta.[4]

John Henry would surely have known about the unusual graves in his cousin Mattie's backyard, as he stayed in the family's home in Jonesboro during the summer of his sixteenth year.

THE HELL BITCH

When Tom McKey, John Henry's favorite uncle, came home from the war, he brought an interesting souvenir with him: a giant knife he called the "Hell Bitch." According to family stories, the knife had started out as a plowshare on the McKey family plantation at Indian Creek in Henry County, then was honed down to a meat cleaver for slaughtering hogs, then was honed down again to a fighting weapon when the war started. The knife was fifteen inches long from swamp oak handle to tip, two inches wide across the blade, and more than one-quarter-inch thick, and kept in a specially made leather scabbard.[5] Later stories of Doc Holliday's Western adventures would mention a huge knife that he carried under his coat for protection when carrying a pistol wasn't allowed. That knife may well have been the Hell Bitch, which disappeared when Doc fled Georgia, leaving behind the empty scabbard still showing the impression of the heavy knife that was once hidden inside.

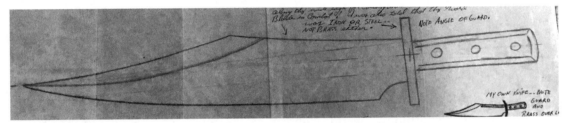

The "Hell Bitch" from a drawing by Jack McKey, grandson of Tom McKey. Author's Collection.

3

PHILADELPHIA & SAVANNAH LINE

Philadelphia started out as a river city, not a railroad city, and John Henry Holliday didn't arrive by train. He came by way of steamship, sailing down the Savannah River to the Atlantic coast, then north past the islands and inlets of the Carolinas, past Virginia's Chesapeake Bay and into Pennsylvania's Delaware Bay, then up the Delaware River to arrive at the biggest city he had ever seen. From the dock at Penn's Landing, the city of Philadelphia stretched for seven miles up and down the Delaware, spread west for two miles to the banks of the Schuylkill River, then crossed the Schuylkill and reached another four miles out into the green Pennsylvania countryside. Even the city market was enormous, covering eighteen blocks from Penn's Landing to 18th Street. Across Philadelphia's expanse of cobbled streets and gaslit lanes lived a population of nearly three-quarters of a million people—making Valdosta, where John Henry could name almost every one of the three-hundred residents, seem like nothing but a bump on a backwoods road.

There were things other than John Henry's rural life that set him apart in that Northern city. He was the son of a former Confederate Army officer, which gave him bragging rights in the South but was something shameful in the Yankee North. He was one of only four Southerners in his class that year and spoke with a drawl, dropping his final "g" and saying "ain't" when his Yankee classmates would say "isn't." Even his manners made him stand out, with his "Yes, Ma'am," and "No, Sir" in answer to even the most trifling question. And he was one of the youngest students at the Pennsylvania College of Dental Surgery, with no background in medicine while many of the other students were already doctors expanding on their professional knowledge, so he would have to hurry to catch up with the book learning. A photograph of him made during his time in Philadelphia shows a young man of nineteen or twenty with the thin beginnings of a mustache covering the small scar from his childhood, a thick wave of hair across a high forehead, and deep-set blue eyes looking with determination toward a respectable future.

The college where he would study for the next two years was located in a four-story brick building at the corner of 10th and Arch Streets, across from the Philadelphia College of Pharmacology, and the two schools shared more than just a street. As both courses of study included an anatomy laboratory, it was convenient for both to share laboratory cadavers as well. The dental students took the heads for dissection, the pharmacology students took the rest of the bodies, and where the remains went from there no one would say—though there was rumored to be a hundred-foot-deep pit in the basement of the Medical College of Pennsylvania where used body parts were thrown.

Cadaver study was one of the more interesting parts of the dental school curriculum that crowded eighteen classroom lectures into six days a week: Chemistry, Dental Pathology and Therapeutics, Dental Histology and Operative Dentistry, Physiology and Microscopic Anatomy, Anatomy and Surgery, and Mechanical Dentistry and Metallurgy. After taking reams of notes in the morning lectures, John Henry spent four hours a day in clinical practice in the operating room, where twenty-eight chairs were arranged to catch the best light from the long windows, gaslight being inferior to daylight for dental work. He had to provide his own instruments and bench tools, keeping them polished and ready for use. He had to purchase his own science textbooks, enough to fill a large personal library. With those costs and the $1,000 program fee, $5 matriculation fee, and $30 diploma fee, attending the Pennsylvania College of Dental Surgery wasn't just an honor—it was an expensive investment.

His evenings were as busy as his days, bent over his science textbooks and cramming by gaslight for weekly exams on *Gray's Anatomy*, *Flint's Physiology*, *Tyson's Cell Doctrine*, *Fownes' Elements of Chemistry*, the *United States Dispensary*, and a dozen others. But his time in Philadelphia wasn't all work and no play—he still had his Saturday afternoons and Sundays free to visit historic sites like Independence Hall with its Liberty Bell, or Christ Church where George Washington had prayed and Benjamin Franklin was buried in the churchyard near the old city wall. And there were other, less reputable historic sites to occupy a young man's time, like the city's famous taverns and ale houses, and the Arch Street Opera House across from the dental college. The theater didn't actually host operas but did have an entertaining lineup of variety acts and dancing girls and was a bargain at seventy-five cents for a matinee.

So, it must have been with some regret that he finished his first year of dental school in Philadelphia, packed away his textbooks, and bought passage on a steamship sailing back to Georgia—and Valdosta must have seemed smaller than ever. But he had work to do there, as well, completing the required internship, called a "preceptorship," with Valdosta dentist Dr. Lucian Frink. An old estate receipt book from that summer shows his pay of $21 for filling six teeth and extracting three teeth for Miss Corinthea Morgan, a former classmate from the Valdosta Institute.

He returned to Philadelphia in the autumn of 1871 for his senior year of studies. Along with the usual long hours in the classroom and the clinic, he would be completing sample cases toward his graduation requirements: a set of teeth mounted in gold and a denture set in the newly patented Vulcanized rubber. The final project of the intensive two-year program was his doctoral thesis, a long research paper on an aspect of dentistry. The only thing he lacked was something beyond his control: He wasn't quite old enough to graduate. The college required that a student be twenty-one years old before receiving a diploma at the March 1872 commencement ceremonies, and John Henry wouldn't turn twenty-one until later that summer. But even if the college had allowed his official graduation, he still couldn't practice in Georgia, where the country's first dental practice act had just been passed, requiring a dentist to be twenty-one years old to receive a license. So, what did John Henry do between the end of dental school in March and his twenty-first birthday in August, when he could officially call himself Dr. Holliday?

There are a couple of clues. One comes from the title of his doctoral thesis, "Diseases of the Teeth"—the same title used by a fellow classmate, A. Jameson Fuchs Jr. of St. Louis, Missouri. John Henry and Jameson were the only two students in the class to submit a thesis on the same topic, and they may well have worked together on the project. Another clue comes from a woman who claimed that she first met John Henry Holliday soon after he completed dental school, when he was practicing dentistry in St. Louis. So it seems that when John Henry finished his college studies he didn't go directly home to Georgia, but took a side trip to St. Louis to practice for a few months with his classmate and friend, Jameson Fuchs—and to meet a woman who would play a large part in his Western life.

GRAVE ROBBERS

An essential course in both the medical and dental school curriculum was human anatomy—the medical students specializing in the body, the dental students in the head—and the best way to study anatomy was by dissection, cutting into an actual corpse. The study cadavers were delivered by "anatomists," who were allowed by law to collect the newly deceased bodies of homeless persons or others for whom no burial arrangements had

Anatomy/Dissection Scene, Jefferson Medical College, ca. 1885. Courtesy of the Archives of Thomas Jefferson University, Philadelphia (Database ID: E-008/CD ID: 6325-3031-1628/CD Sequence: 083).

been made and sell them to the schools for educational purposes. But as a ready supply of legal study corpses wasn't always reliable, anatomists sometimes stepped outside the law and into the cemeteries to find suitable subjects, becoming grave robbers. Historically, grave robbers were more interested in the valuables in the coffin than in the body, but modern medical study had made the bodies themselves a prized commodity, bringing as much as $100 each from a medical school buyer—approximately $3,000 in today's market—one of the reasons a medical or dental education was so expensive.

POMP & CIRCUMSTANCE

Although John Henry wouldn't be officially graduated from the Pennsylvania College of Dental Surgery until a few months later, he likely took part in the school's graduation ceremonies, held on March 1, 1872, in the famed Musical Fund Hall. The ceremonies began at eight o'clock in the evening with the Germania Orchestra playing a rousing overture while the faculty, alumni, and graduates marched in and took their places in rows of seats on the gaslit stage. There was an invocation by the Reverend William Blackwood and a reading of the impressive accomplishments of the graduating class: 5,036 patients treated in the clinic and 1,591 cases mounted in the dental laboratory, with the diplomas awarded by Dean Wildman.

Originally the First Presbyterian Church of Philadelphia, the Musical Fund Hall had been converted into the city's largest auditorium and was noted for its fine

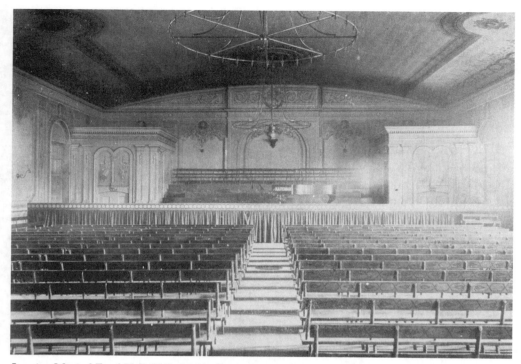

Interior, Musical Fund Hall, Philadelphia, Pennsylvania. Courtesy Free Library of Philadelphia (Item #pdcc00125).

acoustics. World-renowned celebrities appearing at the hall included the Marquis de Lafayette, honored at a reception in 1825 during his tour of the United States, author Charles Dickens reading passages from *A Christmas Carol* on his 1842 book tour, and Swedish songbird Jenny Lind on her 1850 concert tour promoted by showman P. T. Barnum. The last major event held at Musical Fund Hall was the 1856 National Republican Convention, which nominated famed explorer John C. Frémont for president. Frémont would lose the election to Democrat James Buchanan but would later serve as governor of the Arizona Territory when Doc Holliday first arrived there. Following the convention, the larger Philadelphia Academy of Music became the city's premier concert venue, but Musical Fund Hall continued to host smaller events like the College of Dental Surgery graduation. In its declining years, the hall became (among other things) a boxing arena and a tobacco warehouse, then was abandoned. To save the landmark building from the wrecking ball, the auditorium of Musical Fund Hall was removed, and the remaining structure converted into a luxury condo complex and is now preserved as a site on the National Register of Historic Places.

BEN FRANKLIN'S FIRE INSURANCE

In the snowy Philadelphia winters of 1870–1872, when John Henry Holliday was attending dental school, buildings were heated by open fires and coal stoves, and house fires were a constant threat. But Philadelphia was fortunate in having the country's first fire department, founded in 1736 as a volunteer service with assistance from Benjamin Franklin. Ben's plan proposed that homeowners pay for fire insurance from private volunteer fire departments, placing a mark on their home's exterior to show which fire department insured it. If the building caught fire, the insuring fire department would work to save it. If no mark existed, the building was left to burn. In the late 1860s, city officials started plans to transform the volunteer service into a professional fire department that would cover all buildings in the city, and in 1870, the year John Henry Holliday arrived at dental school, an ordinance was passed to create the Philadelphia Fire Department. But the *Philadelphia Gazette* was still filled with fire stories—particularly in the winter when buildings iced over as firehoses poured water on frigid brick.

"Benjamin Franklin, Firefighter" by Charles Washington Wright (1824–1869) on display at the Smithsonian's National Museum of American History. The Picture Art Collection/Alamy Stock (Item #MYB C46).

THE ARCH STREET OPERA

Although the dental students had busy schedules, they surely took time out to visit the newly opened Arch Street Opera, located just across the street from their school. The name "opera" sounded impressive, but the theater mostly hosted minstrel shows, with popular entertainers like singer Andy McKee, banjo player Lew Simmons, and plenty of dancing girls. The Opera House burned down the year John Henry left Philadelphia, being rebuilt and reopened in 1879 as

Arch Street Opera, Philadelphia, Pennsylvania. Courtesy Free Library of Philadelphia (Image #pdcl00103).

the Park Theater. Another fire gutted the theater in 1883 and it was rebuilt again and reopened as the New Arch Street Opera House. By the early twentieth century, the remodeled theater was known as the Trocadero, then the Troc in the 1940s, when it was a movie theater before becoming a burlesque house. In the 1970s, the hundred-year-old site was restored as the Trocadero Concert Hall and added to the Philadelphia Register of Historic Places and the National Register of Historic Places.

4

EADS' FOLLY

The Mississippi River cut the country in half, a thousand-mile-long barrier between the East and the West with only a few railroad bridges spanning its muddy waters. At St. Louis, the Gateway City of the West, there were no bridges yet, and rail traffic had to stop on the east bank of the river and be transferred to ferry boats for the one-mile crossing. But a bridge was coming—if the engineer who had imagined it could get it done. His name was James Eads and the bridge he was building was called "Eads' Folly" by the steamboat companies who hoped he wouldn't succeed. They controlled river traffic and didn't want the competition a railroad bridge would bring, and they set the standard James Eads would have to meet: a bridge so tall that steamboat smokestacks could pass under it, yet so wide that its supports wouldn't impede river traffic. Eads' Folly was to be the answer: the world's first all-steel bridge, built on a pattern of Roman arches with two stone piers sunk into eighty feet of bedrock beneath twelve feet of river water. Nothing like it had ever been attempted and the project was plagued with problems. James Eads had to win a battle with Andrew Carnegie to supply the massive amount of steel needed to build the bridge. A strange ailment afflicted construction workers in the stone chambers deep beneath the river piers, with fifteen men dying of what would later be recognized as decompression sickness, or "the bends." A tornado tore away the newly built superstructure on the east shore of the river, picking up a nearby locomotive and tossing the twenty-five-ton engine up an embankment. But by 1872, when John Henry and Jameson Fuchs arrived from dental school in Philadelphia, Eads' Folly was nearing completion: a graceful structure nearly five hundred feet long with an upper deck for carriages and horse riders and a bottom deck for the railroad. When the bridge was opened to the public two years later, the city would celebrate with fireworks and an elephant parading across to test the strength of the construction.

St. Louis had cause for concern about construction quality. Just twenty years before, most of the wood structured city had been destroyed by a fire that started on a riverboat and swept across the levee to the shore, engulfing fifteen entire blocks. So, the city John Henry entered from the ferry boat landing was newly rebuilt of red brick and black iron with graveled macadam streets—and gutters flowing with beer. That surprising sight was due to the many German immigrants who had come to make new homes and brought their old-world malt recipes along with them, finding that the caves along the river were perfect beer-cooling chambers and making St. Louis the beer capital of America. The city brewed so much lager that the leftovers were poured out at the end of every evening to run through the streets and into the gutters, filling them with fragrant foam.

But St. Louis didn't drink only beer. At the elegant Planter's Hotel on the corner of 4th Street and Pine, the head bartender was the famous "Professor" Jerry Thomas, who in 1864 had written the first book of cocktail recipes. Guests dining and drinking at the Planters included some of the most notable nineteenth-century Americans, with Jefferson Davis, Andrew Jackson, Ulysses S. Grant, and William F. "Buffalo Bill" Cody all signing the hotel's register.

Buffalo Bill was also in town that summer of 1872 with his famous Wild West Show. Young Dr. Holliday may have been in the audience enjoying the sharp-shooting and riding exhibitions, never imagining that he would one day be a Wild West legend himself. There was also P. T. Barnum's Great Traveling Museum Menagerie, billed as the *Greatest Show on Earth*, and the Comique Theater's *Mazeppa*, the popular equestrian drama starring a female rider wearing pink tights that made her look naked on stage. For two young men just graduated from college, St. Louis was full of entertainments.

Jameson Fuchs' home, where he likely also had his dental office, was in the midst of all that activity, on 4th Street near the Planters Hotel and close to the new county courthouse. Two sets of streetcar rails ran past Jameson's home, with the added commotion of horse-drawn carriages and buggies and wagons jostling for space. On the corner was the ticket office for the Vandalia Railroad Line that advertised through-cars to Chicago, Columbus, and Richmond after the ferry ride across the river, making St. Louis a rail center for the whole country.

And somewhere that summer John Henry met a girl named Kate. Wyatt Earp would later remember her as Kate Fisher, a name that appears on the 1870 St. Louis census, though that was likely just one of her many aliases. Her given name was Maria Isabel Katalin Magdolna Horony, born in a German section of Budapest, Hungary, before immigrating with her family to Davenport, Iowa, where her father had a medical practice serving both the English- and German-speaking communities. Maria likely spoke three languages: her native Hungarian and German, and the English of her adopted country. But in 1865, the family's circumstances took a tragic turn when her father dropped dead one spring afternoon and her mother died soon after. Suddenly orphaned, Mary Katherine (the English version of her name) and her four young siblings were shuttled from one home and guardian to another, until she ran off and headed down river to start a new life on her own in St. Louis, now calling herself Kate. In her later memoirs, she gives a confusing history of her time in that city, saying both that she attended the Ursuline Convent school in St. Louis and soon after graduation met a young dentist named John Henry Holliday whom she married, and that she married a dentist named Silas Melvin with whom she had a child and then when both husband and baby died she moved west. There was a Silas Melvin in St. Louis, but he was a guard at the insane asylum, not a dentist, and was married to a girl named Mary Bust, the daughter of a steamboat captain, not to Mary Harony or Kate Fisher. Nor has there been a marriage record found anywhere for John Henry Holliday with Kate Fisher or anyone else. So did Mary Katherine meet John Henry Holliday and begin a romance, then take up with the married Silas Melvin and have a child, then leave St. Louis behind when things got complicated?

Amid the confusion, one point lends credence to Kate's story of meeting Holliday in St. Louis: her mention of where he practiced dentistry, "on 4th Street near the Planters Hotel" where Jameson Fuchs, his college classmate, lived and practiced. It's surely too much of a coincidence to be just coincidence. But whatever the nature of their first meeting, Kate's romance with John Henry Holliday seemed over when he finished his visit with Jameson and took the train back to Georgia.

EADS' BRIDGE

Until the iconic St. Louis arch was erected, the symbol of St. Louis—and the unofficial gateway to the West—was Eads' Bridge, shown here during construction as it would have looked when John Henry Holliday arrived in the city. The bridge would connect the roads and rail lines of Illinois on the eastern bank of the Mississippi River to St. Louis on the western bank, replacing the need for ferry runs across the river.

Eads' Bridge under construction. Library of Congress.

But in 1872, when John Henry made the journey from Philadelphia, the ferry was still the only way to enter the city, mooring at the cobblestoned levee crowded with hundreds of steamboats and lined with factories and saloons. The levee area below Eads' Bridge is now a popular entertainment district known as Laclede's Landing, named after Pierre Laclede Liquest, the French merchant who left New Orleans to open a trading post on the spot he would name St. Louis in honor of King Louis IX of France.

BEER OF KINGS/KING OF BEERS

St. Louis was filled with German immigrants (like the family of John Henry's classmate Jameson Fuchs), many of whom worked in the brewing industry and established St. Louis as the beer capital of the country. Families like the Lemps, Pabsts, Anheusers, and Buschs made fortunes and built mansions above the Mississippi River caves they used as cooling chambers for their trademark lagers. According to family tradition, Eberhard Anheuser was a prosperous soap maker from Germany who won a failing St. Louis brewery in a poker game. He turned the brewery profitable, taking on as partner his son-in-law, beer wholesaler Adolphus Busch. But Eberhard Anheuser wasn't satisfied with the quality of the company's product, so he made trips back to Germany looking for a better recipe. In the Bohemian town of Budweis (now part of the Czech Republic) he found a prized royal lager

Anheuser–Busch refrigerated rail car. FLHC 37/Alamy Stock Photo (Image #MD806G).

the local Budweisers called the "the Beer of Kings," which he took back to St. Louis to create his own "King of Beers," Budweiser. By 1876, Anheuser-Busch had begun shipping out Budweiser on their own fleet of refrigerated railcars, eventually operating 850 cars and founding the Manufacturers Railway Company that operated until 2011. Doc Holliday, fond of his saloons and his drinks, surely enjoyed a Bud.

THE NAKED RIDER

According to the recollections of Wyatt Earp, Doc Holliday's mistress was a woman named Kate Fisher—a name that shows up on the census records in St. Louis when John Henry Holliday was in town. But Kate Fisher was also the name of a noted actress of the time, a theater performer famous for her role in the equestrian spectacle, *Mazeppa*. In the play, a young prince is tied naked to the back of a wild horse as punishment for romancing the wrong woman—the prince always played by an actress wearing pink-colored tights to make her look naked on stage. Cross-dressing was popular in nineteenth-century theater, but the casting was also a good excuse for the audience to see a scantily clad woman, and the show became a huge hit on the Western variety theater circuit. During John Henry's summer stay in St. Louis, *Mazeppa* was showing at the Comique Theater with actress Kate Fisher starring

Adah Isaacs Menken, the most famous "Mazeppa," in her scandalous costume. Courtesy of the Huntington Library, San Marino, California (RB 23851).

in the lead role. So perhaps the elderly Wyatt was just confused in his recollections, remembering Kate Elder as the more famous Kate Fisher—or maybe Doc Holliday managed to romance two Kates in his eventful summer in St. Louis.

"The Poor Soul," c. 1880s (photographer unknown). Courtesy Donald J. McKenna.

THE FACE OF CONSUMPTION?

The September 2015 issue of *True West Magazine* published the story of a mysterious photograph found at an estate sale in St. Louis—mysterious partly because the photo has no identifying mark to give it a name or provenance (trail of ownership), and partly because the subject looks very much like Doc Holliday as an older man, sick with consumption. If the photograph is of Doc, how did it get to St. Louis? There is no history of his being there after his visit as a young man fresh out of dental school. But it's that dental school connection that may explain why such a photo might have found its way to St. Louis: Holliday's dental school classmate Jameson Fuchs, who practiced dentistry in St. Louis before returning to Philadelphia to earn a medical degree from the Jefferson College of Medicine in 1876. Dr. Fuchs then spent the rest of his career as a medical doctor in Mascoutah, Illinois, across the river from St. Louis, but he also inherited property in St. Louis that was willed to his children. Might Doc have had the photo taken elsewhere and sent to his old friend Jameson, to become part of an estate passed down to Jameson's descendants, the photo finally ending up in a St. Louis estate sale? Only Dr. Jameson Fuchs, and the mystery man in the photo, will ever know for sure.

HOLY SISTERS

In her later memoirs, Kate Elder claimed to have attended the Ursuline Convent school in St. Louis, which may have been a bit of historical fiction, giving herself a better history than the facts allow. The school has no records for her during the years when she might have attended, though her name was found on other records listing her as a runaway and possible St. Louis prostitute.[1] But if she had been admitted to a convent school, the Ursuline Academy would have been a proper choice, having been founded in 1848 by three nuns from Austria-Hungary, Kate's homeland.

The Ursuline order, named for Saint Ursula, patron saint of education, began in Brescia, Italy, in the sixteenth century, with a group of twenty-eight women devoted to God and service to the poor. The Ursulines set out to live among the people they served without any distinguishing sign or type of dress, though Church leaders urged them to change their lifestyle into cloistered nuns teaching behind convent walls and wearing the more familiar black habits and long veils. As one of the first Catholic female religious orders to be established in America, the Ursulines founded a convent school in Quebec City that is the oldest educational institution for women in North America, and the Ursuline convent school in New Orleans, the oldest girls' school in the United States.

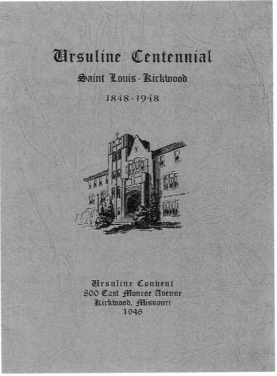

The Ursuline Academy and Convent at 12th and Russell Streets in St. Louis, Missouri, now the site of St. Joseph's Croatian Church. Courtesy Ursuline Archives, Central Province, USA.

The first Ursuline Academy in St. Louis was erected on Fifth Street, near the Old French Market, and two years later moved to larger accommodations at 12th and Russell Streets (the location Kate would have known, now the site of St. Joseph's Croatian Church). The Ursuline Academy continues as a private girls' institution now located in the St. Louis suburb of Oakland and has been named a Blue Ribbon School of Excellence by the US Department of Education. Kate Elder's education, unfortunately, took her in a less excellent direction—and into Western legend.

5

TERMINUS

The city was born of the railroads as the terminating point of the newly chartered Western & Atlantic line, where it would meet with the Georgia Railroad from Augusta and the Macon & Western Railroad from Savannah—all part of an ambitious plan to connect Georgia's coastal port to the Midwest by rail. The year was 1837, and the meeting place was named Terminus, a rough town of railroad workers in the piney woods along the Chattahoochee River. By 1842 the settlement had six real houses and a two-story brick railroad depot, and the thirty residents asked for a more civilized name. The governor suggested Marthasville after his young daughter, but that name only remained for three years before another name was suggested in honor of the railroads that would reach from sea to sea: Atlantica-Pacifica. The name was both descriptive and poetic, but a little long for a road sign, so when the town was incorporated in 1847 it became instead Atlanta.

By 1872, when John Henry Holliday returned to Georgia from two years of dental school in Philadelphia and a summer excursion to St. Louis, Atlanta had grown into a busy city with a population of over thirty thousand. Like the legendary phoenix rising from its own ashes, the city had risen from the ashes of the Battle of Atlanta to become the business center of the "New South," as *Atlanta Constitution* editor and city promoter Henry Grady was calling it. But there were still Federal soldiers stationed at the nearby McPherson Barracks to ensure that Atlanta would comply with the reforms of Reconstruction, and there were still hard feelings against the Yankees.

Until John Henry turned twenty-one in August, he could not practice dentistry on his own, so he took a temporary job working for English-born dentist Dr. Arthur C. Ford, whose office was in a second-floor suite of rooms on Whitehall Street, close to the railroad tracks and Union Station. Dr. Ford announced their association in the professional card section of the *Atlanta Constitution* of Friday, July 26, 1872:

CARD
*I HEREBY inform my patients that I leave to attend the
session of the Southern Dental Association in
Richmond, Virginia, this evening,
and will be absent until about the middle of August, during which time
Dr. John H. Holliday will fill my place in my office.*
Arthur C. Ford, D.D.S.
Office 26 Whitehall Street

Dr. Ford had picked a good time to be gone. August in Atlanta was the hottest month of the year, steamy and sweltering, and for a dentist properly dressed in a vested wool suit and high-collared shirt, it was miserable. But someone had to take care of the patients who stopped by with toothaches or cracked molars and working for Dr. Ford was an auspicious beginning for a young Georgia dentist, despite the discomfort of the weather. As president of the Georgia Dental Association, Dr. Ford had connections that could help Dr. Holliday's new career.

While working for Dr. Ford, John Henry stayed in the home of his uncle Dr. John Stiles Holliday, who had moved from Fayetteville to Atlanta after the war and given up medicine in favor of business and politics. Uncle John's new home was convenient to the downtown, just a street-car ride away on quiet residential Forrest Avenue, and living there allowed John Henry time to discuss dentistry with his cousin Robert, who was planning to attend the Pennsylvania College of Dental Surgery the following year. Robert would name John Henry as his preceptor, planning to serve an internship with his cousin as John Henry had served with Dr. Frink down in Valdosta. The only question was where John Henry would establish his own practice once he turned twenty-one and could finally obtain a dental license.

The answer seemed to lie in the inheritance property he had received from his mother's estate, and which his family had fought over after her death. Along with some land, the most important part of that inheritance was a business building in his old hometown of Griffin. Called the "Iron Front" for its fancy ironwork façade, the building housed shops and vendors—a sort of nineteenth-century shopping mall—and brought in a nice rental income, which explains why the McKey family had not been happy to give it up. The legal fight for possession of the Iron Front had begun soon after Henry Holliday's hasty second marriage and resulted in a Lowndes County court case. Although the records of the case were lost when the courthouse in Valdosta later burned, someone had the judge's decision recorded in the Spalding County Deed Book in Griffin in November 1872—likely John Henry himself, proving his right to possess the building.

As the Deed Book notes, the judge of the Lowndes County court ruled that the Iron Front building would be divided between the Holliday and McKey families, with the south side returning to the McKeys' ownership and the north side remaining with Henry Holliday as guardian for John Henry until his coming-of-age at twenty-one years old. To mark the division of the property, a partition wall was to be erected down the middle of the building. The judge's decision seems especially appropriate to the location of the Iron Front building, on Griffin's Solomon Street. Like the biblical story of the Wisdom of Solomon, in which King Solomon ordered a baby to be cut in half and shared by two women who both claimed to be the mother, the Lowndes County judge ordered the Iron Front building on Solomon Street to be divided in half between the two squabbling sides of the Holliday and McKey families.

Griffin stories say that John Henry moved back to his hometown after graduating from dental school, setting up practice in the Iron Front building in a second-floor room overlooking Solomon Street. It would have been an ideal location for a dental office, with long windows to let in the natural light and enough room to accommodate a heavy iron-footed dental chair. He may have added a private entrance to the office, with a staircase coming up from what was then a small alley next to the building. So, with just a painted sign hung in the window advertising his services, John Henry Holliday, DDS, was in business at last.

At twenty-one years old, he was of average height and slender build, with thick reddish-gold hair and light blue eyes, his father's high cheekbones and his mother's fine narrow nose. His education and professional training gave him a sometimes prideful arrogance, and his adolescent years living under Yankee occupation gave him a distrust of authority and a quick temper when challenged. As family friend Lee Smith would later say of him, he was "one of the best boys that ever lived, if he is let alone, but you mustn't impose on him or you will smell powder burning."[1]

But if John Henry got into trouble in Griffin or Atlanta, there is no record of it. Likely, he spent his time at work or riding the Macon & Western Railroad back and forth between Griffin and visits with his Holliday relatives in Jonesboro and Atlanta.

In the Southern tradition, family came first, and social life revolved around family gatherings, and John Henry had plenty of kin to keep him occupied. If he did have a romance with his cousin Mattie, those months were even busier.

But then came two funerals that shook the family. Mattie's father, who hadn't been well since his time in a Yankee prison camp during the war, died on Christmas Eve at his home in Jonesboro. The weather was icy and the muddy roads difficult, but John Henry surely made the trip to his uncle's graveside funeral in the Fayetteville Cemetery. Then, three weeks later, his foster brother Francisco Hidalgo died of consumption on his farm in Jenkinsburg, near Griffin, and was buried in the County Line Baptist Church cemetery. John Henry was there, as well—and on the same day, he went into Griffin and sold his share of the Iron Front building to Griffin liquor dealer N. G. Phillips for $1,800.[2] As recorded in the Spalding County Deed books, it was the highest price the building would bring for another fifty years.

What made John Henry suddenly sell off his hard-won inheritance, and where did he go from there? He may have stayed in Griffin, paying rent for his office space to the new owner and using the profit of the sale for dental equipment and living expenses. He may have left Griffin and moved back to Atlanta to be close to his Holliday cousins. Or he may have left north Georgia entirely and taken the train south to Valdosta to spend some time with his McKey relatives there. Whatever his plans, it was there in Valdosta that the final chapter of his Georgia life played out.

According to popular legend, Doc Holliday left home and went west because he was diagnosed with consumption and told that he had to go to a kinder climate to save his life. And that's partly true. He was eventually diagnosed with consumption (though when or where, we don't know) and he did go to the western Territory of New Mexico for his health. But that was years after he left Georgia, after he'd already made a name for himself in several other states. The first place he went after leaving home was Dallas, Texas, which is in the South, not the West, and which did not have a kinder climate. Dallas weather was much like Georgia, hot and humid in the summer, cold and humid in the winter. It had also been recently closed down by a yellow fever epidemic and was famous for being the second least healthy place in the country to live, right behind the bayous of Louisiana. No one would go there for his health.

So, what was it that made John Henry Holliday leave home? The more likely cause of his western exodus wasn't sickness, but a shooting—a story told in various versions by people who knew him personally, most notably by lawman Bat Masterson. As Masterson tells it, near the south Georgia village where Holliday was raised ran a little river where a swimming hole had been cleared, and where he one day came across some black boys swimming where he thought they shouldn't be. He ordered them out of the water and when they refused to go, he took a shotgun to them and "caused a massacre." In the troubled days of Reconstruction, his family thought it best that he leave the area, so he moved to Dallas, Texas. The village, of course, was Valdosta, and the river was the nearby Withlacoochee.

Bat Masterson's story first appeared in *Human Life Magazine* in 1907 and was repeated in newspapers across the country at a time when most of the men who'd known Doc Holliday were still alive and could have refuted the story—but no one ever did. And there were other versions of the story told by people who lived in Valdosta at the time of the shooting, although they disagree on the number of casualties. None of the locals mentioned sickness as a reason for his leaving Georgia, but they were still talking about the shooting on the Withlacoochee decades after his death. The following report is from the *Valdosta Times*, August 29, 1931, based on the recollections of John Henry's favorite uncle, Tom McKey:

> *Accompanied by Mr. T. S. McKey . . . John one day rode out to a point northwest of the city which was noted throughout this section for its fine "washhole." Arriving there, they discovered that several negroes had been throwing mud into the water and stirring it up so that it was unfit to swim in. Holliday began scolding the negroes and one of them made threatening remarks back to him. John immediately got his buggy whip and proceeded to punish this hard-boiled negro. The negro fled and returned in a few minutes with a shot gun. He shot once and sprinkled Holliday with small bird shots. Holliday promptly got his pistol and pursued the fleeing negroes. When the negro who had shot at him saw that the youth meant business, he took to his heels and could not be caught.*

No matter the body count, the story is generally consistent in the events, and although disturbing for its racist overtones, it's true to the tenor of the times of Reconstruction. And it's not surprising that, given those times, the family would report a less violent version. What is surprising is that, given the opportunity to deny the story completely and blame Holliday's exodus from Georgia on a case of consumption, they did not.

But whatever sent him west, whether sickness or a shooting, John Henry Holliday's life in Georgia had come to an end.

UNDERGROUND ATLANTA

Atlanta's first railroad depot was blown up by the Yankees after the Battle of Atlanta, an event depicted in one of the most dramatic scenes of the film *Gone with the Wind*, as Rhett Butler escorts a terrified Scarlett and Melanie out of the city and leaves them on the road to Tara. The movie fire was actually the burning of the old *King Kong* set in Culver City, California, and "Scarlett" was actually a stunt woman—actress Vivien Leigh had yet to be cast in the film.

The burning of Atlanta as portrayed in Gone with the Wind *(1939). World History Archive/Alamy Stock Photo (Image #57304865).*

For a half-dozen years after the war, Atlanta had no official train depot until a new Union Station was built in 1871. It was this station that John Henry Holliday would have known during his train travels to the city, the building standing in the middle of Whitehall Street, now Peachtree Street. But as railroad traffic increased to six sets of tracks to accommodate the several railroad companies that used the station, crossing Whitehall became dangerous and sometimes deadly. The city responded by building a pedestrian bridge over the tracks, which was widened to become a vehicle bridge called a viaduct, which was finally replaced by an entire elevated street system—leaving the original track area "underground" while the businesses moved up to the newly built second-floor street level. In the Prohibition years of the 1920s, the old underground stores became a neighborhood of speakeasies and illegal drinking, with the nineteenth-century architecture remaining intact with decorative brickwork, granite archways, ornate marble, cast-iron pilasters, hand-carved wooden posts, and gas streetlamps. In

Union Depot, Atlanta. Courtesy Kenan Research Center at the Atlanta History Center (Atlanta History Photograph Collection (VIS 170.835.001).

the 1970s the historic area was developed as a shopping and entertainment district called Underground Atlanta. The area is currently under redevelopment for mixed use with apartments above ground and retail below ground—including the corner of Whitehall and Alabama Streets where a young Dr. Holliday worked in Dr. Arthur C. Ford's office in the summer of 1872.

Church of the Immaculate Conception. Courtesy Kenan Research Center at the Atlanta History Center (Atlanta History Photograph Collection (VIS 170.420.001).

KISSING COUSINS

Across the road from the former Union Station stands the Shrine of the Immaculate Conception, still under construction in John Henry's day but already holding services in the basement while the soaring stained glass-windowed towers were completed. Known then as the Church of the Immaculate Conception, it was the only Catholic church in North Georgia, and the home parish of Mattie Holliday's Catholic family, with the names of her Fitzgerald and Catholic Holliday relatives filling the church register's baptism and marriage records. But until her family moved from Jonesboro to Atlanta, they did not often attend services at the church and would have welcomed Father John Duggan in his travels to offer the Sacraments and Last Rights to his far-flung parish. As for Mattie and John Henry's rumored romance, it would have been fated to fail by her Catholic faith, which did not allow marriages between first cousins. The closest family marriage allowed was second cousins, the children of first cousins, appropriately called "kissing cousins." If Mattie had chosen to marry her first cousin John Henry Holliday, the ceremony could not have been performed by the Church or recognized by the Church if performed in some other denomination, and Mattie would have been considered "living in sin." For the saintly Mattie Holliday, that would have been unthinkable.

FOUNTAIN OF YOUTH

Located in the hilly countryside two miles from downtown Atlanta, the Ponce de Leon Springs offered mineral waters and outdoor recreations like picnics, promenades, and target shooting. Although named for the famous Spanish explorer who searched for the legendary Fountain of Youth, the area was officially discovered by railroad workers who came across two small cold-water springs at the base of a steep hill near to the road construction. The railroaders said the spring water had a "sulfurous, nasty taste" but

Ponce de Leon Springs. Courtesy Kenan Research Center at the Atlanta History Center. Atlanta History Photograph Collection (VIS 170.915).

it soon gained a reputation for giving miraculous medical cures—including cures for consumption. During John Henry's stay in Atlanta, families made day-long excursions to the springs, and hotels had scheduled horse-drawn taxi service for their guests.

The dirt road leading to the springs eventually became a fashionable residential street called Ponce de Leon Avenue, lined with mansions and fine churches. In this 1890s photograph, the Knowles children (Constance and Clarence) are being driven along Ponce near their home in a carriage pulled by Daisy and Dandy. Constance and Clarence were the grandchildren of John Henry's cousin George Holliday—giving an idea of the kind of life he might have enjoyed if fate hadn't taken him west.

Daisy and Dandy with the Knowles Children. Courtesy Kenan Research Center at the Atlanta History Center. Atlanta History Photograph Collection (VIS 170.68.22).

JUST BECAUSE YOU SAY IT A LOT DOESN'T MAKE IT SO

All legends start somewhere, and the legend of Doc Holliday going west for his health began not in his own lifetime, but nearly fifty years after he died, in 1931's *Wyatt Earp: Frontier Marshal* by Stuart Lake. Until then, the story of his exodus told by all the people who knew Holliday was that he'd shot a black man—or several—in south Georgia. Even a report of his death in a Montana newspaper published the week he

Wyatt Earp: Frontier Marshal *by Stuart N. Lake, Houghton Mifflin Company, original cover of 1931 edition.*

died told essentially the same story. But when author Stuart Lake set out to write a biography of famed lawman Wyatt Earp—including stories of his friend Doc Holliday—he found Wyatt to be the strong, silent type without much to say. Over the course of their eight interviews, he remembered the eighty-two-year-old Earp as being "illiterate" and his speech "at best monosyllabic." In other words, Wyatt Earp was a terrible interview and Lake had to elaborate much of the story himself to create a truly heroic epic. There was also the issue of Wyatt's and Doc's living relatives: they wanted a "good, clean story," and that likely did not include scenes of racial violence. So, the Doc Holliday we find in *Wyatt Earp: Frontier Marshal* is partly fact and partly Stuart Lake's creative writing. But although the book was essentially a historical novel it was promoted as Wyatt Earp's firsthand account of the Wild West and became a wildly popular best-seller, spawning movies like *Frontier Marshal* (four versions) and even the John Ford classic, *My Darling Clementine*. Then came radio dramas and TV shows like *Wyatt Earp* and comic books like *Wyatt Earp* and Doc Holliday biographies based mostly on *Wyatt Earp: Frontier Marshal*, then more movies and more biographies, all spouting the by-now accepted history: Doc Holliday went west to Texas because he was dying of consumption and needed the "high, dry plains of the Western plateau," as Stuart Lake put it, to heal himself. Even a modern biography written by a Holliday family relative recounted the same tale—likely based on the family's reading of *Wyatt Earp: Frontier Marshal* and remembering that it happened just that way. But just because something has been said over and over again doesn't make it true—though it can make it legend.

6

HOUSTON & TEXAS CENTRAL

There are no nineteenth-century reports of what route John Henry Holliday took to Texas, only educated guesses. But if the story of a shooting on the Withlacoochee River is true, then he likely made a fast escape from Georgia, traveling twenty miles south to the Florida state line and crossing over into Hamilton County, where his mother's brothers—William, James, and Tom McKey—owned Banner Plantation, and the Pensacola & Georgia Railroad had a depot at the nearby town of Live Oak. From there, the train ran west to the state capital of Tallahassee and on to the edge of Escambia Bay, a two-bit ferry ride away from the Gulf Coast port of Pensacola. And Pensacola had regular sailings to New Orleans and Galveston, Texas.

The island city of Galveston was the gateway to Texas, the richest port on the Gulf of Mexico and the second richest port in the United States. The streets were paved with crushed oyster shells that sparkled in the summer sun and gleamed at night under the glow of gaslights. The mansions of the leading men of Texas society lined Broadway Street, surrounded by gardens of flowering oleander and fragrant groves of orange and lemon trees. The strand on the north side of the island, where the wide harbor faced the mainland, was crowded with brick business houses and the traffic of port commerce, while the sand beach on the south of the island was filled with the carriages of pleasure-seekers enjoying the balm of Gulf breezes. Galveston even had a railroad, the Houston & Texas Central Railway that ran across a trestle bridge over Galveston Bay to the mainland, and from there to Houston and Dallas.

The coming of the railroad had turned the farm town of Dallas into the newest boomtown of Texas, but not without a little legal sleight-of-hand. When the Houston & Texas Central announced the proposed route, with the rails to pass eight miles to the east of Dallas, local boosters came up with a scheme to bring the train closer: They bribed the railroad with a $5,000 donation and a right-of-way for the roadbed, then raised $10,000 in gold for a mule-drawn streetcar system to connect the new depot to the center of town. Then, when the Houston & Texas Central deal was done, they made a similar offer to the new Texas & Pacific Railroad that was building east to west across the state but planning to bypass Dallas by fifty miles to the south. If Dallas could wrangle the meeting of the two railroads, the city would become the shipping center of the entire state. But when the Texas & Pacific declined a lucrative offer, the Dallas boosters tried another, less transparent, approach. They had their state representative attach a rider to the railroad bill requiring the Texas & Pacific to pass within one mile of a watering hole called "Browder Springs." Since no one knew or cared where Browder Springs was, the bill passed without objection—until the railroad engineers went to work and discovered that Browder Springs was one mile from the Dallas County Courthouse, and they had been duped into building where they hadn't wanted to go. To make amends, Dallas put up $200,000 in bonds, land access, and a $5,000 cash donation to the railroad. And thus, began the railroad boom of Dallas. As an early resident described it:

> Dallas was then a tough town with two railroads, population about 8,000. There was a street car line on Main Street to the Court House. The cars were driven by a small pair of mules. When a car got off the track the passengers got out and lifted it on again. The stores had begun to reach east about two or three blocks from the Court House along Main and Elm. The residences were a few frame houses, and as many of plank, upright, called Shot Gun Houses. The water supply was furnished by wagons, 2 buckets for 5 cents. On Main Street there was a mesquite thicket, where browsed a drove of burros, that had been abandoned by a man from New Mexico. The boys would sometimes rope one and the market price was 50 cents.[1]

For John Henry Holliday, newly arrived that summer of 1873, the tough town of Dallas looked like a good place for a fresh start. Despite his recent troubles, he had the makings of a proper professional man and he accepted a position in the dental practice of Dr. John Seegar, originally from Fayette County, Georgia, and an old acquaintance of the Holliday family. The partnership was listed in the new *Dallas City Directory* as Seegar & Holliday, with offices above Cochran's Drug Store on Elm Street, halfway between Main and Austin.[2] To advertise his arrival, young Dr. Holliday entered three displays of dental work, likely his dental school sample cases, in the scientific exhibits at the first Texas state fair. Called the North Texas Agricultural, Mechanical, & Blood Stock Association Fair, the event was held in a grove of hardwood trees beyond the tracks of the Houston & Texas Central and the Texas & Pacific Railroads. Dr. Holliday's entries won three first place awards, as reported in the October 11, 1873, *Dallas Weekly Herald*:

> *Best Set of Artificial Teeth and Dental Ware, prize $5*
> *Best Set of Teeth in Vulcanized Rubber, prize $5*
> *Best Set of Teeth in Gold, prize $5*

The last case would have cost a patient about $200 at a time when an average worker earned just $400 a year, making Dr. Holliday's prize-winning dental work very pricey, so he seemed set for a prosperous career in his new hometown. And as a professional man he needed to "walk the paths of rectitude," as he would later call it, so he joined the congregation of the Methodist Episcopalian Church, his mother's denomination, and attended meetings of the local Temperance Union, fighting against public drunkenness. And for a few months, things went along well for him. But Dr. Holliday had a habit that would get in the way of his being a respectable Dallas businessman. He liked to play cards, a gentlemanly pastime back home in Georgia, but problematic in Dallas where there was a law against "Gaming in a House of Spirituous Liquors." A man could bet on cards, or he could drink liquor, but he couldn't do both in the same place at the same time.

To comply with the law, the forty saloons along Main Street were all arranged with a drinking room at the front of the building and a card room at the back of the building, keeping the liquor away from the games. But if a man happened to carry his drink from the bar to the card room, or his poker chips from the card room to the bar, he was breaking the law and subject to arrest by the ever-vigilant Dallas City Police. And that was how Dr. Holliday first got into trouble with the law in Texas: He was arrested for playing keno in a saloon and had to stand before the judge, who set his court date out for a year, essentially putting him on probation for bad behavior.[3] Perhaps showing the kind of bad company Dr. Holliday was keeping, his $100 bond was posted by Thomas M. Miers, a Dallas liquor dealer. And it may have been the gambling and the drinking that caused the early end of the dental partnership of Seegar & Holliday. On March 2, 1874, the *Dallas Daily Commercial* ran the following card:

Upon mutual consent, the firm of Seegar and Holliday have dissolved. J.H. Holliday will be responsible for the two debts against the firm. J.A. Seegar will remain at the old office over Cochran's Drug Store, Elm. J.H Holliday's office is over Dallas County Bank, corner of Main and Lamar.

It was a bad time to be starting up a dental practice, or any other kind of business. The national railroad boom that had started after the war had finally slowed, with nearly every railroad in the country cutting back or closing down, and when the big New York investment house of Jay Cooke & Company collapsed a string of banking failures followed, bringing the deepest depression the country had ever seen. In the aftermath of the nationwide Panic of 1873, five-thousand businesses closed and whole towns seemed to just dry up and blow away altogether, and Dallas had money worries like the rest of the country. If folks had trouble making ends meet, they likely weren't interested in paying for Dr. Holliday's pricey dental work. That may have been what convinced him to leave Dallas for a while—buying another ticket on the Houston & Texas Central Railway, heading north toward the Red River and the last boomtown in Texas.

FLORIDA–GEORGIA LINE

The fastest escape route from Valdosta, Georgia, was south across the state line to Florida. But for John Henry Holliday, Florida would still be too close for comfort if the martial law of Georgia came calling, so his McKey uncles' plantation in Hamilton County was just a layover on a much longer journey to Texas, a journey complicated by the aftereffects of Civil War and Reconstruction—and a Yankee railroad swindle.

Florida was the South's least populated state when the Civil War began, with a scattering of sugar and cotton plantations across a remote interior, a few small towns along the coast, and its largest city on the island of Key West. The goal of most travelers was to get around Florida as fast as possible, sailing down the Atlantic Coast and through the treacherous Florida Straits to the Gulf of Mexico. So that was the purpose of Florida's first major railroad, carrying goods and passengers over land from the Atlantic Coast to the Gulf Coast, saving three days over the sea route. The benefit to the state would be the income and goods brought into the new ports at Amelia Island on the Atlantic and Cedar Key on the Gulf, the two ends of the road. But the Florida Railroad had just opened for business when the Civil War began, putting a temporary end to its travels.

There were some short-line roads predating the coast-to-coast rails, like the mule-drawn Tallahassee Railroad that opened in 1834 during Florida's territorial days. The capital of the territory had been planted at Tallahassee, halfway between the old Spanish towns of Pensacola and St. Augustine, to give legislators from either coast a shorter trip for official business. But the officially convenient location left the new capital landlocked, so twenty miles of wooden rails were laid from Tallahassee south through oak and pine forests to the St. Marks River and its outlet to the Gulf. The road served for twenty years until it was taken over by the Pensacola & Georgia Railroad, which replaced the wood rails with iron and retired the mule power in favor of locomotives, with a plan to connect the road to a new line reaching from Pensacola to St. Augustine. But like the ambitious Florida Railroad, the Pensacola & Georgia also became a victim of the end of railroad building during the Civil War.

Then came Reconstruction and a former Union general with a plan to profit off the capital's need of rail service by creating the Florida Central to complete the line to Pensacola. He sold his plan to investors, laid twenty miles of rail west from the city, then skipped town with the rest of the money. The swindle left Tallahassee wiser but still without a completed railroad line—which is why John Henry Holliday's trip across Florida started on horseback, then moved to a train, then finished by ferry boat.

THE DROWNING OF GALVESTON

When John Henry Holliday arrived in Texas, Galveston was the largest port city on the Gulf of Mexico, and second only to New York in commerce. The city's location on a barrier island seemed ideal for shipping, and promoters claimed the area was naturally protected from the ravages of the hurricanes that swept other Gulf cities as high tides would wash around the island into the harbor on the mainland side. The great storm of September 1900 proved that theory deadly wrong. The monster hurricane brought a storm surge of eight to twelve feet that swept over the entire island, drowning a reported eight-thousand residents and leaving the remaining thirty-thousand

Seeking Valuables in the Wreckage, Galveston, Texas. Library of Congress.

homeless when most of the buildings on the island were destroyed. Called the Great Galveston Hurricane, it remains the deadliest natural disaster in US history and ended the golden era of Galveston as investors turned instead to the little town of Houston, situated more safely inland on Buffalo Bayou. Galveston rebuilt, putting every building on raised foundations and erecting a sturdy seawall that has saved it from other hurricanes, but it never regained its status as a major port and business center and is now a beach resort town with a dramatic, and cautionary, history.

POSTMARKED PENSACOLA

While there is no proof of what route John Henry Holliday took west, an old story out of Waycross, Georgia, may hold a clue to his travels. In the 1980s a Waycross gentleman contacted an antiques dealer in Florida with an offer of an old box for sale, a box he'd discovered in the attic of the home he'd recently moved into. Inside the box were some old photographs, a wooden cross that might have been a grave marker, and letters with the postmark Pensacola. Only the signature on those letters made them at all interesting: *John Henry Holliday*, which the antiques dealer recognized as the name of Georgia's most famous Western character. But the legend of Doc Holliday had never mentioned Pensacola or any other Florida town, so the dealer passed on the offer. What he didn't know was that John Henry's cousin Clyde McKey, his uncle

Tom McKey's youngest daughter, had family that had lived in Waycross, and the letters had likely once been hers, sent by John Henry Holliday to the family as he stopped over in Pensacola on his way to Texas, and into legend.

BROWDER SPRINGS

The artesian springs located a mile southeast of the Dallas County Courthouse were named for Lucy Jane Browder and her two sons, who acquired the property before 1850. The springs served as a fresh water source for the new community, while the picturesque location was a popular site for picnics. In 1871, Browder

Browder Springs Hall at Old City Park, Dallas, Texas. Author's Collection.

Springs also served as a ruse by which Dallas captured the Texas & Pacific Railway and became the shipping center for north Texas, but by 1886 the water needs of Dallas had surpassed the capacity of the springs and alternate water sources were developed. The area of Browder Springs is now home to Old City Park, a living history museum with a collection of historic buildings from all over north Texas and a restored mercantile called Browder Springs Hall.

LAST OF THE MCKEYS

Although John Henry was far from home when he arrived in Texas, he wasn't far from family. His uncle Jonathan McKey, his mother's oldest brother, lived near the town of Brenham in Washington County, 120 miles past Galveston on the Houston & Texas Railroad. Uncle Jonathan had been a wealthy planter in Henry County, Georgia, with fifty-six slaves on his property, before going west to Texas to take up land along the Brazos River. It was an area rich with history—Washington County was first known as Washington-on-the-Brazos, the birthplace of the Texas Declaration of Independence from Mexico following the massacre at the Battle of the Alamo. When the Texans won their freedom at the Battle of San Jacinto, the Brazos River country started to fill up with settlers—like Jonathan McKey, who came to grow cotton and corn in the rich river bottoms and raised a family near Brenham. During the Civil War, Jonathan served in the 3rd Texas Regular Cavalry, but Reconstruction put a temporary end to the area's prosperity, as the big slave-run plantations were broken up by the Federal government and the land was given away to former slaves and newly arrived German immigrants. If John Henry Holliday had imagined his Uncle Jonathan McKey living in Texas in his former Old South glory, he must have found the truth to be disappointing.

7

THE KATY

The Red River divided Texas from the Indian Nation—Seminole, Cherokee, Choctaw, Chickasaw, Creek. The Nation was meant to be a refuge for the tribes that had been driven from their ancestral homes in the East and the West, but an Indian refuge couldn't stop commerce. Soon Texas cattlemen were trailing their herds north across the Nation to the railheads in Kansas and Missouri for shipment to meat markets in the east. And soon after that, the Missouri, Kansas & Texas (MK&T) Railroad began laying rails south from Junction City, Kansas, and across the Indian Nation to Red River City, Texas, to profit off the cattle business by creating the first Texas cattle shipping center.

Though the name Red River City sounded impressive, the place was hardly even a village—just a scattering of shacks along the river waiting for the railroad to arrive to bring business and make the place boom. So there weren't enough citizens of Red River City to make much of a protest when the MK&T Railroad, nicknamed "the Katy," decided to build its depot four miles farther south, in another newly made town named in honor of the railroad's vice president, George Denison. And that was how Denison, Texas, the town called "Katy's Baby," was born.

By the time Dr. John Henry Holliday arrived in the summer of 1874, Katy's Baby was two years old, past its infancy and growing fast. The town now had two railroads, with the tracks of the Houston & Texas Central coming north to meet the Katy, with two railroad depots, two roundhouses, and a hundred acres of cattle pens beyond the tracks. Across from the Katy depot sprawled the Alamo Hotel and Restaurant, and down Main Street were the Grand Southern Hotel, the Planters Hotel, the Lindell Hotel, and several boardinghouses. There were five restaurants in town, eight church congregations, and the first free graded school in Texas just opened in an impressive two-story red brick building. There was even a baseball team—the Denison Blue Stockings, who were already in a hot rivalry with the team from nearby Sherman.

The baseball scores, along with all the other Denison news, were reported in the two newspapers already in print: the weekly *Denison Journal* and the *Denison Daily News*, whose editor also ran the *Dallas Daily Commercial*. And it may have been in that paper that Dr. Holliday first learned of the boomtown on the Red River and the business that would make it boom even bigger—the founding of the Texas & Atlantic Refrigeration Company with its newly patented refrigerated railcars that allowed cattle to be slaughtered in Texas and the meat dressed and packed on ice for a fast trip to dinner tables in the East. No longer would cattle have to be driven on the hoof to railheads in Kansas and Missouri for shipping to markets in the East, and the Katy's depot at Denison, the northern end of the rails in Texas, was the shipping point for the new industry.

Dr. Holliday joined hundreds of other young men arriving in Denison that depression year looking for a job—of the nearly four thousand residents fewer than seven hundred were even old enough to vote—and settled into the sporting life of a railroad boomtown. He may have taken a room at the Alamo Hotel across from the train depot or at one of the less expensive hotels or boardinghouses and used his room as a dental office. He didn't pay for an advertisement in the local papers, so it's likely he just put a sign in his window, as many businesses did, and went to work. As there were only two other dentists in Denison at the time, there were plenty of teeth to keep them all busy.

When he wasn't working, John Henry could attend services and socials at the Methodist Episcopal Church that met in a white frame building on Woodward Street, or take in a variety act at the opera house on the second floor of the Planters Hotel. And he surely enjoyed the rowdier entertainments at the saloons and dance halls on Skiddy Street, a muddy ravine just below Main Street. Though the saloons had elegant names like the Palace, the Park and the Sazerac (named after a famous New Orleans cognac cocktail), they were rough buildings in a rougher place. The local law was former schoolteacher-turned-deputy Jesse Leigh "Red" Hall, who understood that young men needed exercise, so he fined—but didn't close down—the Skiddy Street bordellos. For Dr. Holliday, the liberal life of Denison must have seemed a relief after the constraints and embarrassments of Dallas.

But his dual career of dentistry and gambling came to an early end when the depression finally reached booming Denison and the Texas & Atlantic Refrigeration Company lost its financial backers and closed down. With no refrigerated rail cars to carry dressed beef, the slaughterhouse and the packing plant beside the tracks closed down, as well, and suddenly it seemed that everyone in town was out of work. For Denison's newest dentist, business wasn't going well, and by the end of the year he packed up his things and bought a ticket on the southbound Houston & Texas Central, headed back to Dallas.

He arrived in time to take in the New Year's festivities—and to make some fireworks of his own. On New Year's Day of 1875, he went into a saloon across the street from the new Dallas City Hall and got into a shooting affray with a bartender named Charlie Austin. According to the *Dallas Herald* of January 2, 1875: "Dr. Holliday and Mr. Austin, a saloonkeeper, relieved the monotony of the noise of fire-crackers by taking a couple of shots at each other yesterday afternoon. The cheerful note of the peaceful six-shooter is heard once more among us. Both shooters were arrested."

Although the light tone of the newspaper story made the affray seem a minor affair, it wasn't treated lightly by the local law. Charlie Austin was charged with carrying a pistol and his case later dismissed, but Dr. Holliday was indicted by the Dallas County Grand Jury with Assault with Intent to Murder.[1] If found guilty, he would face two to seven years in the State Penitentiary.

The case came to trial on January 25 in the new Dallas County Courthouse, where Dr. Holliday pled not guilty to the charge. Though the records unfortunately don't give his testimony, he must have made a good case, because the jury verdict agreed and found him not guilty. But he still had one more legal issue to attend to: the final court date for his old keno charge from the year before. So, he stayed in Dallas until the spring to settle the case and pay his $10 fine—and one would have thought that would be the end of his trouble in Texas. But within a month he was gone from Dallas and Denison both, beyond the reach of the railroads and wandering the frontier towns of west Texas, where there were more gambling arrests and warrants—and another rumored shooting.

What was it that made Dr. John Henry Holliday suddenly leave his professional life behind and travel down dark and dangerous trails? Might it have been in Texas that he learned he had consumption, or finally faced the fatal diagnosis? And how would a twenty-three-year-old young man react to such devastating news—with sarcasm and careless resignation, the supposed character traits of the legendary Doc Holliday? Or would he flail at the fates that had stolen his life away?

Fort Griffin was his first documented stopover in that desperado year, a hundred miles beyond Dallas on a bluff overlooking the Clear Fork of the Brazos River. The military post occupied the high ground, with soldiers from the 10th Cavalry assigned to defend the nearby Dodge City Cattle Trail against raids by the fierce Comanche and Kiowa. The low ground along the river was called "The Flats," a single muddy street occupied by trail outfitters, saloons, and whorehouses that served the buffalo hunters, cowboys, and crowds of sporting men—including one "Dock Holliday" who was arrested twice in June 1875 for "playing at a game of cards at a house used for retailing spirituous liquor," along with Hurricane Bill Martin, Mike Lynch, and one "Curly."[2] Hurricane Bill and Curly stayed to pay their fines and play again, but Holliday and Lynch skipped town, and on June 30 an *alias capias* warrant was issued for their arrest and forwarded to the sheriff at San Angelo. But by the spring of 1876, Doc Holliday was back in Fort Griffin and getting into even more dangerous trouble.

As Bat Masterson tells it, Doc Holliday killed a solider in a military post town before making a fast run from Texas for points north.[3] The soldier may have been Private Jake Smith, a black buffalo soldier "absent without authority from his post" at Fort Griffin, who was shot and killed by an unknown party on March 3, 1876.[4] Shortly after that event, Doc Holliday disappeared from the historical record in Texas. When he showed up again, he had a new home, a new career—and an alias.

STEAK ON ICE

In 1873, the Texas & Atlantic Refrigeration Company of Denison made the first successful rail shipment of chilled beef from Texas and the Great Plains to markets in the East. The technology used was based on the work of Thomas L. Rankin of Dallas and Denison, who held patents in refrigeration and worked on the development of refrigerator and abattoir (a polite term for "slaughterhouse") service for rail shipping. No longer would beef have to be shipped on the hoof in crowded cattle cars to be slaughtered and dressed in distant markets, but could be first processed in Texas, saving space and money on transportation. To support the new industry, cattle-holding pens and slaughterhouses were built near the Denison train depot, and the Arctic Ice Manufacturing Company was established along the tracks of the MK&T, with ice carved from a frozen bay in Quincy, Illinois, and hauled in refrigerated cars to ice vaults in Denison. But after an impressive first year of booming business, Denison's Texas & Atlantic Refrigeration Company became another victim of the

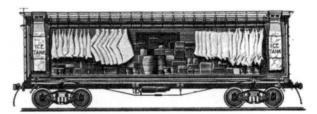

Early Refrigerator Car. FLHC Y1/Alamy Stock Photo (Image #RYC726).

Panic of 1873 and closed its doors, putting hundreds of young men—and one young Georgia dentist—out of work.

President George Washington's First Inauguration. Library of Congress.

GEORGE WASHINGTON'S SWORD SLEPT HERE

Doc Holliday is part of the colorful story of Denison, Texas, but it was another doctor who gave the town a lasting place in American history: Dr. Lawrence Augustine Washington Jr., who left his medical practice in Virginia to settle in Denison is its infant years. Dr. Washington was the great-nephew of that most famous of all Americans, General George Washington. When George's younger brother Samuel died (like Doc Holliday, of consumption) a few months after the decisive Battle of Yorktown, General Washington took over guardianship of Samuel's children, raising them in his home at Mount Vernon and sending them to the College of Philadelphia. As George Washington had no children of his own, he willed to his brother Samuel's oldest son, Lawrence, the sword and suit of clothing worn at the first presidential inauguration, items then willed to Lawrence's oldest son, Lawrence Augustine Washington Jr., who took them with him to Texas. In 1874, the editor of the *Denison Daily News* told of visiting Dr. Lawrence Washington Jr.'s home and seeing a packet of letters that George Washington had written to his brother, Samuel; a sword once carried by the first president; and a suit of clothes of dark brown "repp" silk worn by General Washington. The Denison reporter got one thing wrong in his story: the brown suit was not repp silk (a term for a fabric with a raised weave), but a domestic broadcloth shrunk and napped to resemble velvet, manufactured in Hartford, Connecticut, and proudly worn by President Washington at his first inauguration as a symbol of his hope for the development of American manufactures. After Dr. Lawrence Washington Jr.'s death in 1882, his widow sold the items to the Washington Association of New Jersey for display at Washington's Headquarters. She wrote: "My husband . . . always told me and our children that his father told him General Washington in person gave him the suit, etc., when he was living at Mount Vernon because of their being worn on the day of his inauguration, and that they have never been out of the possession of the Washington family." The suit and sword that resided in Denison during Doc Holliday's Texas years are now displayed in the museum at George Washington's Mount Vernon.

"CHAMPAGNE CHARLIE" AUSTIN

In the New Year's Day 1874 shooting affray in Dallas, Dr. Holliday's opponent was a bartender named Charlie Austin who, according to an advertisement in the *Dallas Daily Commercial* of August 12, was known as "Champagne Charlie . . . a rollicking fellow . . . who fixes up the 'smiles' and hands them out smilingly."

It was a common nickname for a bartender, taken from a popular song of the time, "Champagne Charlie," by English music hall star George Leybourne, who also wrote "The Daring Young Man on the Flying Trapeze." Leybourne's songs crossed the pond and became huge successes on the American variety theater circuit, with lyrics that appealed to the saloon crowd. In the first verse of "Champagne Charlie," the "P.R.F.G.

game" meant "Private Room for Gentlemen"—a secluded spot where a sporting man and a saloon girl could entertain themselves away from the public eye. No doubt Doc Holliday found Dallas's "Champagne Charlie" to be a little less friendly than the chap in the song:

I've seen a deal of gaiety throughout my noisy life
With all my grand accomplishments I never could
   get a wife
The thing I most excel in is the P.R.F.G. game
A noise at night, in bed all day, and swimming in
   Champagne.
Champagne Charlie is my name
Champagne drinking is my game
Good for any game at night my boys
For Champagne Charlie is my name
Who'll come and join me in a spree?

Courtesy of Lester S. Levy Collection of Sheet Music, Sheridan Libraries, Johns Hopkins University.

BUFFALO SOLDIERS

The military post of Fort Griffin, Texas, was home to soldiers of the 10th Cavalry Regiment of the US Army—the
famed African American "Buffalo Soldiers." The nickname
was given by the Comanche and Apache, who thought the
tightly curled hair of the black soldiers resembled the curly
hair on a bison's face. As the bison was revered by the Indians, the nickname was considered a term of respect, and
the Buffalo Soldiers proudly featured a bison on their regi-
mental crest. The proud black troops built and renovated
dozens of forts, strung thousands of miles of telegraph
lines, and escorted wagon trains, stagecoaches, railroad
trains, cattle herds, railroad crews, and surveying parties.
They opened new roads and mapped vast areas of the West,
recovered thousands of head of stolen livestock, brought
dozens of horse thieves to justice, and pursued Indian raiders. In twenty-four years of active service, the Buffalo Soldiers earned twenty-three Medals of Honor and numerous

*Shield of the US Army 10th
Cavalry "Buffalo Soldiers."
Courtesy The Institute of
Heraldry and the Army
Trademark Licensing Office.*

commendations. But there was sometimes friction and violence between the black
troops and civilians in Texas, which had been a slave-holding state during the war,
and under federal occupation during Reconstruction any face in a hated blue uniform
was resented, especially a black face. If Private Jake Smith, a Buffalo Soldier shot and
killed at Fort Griffin, was the same soldier Bat Masterson had accused Doc Holliday
of shooting, it would be Doc's second episode of racial violence—perhaps a vestige of
his family's slave-holding heritage.

THE RAILROAD RAG

When the Missouri, Kansas & Texas Railroad (the Katy) built on from Denison to
Houston, its joint ownership of the Galveston, Houston & Henderson Railroad gave
it immediate access to the Port of Galveston and its ocean-going shipping on the Gulf
of Mexico. To promote the new route, the Katy's agent William Crush, noting how
many spectators showed up at train wrecks, decided to stage a planned train wreck
and invite the public. Drawn by months of advertising on posters spread across northern Texas, a crowd of forty thousand gathered on September 15, 1896, on an empty

"Crush, Texas Before," The Texas Collection, Baylor University, Waco, Texas.

stretch of land named for the day "Crush, Texas" to watch the collision. The two steam engines, painted red and green and towing cars filled with railroad ties, touched noses, then each backed up a mile or so, the crews jumping out after setting the trains at full throttle. The ninety-mph collision (each train was traveling at forty-five mph) was spectacular, as promised— both boilers exploded and three spectators were killed while many more were injured from debris, including the photographer for the event who lost an eye from a flying bolt. Although agent William Crush was fired that evening, he was rehired the following day, having clearly accomplished his goal of drawing attention for the railroad. Famed ragtime composer and pianist Scott Joplin, who was performing in the area at the time, commemorated the event in his song "The Great Crush Collision March," which musically reenacts the crashing of the locomotives.

8

DENVER & KANSAS PACIFIC

For most Western towns, the railroads brought a boom. For frontier Denver, the railroads almost brought doom, when the Union Pacific, building west from Kansas in 1866, platted its terminus at Cheyenne, Wyoming, clipping the northern edge of the Colorado Territory and missing Denver by a hundred miles. Business soon followed the rails, as half of Denver packed up and moved north to Cheyenne, leaving Denver a city "too dead to bury."[1] But the remaining citizens decided to fight back, forming a Board of Trade to build their own railroad, the Denver Pacific Railway, to head north and meet up with the Union Pacific in Cheyenne. Then Denver's neighboring city of Golden—at the time, the territorial capital—organized its own railroad, the Colorado, Clear Creek & Pacific Railway to beat the Denver Pacific to Cheyenne, and the race to become the transportation hub of the Colorado Territory was on. After two years of struggles, the Denver road had won more investors, along with the backing of the US Congress, and in June 1870 completed the first northern route to Cheyenne. Two months later, the Kansas Pacific Railroad completed an east-west line to Denver, connecting with the Denver Pacific and assuring the central role of Denver in Colorado transportation and commerce. By 1876, Denver had four railroads and four depots, and had become the "Queen City of the Plains" and the capital of the new State of Colorado—which had almost been named the State of Centennial in honor of America's one hundredth birthday.

Doc Holliday had a new name that year, as well, borrowing Tom McKey from his favorite uncle back home for his new career as a Denver City card dealer. The fact that he used an alias in Denver lends credence to Bat Masterson's story of his shooting a soldier in Texas and making a fast exit from that state. Until he was sure the army wasn't looking for him, being Tom McKey was a safer bet, and working in a gambling house was a logical career choice for a gambling dentist who had left his tools and equipment behind. So, he took a job as a faro dealer at John Babb's variety house on Blake Street, and rented a room above Long John's Saloon a few doors away.

An 1870s-era photograph of Babb's place shows an elegant two-story brick building with French doors, arch-topped windows, and a graceful balcony. In front of the building, a group of men gaze casually back at the photographer, most of them wearing vested suits and boots and one man sporting a black top hat. As a dealer for the house, Tom McKey surely dressed in similar genteel fashion, though even properly attired and gainfully employed, he couldn't stay out of trouble for long. As the *Denver Republican* later reported, "One night he electrified the town by nearly cutting off the head of Bud Ryan, a well-known Denver gambler."[2]

Bat Masterson later gave his own version of the incident:

> *While Denver, in many respects in those days was a rough and ready town, it nevertheless enforced to the very letter the ordinance against the carrying of fire arms, and Holliday, for the nonce becoming prudent, put his canister aside, but straightway went and bought himself a murderous looking knife. Thus heeled, he did not long delay in getting into action, and in so doing, carved up the face and neck of one Bud Ryan.*[3]

The unlucky Bud Ryan was still living in Denver years later when the 1890 census recorded his name and address, and still carried the scars of the knife fight with Tom McKey. And according to members of the McKey family, the "murderous looking knife" was likely the Hell Bitch, the homemade blade that Doc's uncles had carried during the Civil War and that disappeared with him when he went west. But as in Dallas, no record remains of what caused the affray, so we don't know if Tom McKey was in the right or in the wrong, though as Bat mused:

> *Holliday seemed to be absolutely unable to keep out of trouble for any great length of time. He would no sooner be out of one scrape before he was in another, and the strange part of it was he was more often in the right than in the wrong, which has rarely ever been the case with a man who was continually getting himself into trouble.*[4]

The Bud Ryan trouble put an end to his quiet refuge in Colorado, so although the dry mountain air was bracing and the view inspiring, he was soon on the road again, leaving his alias of Tom McKey behind and leaving unclaimed letters for T. S. McKey at the Denver post office.[5]

According to one Holliday family historian, he next bought a ticket on the Kansas Pacific Railroad and headed east. A hundred miles or so before Kansas City, he got off the train and made a side trip to the little farm town of Laclede, where his Aunt Annaleeza Holliday McCoin was living with her family.[6] "Annaleezie" was his father's youngest sister, only twelve years older than John Henry himself and more like a cousin than an aunt. She'd been a young mother when the Civil War began and was a young widow after, then had remarried and moved to Kansas with her family, looking for a new life and a fresh start—something John Henry understood too well. And being so far from Georgia, she surely enjoyed an unexpected visit from her nephew on his way back from Denver to Dallas and shared what news she had from home, including his father's plan to run for mayor of Valdosta in the next election.

If John Henry shared much of his own news, Annaleezie didn't pass on the stories. And why should he worry the family with sordid tales of gambling arrests and shootings and a knife fight with Bud Ryan? As far as his aunt knew he was simply traveling for his health, having taken in the dry air of Colorado before going back to his busy professional life in Dallas.

DENVER'S PALACE

> *I dealt cards for Charley Foster in Babb's House, where Ed Chase's place is now.*
> —Doc Holliday

The king of gambling in Centennial Denver was Big Ed Chase, who opened his first saloon when the city was still a frontier town, bringing Denver's first billiard table across the plains by oxen. His business flourished, with the Arcadia Club, the Cricket Club, and the Progressive offering gambling, liquor, and variety acts. Ed Chase's biggest competitor was also his friend John A. Babb, who owned the Canterbury Hall on Blake Street. The Canterbury was popular with the sporting class but had a bad reputation with the law, as John Babb didn't always bother to get the proper licenses for operating a saloon and keeping a dance hall, and added to his crimes by using female waiters and allowing gaming in the same room with the drinking. The Denver papers of 1875 were filled with reports of Babb's days in court, and by December he'd given up on Denver and taken the train north to Cheyenne where the *Cheyenne News* gave him a tongue-in-cheek welcome: "Mr. Babb is well known as a theatrical manager and a gentleman of high moral standing."[7] But having let the dust in Denver settle a bit, Babb returned to

Palace Variety Theater. Denver Public Library, Western History Collection (X-24703).

the city in early 1876 to reopen his Canterbury Hall as the Theatre Comique, a tony varieties house with Charley Foster running the gaming room and a young Georgian named Tom McKey dealing faro. John Babb eventually sold the Theatre Comique to his friend Ed Chase, who reimagined it as the Palace Theater, making it a centerpiece of the sporting community. In addition to its 750-seat theater with private boxes where beer was sold for $1 a bottle, there was a gaming room with space for two hundred players and twenty-five dealers, a well-stocked bar behind a sixty-five-foot mirror, and a midnight lunch of roast beef, pork, venison, antelope cutlets, breast of prairie chicken, wild turkey, quail, salads, and sandwiches. Although the Palace Theater declined in the twentieth century and was replaced by a nondescript business building in the shadows of the Coors' Field Baseball Stadium, the property's history was remembered in the twenty-first century in the naming of the new Palace Lofts, a luxury condo complex with units going for a million dollars and more. Ed Chase, John Babb, and Doc Holliday—alias Tom McKey—would have called that a winning wager.

BUCKING THE TIGER

Dr. John Henry Holliday left more than his name in Texas—he left his career, as well. Living under the alias Tom McKey, without his real name and title, he couldn't practice dentistry and had to find another profession to pay his room and board in Denver. Luckily, his skills at the card table suggested another source of regular income: as a faro dealer at John Babb's Comique Theater.

Faro was descended from the late seventeenth-century French card game called pharaon in which several players made bets against the "bank." The game was easy to learn, fast action (a round took only ten to fifteen minutes), offered better odds than most other card games—and became wildly popular in the American West. Playing faro was called "bucking the tiger" because early card decks featured a drawing of a Bengal tiger on the back. "Tiger Town" was a common nickname for city gambling districts, and smaller towns had "tiger alleys." A picture of a tiger hanging in a saloon window showed that faro was played there.

Although the game looked elaborate, with its own green baize playing table that displayed a deck of cards called a "layout," the play proceeded simply. Players, called "punters," placed a chip on which layout card they thought would be pulled next from the dealer's card box, called a "shoe."

"Faro Game at Bisbee, Arizona" by Camillus Fly (c. 1900). National Archives.

Once all bets were down, the dealer pulled two cards from the shoe, the first laid to the right of the box for the bank, the next laid to the left of the box for the players. If a punter's bet matched the player's card pulled, he won even odds. If a punter's bet matched the dealer's card, the bank won the bet. If a bet neither won nor lost, it could remain on the table for the next draw from the dealer's box. To keep track of which cards had been played and theoretically give the player a better chance of making a good bet, a "casekeeper" kept tally on an abacus-like device. There were ways for a player to alter a bet for better odds: placing the chip on a particular spot on a card, or "coppering" the bet by placing a copper token on it to reverse the original bet. But the game remained simple: bet on the cards, see which cards come up next. And like all banking games, faro could be rigged for the house. *Hoyle's Rules of the Games* began the faro section warning that no honest faro bank could be found in the United States, and prosecutions of crooked faro bank cases went all the way to the US Supreme Court.

For Tom McKey, as an employee of the house, artful cheating was an important job skill. He needed to keep the customers winning enough to keep them coming back, while keeping the games profitable for the house. There were several standard ploys, including using stacked decks with extra pairs of cards, rigged decks with textured cards that let the dealer arrange cards while appearing to be shuffling, and rigged dealing boxes with windows or prisms that allowed the dealer to see the cards coming up next.

In concert with all of these, a good dealer could use a little sleight of hand to switch cards or even move a punter's bet on the layout. Tom McKey would later use the lessons he learned in Denver when, as Doc Holliday, he opened his own faro bank in Tombstone.

LOCOMOTIVE MAN

Doc Holliday was a Southern man from a slave-holding family, but his ideas of the world were challenged when he went west and met black men in positions of authority and power—like Mr. Barney Ford, millionaire owner of the Inter-Ocean Hotels, the finest hotels in Cheyenne and Centennial Denver.

Barney L. Ford, 1885–1895. Photo by Walter H. Foreman. History Colorado, (95.200.183).

Born into slavery on a Virginia plantation in 1822, Barney grew up working in the tobacco fields and dreaming of freedom. But freedom was just a dream, until his master sold him to a hog farmer in Georgia, who hired him out to a Mississippi riverboat, and Barney jumped ship at Quincy, Illinois, taking the Underground Railroad to Chicago.

He was twenty-six years old when he started life as a free man with no surname—slaves didn't need them, being considered property instead of people—so his first task was to choose a name for himself. Near the house where he was staying in Chicago was the Baldwin Locomotive Company, which had just unveiled its newest engine, the Lancelot Ford. Barney liked the idea of naming himself after something that was going places like that locomotive engine, so the slave boy named Barney became a man named Mr. Barney Lancelot Ford.

In 1849, he followed the gold rush to California, sailing from New York to the Nicaragua crossing before taking sick in the jungles. Too ill to travel on, he stayed in Panama and opened a hotel for other travelers. When Nicaragua rescinded its anti-slave laws, he went back to Chicago, where he heard about the gold strikes in Colorado and headed west again. He prospected the diggings around Central City and was rumored to have found a promising strike, until a band of armed white miners informed him that territorial law didn't allow a black man to file a mine claim. But Barney knew there were other ways to make it rich in a gold rush. Denver was in its first boom and almost

16th St. Inter-Ocean. Courtesy Denver Public Library, Western History Collection (X-18608).

every kind of business was turning an easy profit. Barney started out by opening a barbershop, then took the money he made from that to open a restaurant, and when the restaurant proved a success, he turned his money around again and used his experience in Nicaragua to open a string of hotels, culminating with the elegant Inter-Ocean Hotel.

When Colorado first sought statehood in 1865, Barney went to Washington, D.C., to lobby against its admission, as Colorado did not yet allow African Americans to vote, then he worked to help pass the Fifteenth Amendment to the Constitution, giving all men the right to vote. When the Amendment was ratified, Barney threw his support to Colorado's statehood. The state now honors Barney Ford's accomplishments with a stained-glass window at the state capitol and a hill near the former mining camp of Breckenridge called Barney Ford Hill—the place where his first mining claim was stolen away now gives him a permanent claim to Colorado's gold country.

PINKERTON'S DETECTIVES

It's an iconic image of the Wild West: a daring train robbery by masked bandits, and a doggedly determined chase by Pinkerton's detectives. And according to one family story, the Pinkerton's once trailed Doc Holliday, as well.

The Pinkerton's National Detective Agency was founded in 1850 by Scotsman Allan Pinkerton, who'd started his law enforcement career by stumbling on the lair of a gang of Chicago

Pinkerton's Detective Agency logo. Library of Congress.

counterfeiters, leading to their arrest. The resulting celebrity won him an appointment as a deputy sheriff and then special agent for the US Post Office and led to the formation of his own agency hired to protect President-elect Abraham Lincoln during his trip to Washington for his first inaugural. During the Civil War, Pinkerton served as chief of intelligence for Union General George McClellan. The agency continued to grow, and in 1874 the Adams Express Company hired Pinkerton's to find train robbers Frank and Jesse James and bring them to justice. But instead of arresting the James brothers, the detective assigned to the case was murdered, and Pinkerton wrote, "There is no use talking, they must die."[8] In January 1875, a group of Pinkerton's detectives and sympathetic locals raided the James farm in Kearney, Missouri, and tossed a fire bomb into the kitchen of the farmhouse. The explosion wounded the mother, Zerelda James, so badly that the lower portion of her right arm had to be amputated, and killed her eight-year-old son, Archie. The debacle changed public opinion across the country to side with the James Gang and turn against the detectives, and Pinkerton gave up the chase.

It may have been during that time of public disaffection that the Pinkerton's took on a smaller case: finding the man who killed a black buffalo soldier in a Texas military post town. According to Mattie Holliday's niece, the late Regina Rapier of Social Circle, Georgia, the Pinkerton's detectives paid a call on the Holliday family home in Atlanta, looking for information on their cousin John Henry Holliday—in particular, a photograph to help in their investigation. Mattie had a photograph of John Henry, the one he'd had made in Philadelphia while he was in dental school there, but she wasn't about to let the Pinkerton's have it. So, while Mattie was talking with the detectives, her clever sister Lucy quietly took the photograph and hid it down the laces of her corset where they were not likely to look. The Pinkerton's never got the photo or their man, and John Henry Holliday was free to leave his alias of Tom McKey behind and return to his professional life in Texas.

9

TEXAS & PACIFIC

After a season on the run as Tom McKey, faro dealer in a Denver, Colorado, variety house, Dr. John Henry Holliday arrived back in Dallas, Texas, in January 1877 with another chance to walk "the paths of rectitude" and return to a life of respectability. But if that was his plan, he got off on the wrong foot. Within weeks of his return he was in trouble with the law again, arrested on three counts of gambling.[1]

Dallas may not have wanted a gambling dentist, but there were other towns less judgmental of a man's recreations. After doing his day in court, Dr. Holliday bought a ticket on the Texas & Pacific Railroad for a ride on its newly completed extension from Dallas to Fort Worth, then took a stage the rest of the way to the town of Breckenridge, Texas, celebrating its first birthday and the Fourth of July with fireworks and picnics and wide-open poker games.

Breckenridge was mostly mesquite with a couple of saloons and gambling halls, a small hotel, a general store, and a Law & Land office. The Independence Day picnic and fireworks were held in the empty lot set aside for the not-yet-built county courthouse. The poker, along with all the usual games of chance, occupied the Court Saloon. And amid the celebrations, Dr. Holliday got into a saloon fight with a card dealer named Henry Kahn. Holliday's weapon of choice this time was a walking stick—a fashionable gold-headed cane, dangerous but not deadly. As in his other altercations, no record remains of what caused the fight, but we know what happened after: Both men were hauled into court and fined for the disturbance, and Kahn took his revenge by pulling a pistol and shooting Holliday. According to the *Dallas Daily Herald* of July 7, 1877: "Our reporter was told in Fort Worth yesterday that a young man named Doc Holliday, well known in this city, was shot and killed at Breckenridge last Wednesday."

As Mark Twain said of himself, "The stories of my death have been greatly exaggerated," and so were the reports of Holliday's death. He wasn't dead, but he was seriously wounded, enough to bring his cousin George Henry Holliday from Atlanta to care for him. As noted in the *Fort Worth Democrat* of July 21, George Holliday arrived in Fort Worth on the Texas & Pacific and checked into the Transcontinental Hotel, where he stayed with the still-healing John Henry and tried to convince him to return to Georgia. But "Doc Holliday," as the papers called him, was now a confirmed sporting man, and once he was well enough to take care of himself again, he sent George home alone and went back to Dallas. He may have been giving the town one last try, or just packing up his dental equipment before finally moving on, but his last legal record in Dallas was one more gambling arrest, and that was the end of his career as a Dallas dentist.[2]

But he wasn't giving up on life just yet. He would struggle, he would fight, and he would survive as long as the consumption would let him. And having played his last hand in Dallas, he soon found another locale with more promise: Fort Griffin on the Brazos River, where he'd been arrested two years before. In his time away the town had grown into a gambler's paradise as the central supply stop on the Dodge City cattle trail. The military post on the bluff was still in service, but the soldiers were busy chasing Comanches and didn't bother the denizens of the Flat down below. The local law was Shackelford County Sheriff John Larn, a cattleman suspected of hiring rustlers to supply his own ranch with stolen cattle. The social scene was hosted by a lady gambler named Lottie Deno and an Irish saloon-keep named Johnny Shaughnessey.

As the register of Fort Griffin's Occidental Hotel for September 14, 1877, recorded, J. H. Holliday took a room and promptly opened a bar tab at the hotel's restaurant. His first week at the hotel cost him $20 for room and board and another $120 for liquor. So not only was he now a confirmed gambler, he seemed on his way to becoming an alcoholic, as well, drowning his troubles in more trouble. According to one Fort Griffin resident:

> *This fellow Holliday was a consumptive and a hard drinker, but neither liquor nor the bugs seemed to faze him. He could at times be the most genteel, affable chap you ever saw, and at other times he was sour and surly, and would just as soon cut your throat with a villainous looking knife he always carried, or shoot you with a .42-calibre double-barreled derringer he always kept in his vest pocket.[3]*

It may have been during one of his more genial moments that he renewed an acquaintance with a woman from his past—Kate Fisher, the actress from St. Louis, now working as a Fort Griffin dance hall girl named Kate Elder. How they met again isn't recorded, but Kate did note where they went from there: They left Fort Griffin together and took the stage roads into West Texas, stopping "at every place where there was money to be made at his profession." So, Doc Holliday hadn't given up on dentistry, he just found a new place to practice. According to Kate, at Eagle Pass on the Rio Grande he crossed over the river into the Mexican military post town of Piedras Negras and offered his services to the commandant:

> The commandante told Doc he would arrange quarters for him to practice in, and asked him to report next morning at 10 a.m. We remained at Eagle Pass for more than three months, and Doc went across the river every morning . . . the commanding officer would not accept anything in the way of rent for the office Doc had occupied.[4]

They made their home in Eagle Pass at the National Hotel while Doc spent his evenings gambling at Blue Vivian's saloon, according to a story passed down through the Vivian family.[5] But after wintering on the border Doc and Kate were ready to move on again, from Eagle Pass to San Antonio, Brackettville, Jacksboro, and back to Fort Griffin—all places where a gambling dentist was more welcomed than in Dallas.

Although the iconic Doc Holliday is a dark and brooding man with a long mustache, he's described differently by buffalo hunter Sam Baldwin, who knew him during his Fort Griffin days. "He was a tall, slim fellow; was a dentist by trade and had a Southern drawl. His hair was almost red and he was blue-eyed. Didn't have a mustache." Sam wasn't charmed by the drawl, however, saying he had "kind of a whining voice."[6]

Another Fort Griffin resident that spring of 1878 found Holliday to be better company. Wyatt Earp was a lawman from Dodge City who was spending the quiet winter months working as a detective chasing after stolen cattle. In January he visited Fort Worth, where he got involved in a saloon altercation, then moved on to Fort Clark. By the time he landed in Fort Griffin he'd lost the trail of the stolen cattle. As the story goes, Earp was in Johnny Shaughnessy's saloon looking for someone who might know the lay of land and may have heard something of the missing cattle. Shaughnessy called to a young man in the card room and introduced him as Doc Holliday, who played cards with all sorts and might have some information to share. And that simple meeting was the beginning of a legendary friendship. Although Doc couldn't lead Wyatt to the cattle, he did have questions of his own about Dodge City, the most famous of the Kansas cowtowns.

Several stories have been told about why Doc Holliday left Fort Griffin that year—the most dramatic being a knife fight with a gambler named Ed Bailey whom Holliday killed over a disputed poker hand. According to the story, Doc was quickly arrested and put in a temporary jail cell in Fort Griffin's new Planter's Hotel, where Kate helped him to escape by lighting a fire in the woodpile out back, distracting the jailor. But as Kate later wrote, "It reads fine, but there is not a word of truth in that fairy story."[7] Nor is there any historical proof to the story: no reported fire behind the Planter's Hotel, no arrest record or warrant for Doc Holliday in a Fort Griffin knife fight, and no bloodied Ed Bailey anywhere to be found. More likely, the Ed Bailey knifing was the invention of a San Francisco newspaper reporter who first broke the story after doing an interview with Wyatt Earp years later.[8] And it may have been that fictionalized history that Wyatt was thinking of when he said, "After Holliday died, I gave a San Francisco newspaper reporter a short sketch of his life. Apparently, the reporter was not satisfied. The sketch appeared in print with a lot of things added that never existed outside the reporter's imagination."[9]

But even without the Ed Bailey affair, there was plenty of drama in Doc Holliday's life—and his next stop would take him to Dodge City, and into legend.

FAMILY BUSINESS

When George Henry Holliday went to Texas to see his wounded cousin John Henry, he had to take some time off from the family business: the Atlanta Dental Depot, owned together with his brother, Robert Holliday. The company supplied tools and equipment to dentists—a field the brothers understood well, as Robert was also a practicing dentist, having followed Cousin John Henry to the Pennsylvania College of Dental Surgery. Robert graduated from the school in 1874 before entering practice in Atlanta and had originally planned to serve his preceptorship with his cousin John Henry until Doc's life took unexpected turns. Later, Dr. Robert Holliday helped to found the first dental school in Georgia and the Tulane University Dental School in New Orleans.

▷ESTABLISHED 1858.◁

Only Dental Depot in the C'ty.

HOLLIDAY BROTHERS,

ATLANTA DENTAL DEPOT,

28 Whitehall st., Atlanta, Ga.   P. O. Box 304.

Holliday Brothers Dental Depot advertisement in The Atlanta Constitution, *Atlanta, Georgia, October 2, 1887, page 12. Author's Collection.*

The Atlanta Dental Depot was renamed the Atlanta Dental Supply Company, with George's son George Henry Holliday Jr. becoming President, and George Jr.'s son, Dr. Franklin Caldwell Holliday, also becoming a respected Atlanta dentist. Today, Atlanta Dental remains a major supplier to dentists around the South and the Holliday family dental tradition continues with Dr. Tammy Bailey, the great-great granddaughter of Dr. Robert Holliday, and cousin to the original Doc Holliday, DDS.

Amanda Blake as "Miss Kitty," a character modeled after Lottie Deno, with Milburn Stone as "Doc" in the TV Western *Gunsmoke. Archive PL/Alamy Stock Photo (Image #KKHTM).*

LOTTIE DENO, LADY GAMBLER

One of the most colorful characters of Fort Griffin, Texas, while Doc Holliday was in town was the lady gambler known as Lottie Deno. Born Carlotta "Lottie" Thompkins in Warsaw, Kentucky, in 1844, she'd left home after her family fell on hard times during the Civil War, taking up with a gambler who worked the riverboats on the Ohio and Mississippi rivers. At nineteen years of age, she split from the gambler and headed for San Antonio, Texas, where she met and fell in love with gambler Frank Thurmond, with whom she had a long on-again off-again relationship.

During one of the off times, she moved alone to Fort Griffin, where local lawman John Jacobs remembered her as being "on the portly side, a fine looker, and in manners a typical Southern Lady, but she didn't always live up to her appearance."[10] Jacobs was being diplomatic in his comments. In addition to playing cards, Lottie ran a bordello, being fined $100 for Maintaining a Disorderly House and paying $65 for legal representation.[11] The real ladies in town called her "wicked," a polite way of saying "whore."

A Fort Griffin legend involves Lottie Deno with another wicked lady, Doc Holliday's mistress, Kate Elder. According to the story, Doc and Lottie were in the middle of a poker game when Kate showed up, accusing Lottie of stealing her man. Angry words flew and Doc had to put himself between the two women to keep them from doing violence to one another.[12] If there is any truth to the story, it may be that incident that Kate later described to a friend: "I went in once to see where he was with another woman. I had a big knife with me and said I'd rip her open. Doc came away from her."[13]

The incident may have happened in Johnny Shaughnessey's saloon, where Lottie did most of her gambling and where Doc Holliday met Wyatt Earp. Lottie had been Shaughnessey's mistress before a young man named Johnny Golden came to town. Golden was ten years younger than Lottie, the black sheep of a rich Boston family, and when she turned her affections his way, Johnny Shaughnessey paid the town marshal $250 to have his rival "removed" from Fort Griffin. The marshal brought a charge of horse theft against Golden, who denied the accusation, then hauled him away to the military guardhouse at the fort. Along the way, someone shot Johnny Golden in the back, leaving his body in the wagon yard of Hank Smith's Occidental Hotel, where Doc Holliday had stayed when he first arrived in town. Blaming herself for the killing, Lottie spent a month alone in her shanty by the Brazos River before leaving Fort Griffin on the stage to Jacksboro. A few months later, Shaughnessey also left town.

Lottie eventually reconciled with her former flame Frank Thurmond and moved with him to New Mexico, where they operated gaming rooms and restaurants and married in Silver City on December 2, 1880. They made their new home in the railroad town of Deming, where Frank went into mining and land sales, becoming a bank president, and Lottie got religion and became a founding member of St. Luke's Episcopal Church of Deming, proof that even the wickedest of women could change for the better.

THE FORT GRIFFIN GANG

Doc Holliday would remember that the troublesome cowboys of southern Arizona had been troublemakers in Texas, as well. As he later told a Denver newspaper: "The Tombstone Rustlers are part of this Fort Griffin gang."[14]

The gang Doc referred to was a cattle rustling ring run by, of all people, the sheriff of Shackleford County, Texas, John Larn. Like Doc Holliday, John Larn was a Southerner, born in Mobile, Alabama. But it was a move to Colorado that set him on a deadly trail, when he took a job on a cattle ranch and shot the owner to death in an argument. Fleeing to New Mexico, Larn reportedly shot a sheriff he thought was trailing him, before he landed in the Texas town

Thought to be a portrait of Sheriff John Larn. Courtesy Robert K. DeArment.

of Fort Griffin, where he took a job working for rancher Bill Hays. Larn's troubles seemed to be behind him when he married the daughter of a prominent ranching family, then served with the local vigilance committee hunting down cattle rustlers and won election as sheriff of newly made Shackleford County. But when he entered into a deal to supply the local garrison with three beeves a day, folks began to suspect that the sheriff was up to something. While Larn filled his contract with the garrison without losing any cattle out of his own herd, his neighbors' herds kept getting smaller. Soon, it was clear that the sheriff of Shackleford County was also the head of a rustling ring, stealing from his constituents and selling rebranded cattle to the military. Local stories say the men who worked for him included the likes of Johnny Ringo, Pony Deahl, and one "Curly," who may have been Curly Bill Brocious. The rustling came to a sudden end when the sheriff was arrested, though he never made it to trial—the old vigilance committee that had been the law before the real law arrived in that part of Texas raided Larn's jail cell and shot him dead. As for Ringo, Deahl, and Curly Bill, they disappeared from Fort Griffin—and showed up again in Tombstone, Arizona, where they rustled cattle and lent their support to another crooked lawman: Cochise County Sheriff Johnny Behan.

Mary Catherine Cummings.
Courtesy of the Sharlot Hall
Museum and Library and Archives,
C-230-Item 3, Folder1, Box 7.

THE MEMOIRS OF KATE ELDER

Doc Holliday's mistress Kate Elder was an old woman living at the Pioneers Home in Prescott, Arizona, as Mary Cummings when she began sharing her memories, and they weren't always reliable—and adding to her memory lapses, she had an agenda, as well. Newspaper reporter Anton Mazzanovich had sent her a copy of Stuart Lake's 1931 novelized biography *Wyatt Earp: Frontier Marshal* and she was incensed by its portrayal of her life, especially the story of Doc Holliday knifing Ed Bailey in a Fort Griffin saloon. To refute Lake's book, she wrote Mazzanovich a long letter detailing her life with Doc Holliday, including her unique observations on events at Tombstone. She may have left some things out and gotten dates confused, but she sure had a lot to say. The reporter went on to publish selections from the letter in a series of columns in the Bisbee, Arizona, *Brewery Gulch Gazette* in April and June 1932. Mazzanovich talked of plans to publish what he termed her "memoir" in some other form as well, letting her words speak for themselves, but died before the project was published. After Mazzanovich's death, author Joseph Chisholm gained access to Kate's correspondence and visited with her to "verify the data" as he put it, then included it in his unpublished manuscript *Tombstone's Tale*, saying, "it required no editing for the lady is well-educated and intelligent." Kate, however, decided against Chisholm using the material in the hopes that some publisher might pay her for her words. So, in the fall of 1935, she had a friend, Mrs. W. J. Martin of Prescott, contact Arthur W. Bork, a graduate student at the University of Arizona, to ask his assistance in preparing a manuscript based on her reminiscences. Mrs. Martin had spent four years helping Kate work on the project but knew that it needed a more trained writer to make it salable. On Thanksgiving Day, Arthur Bork joined Mrs. Martin to begin interviewing Kate for additional information, and Bork's wife typed the manuscript. For the next three years, Bork tried unsuccessfully to find a publisher for the material, and in 1940, Kate wrote another account of her life in a letter to her niece Lillian Raffert. There were now three Kate Elder memoirs written for three different purposes: the Mazzanovich correspondence to refute Lake, the Bork manuscript to find publication, and the Raffert letter to give a more sanitized version of her life to her niece. Because they were intended for three different audiences, the memoirs had substantive and sometimes contradictory differences that made many historians doubt the truth of any of them, and for thirty years they remained unpublished. Then in 1977, *Arizona and the West* magazine published an article based on portions of the Bork manuscript and notes and the Raffert letter, with editorial commentary and additional information by author Glenn Boyer. Unfortunately, Boyer also added some fictional elements to the history, tainting the facts and further confusing Kate's already complicated memoirs. Historian Anne Collier's solidly researched paper "Big Nose Kate—Mary Catherine Cummings: Same Person, Different Lives" in the October 2012 *Journal of the Wild West History Association* corrected Boyer's fictions and added newly discovered biographical information to Kate's story. But the memoirs themselves—Kate's life in her own words—remain unpublished.

10

ATCHISON, TOPEKA & SANTA FE

Fort Dodge, Kansas, was established to guard wagon trains traveling on the Santa Fe Trail, and Dodge City grew up in its shadow as a supply station, with the first business in town a tent saloon to serve the soldiers at the fort. When buffalo hunters found the place, Dodge City began to grow, and when the Western Cattle Trail met the newly laid tracks of the Atchison, Topeka & Santa Fe Railway, Dodge City boomed. Mountains of buffalo hides piled up beside the railroad tracks, waiting for shipment east; mounds of buffalo bones dried in the sun waiting for eastern factories to turn them into bone china; hundreds of herds of Texas cattle arrived with thousands of trail-weary cowboys ready for rest and recreation. And Dodge City, the town born to serve booze, was happy to help out. Before long, papers in the east were calling Dodge the "Beautiful, Bibulous Babylon of the Plains"—*bibulous* coming from the Latin verb *bibere*, to drink. Which meant that Dodge City was one well-distilled town.

The most famous saloon in Dodge City was the Long Branch, named after the most famous breed of Texas cattle in homage to the Texas cowboys who crowded the bar. The saloon even had the "long branched" head of a Longhorn steer mounted over the bar. But although a six-piece orchestra played nightly, the real entertainment was the games. Like the dozen other Texas-themed saloons in town, the Long Branch hosted everything from dice and roulette to $1,000 poker games, making Dodge City just the sort of place that Doc Holliday would feel at home.

He and Kate Elder arrived in Dodge in the spring of 1878, just in time for the annual cattle drive, and took a room together at the Dodge House Hotel. On June 8, Doc placed an ad in the *Dodge City Times*:

J.H. Holliday, Dentist, very respectfully offers his professional services to the citizens of Dodge City and surrounding country during the summer. Office at room No. 24, Dodge House. Where satisfaction is not given money will be refunded.

Wyatt Earp had arrived back in Dodge soon after Doc got there and reclaimed his former job as assistant to City Marshal Charlie Bassett, and was soon busy arresting drunks and cowboys who carried their pistols with them over the "deadline," the boundary between the red light district south of the railroad tracks and the business district north of the tracks. Bat Masterson was in town, too, as the new sheriff of Ford County, and it was there that he first met Doc Holliday. As he later wrote of Doc during his time in Dodge:

> *He was slim of build and sallow of complexion, standing about five feet ten inches, and weighing no more than 130 pounds. His eyes were of a pale blue and his moustache was thin and of a sandy hue. Dodge City was then very much like Dallas and Denver, only a little more so, and the doctor did not express regret at having come. It was easily seen that he was not a healthy man for he not only looked the part, but he incessantly coughed it as well. During his year's stay at Dodge at that time, he did not have a quarrel with anyone, and, although regarded as sort of a grouch, he was not disliked by those with whom he became acquainted.*[1]

One of the Dodge City denizens who thought well of Doc was Vaudeville actor Eddie Foy, in town for the season and performing at the Comique Theater. When he wasn't on stage, Eddie got to the know the regulars—including Doc Holliday, whom he mentioned in a story about cowboys firing shots into the theater one hot summer night:

> *Everybody dropped to the floor at once, according to custom. Bat Masterson was just in the act of dealing a game of Spanish monte with Doc Holliday, and I was impressed by the instantaneous manner in which they flattened out like pancakes on the floor. I had thought I was pretty agile myself, but those fellows had me beaten by seconds at that trick. The firing kept up until it seemed to me that the assailants had put hundreds of shots through the building. . . . The marvelous part of the whole affair was that aside from a few harmless scratches and some perforated clothing, nobody in the dancehall was hurt.*[2]

The cowboys were not so lucky, with a drover named George Hoy caught in the crossfire between his cowboy friends and the Dodge City police officers and dying a month later of his wounds. And soon after that it would be Wyatt Earp taking fire and Doc Holliday coming to his aid, an event that made and sealed their friendship, according to Wyatt: "I am a friend of Doc Holliday because when I was city marshal of Dodge City, Kansas, he came to my rescue and saved my life when I was surrounded by desperadoes."[3]

Though Wyatt didn't state the particulars, it's likely that the incident occurred in September of that year, when the weather was cooling and the cattle season was winding down, but the Indian troubles were heating up. A thousand Cheyenne had broken away from the reservation at Fort Reno in the Indian Territory and were headed to the Dakotas by way of Kansas. The Cheyenne were led by the infamous Chief Dull Knife who was intent on returning his people to their ancestral lands no matter what stood in the way. The killing started soon after they crossed over the Kansas line, where two ranchers were murdered and left for the buzzards. In Comanche County, a gang of cowboys was shot down as they sat unarmed around their campfire. On the Salt Fork of the Cimarron River, a settler was shot in the neck, his wife was wounded, and their baby had a bullet put through its breast. In Meade County, a man's throat was slit from ear to ear. In Ford County, a man cooking breakfast for a cattle crew was butchered. Then just south of Dodge City, Dull Knife's band made a massacre, killing ten people and wounding five more, and slaughtering most of six hundred head of cattle.

The residents of Dodge City were in a terror, expecting to be overrun at any moment by bloodthirsty Cheyenne. And as the firehouse bell rang to call the citizens to arms, Mayor James H. "Dog" Kelley telegraphed the governor to send weapons, writing, "The country is filled with Indians."[4] By the morning of September 20, every farmer within thirty miles of Dodge had come into town for safety, and in response to Mayor Kelley's telegram, the adjutant general arrived with the first shipment of six thousand carbines and twenty thousand cartridges. His train was met by a mob of citizens and the Dodge City Silver Cornet Band, and the local paper reported: "The scene at the depot reminds us of rebellion times."[5]

With the cavalry from Fort Dodge called out to help quell the uprising and only nineteen men left at the fort to help defend the nearby town, Dodge City became an armed camp. Bawdy houses became shelters for the families of farmers that came into town for protection, and good citizens joined in with cowboys and gamblers to go out in support of the army. The Santa Fe Railway even outfitted a special locomotive to carry the civilian soldiers to suspected attack sites, with Dodge's assistant marshal, Wyatt Earp, leading a posse that rode the train to put out a range fire set by the Indians. So Doc Holliday was one of the only able-bodied men still left in town when Wyatt returned with some Indian prisoners, and Wyatt was the only lawman in town when cowboy boss Tobe Driskill and his drovers hit Dodge a short time later, expecting to find the place empty and open for the taking. Instead, they found Wyatt alone on Front Street near the Long Branch Saloon and threatened to shoot him on the spot. As the event was retold in *Wyatt Earp: Frontier Marshal*:

> It happened that Doc Holliday was seated at a monte table and glancing through the window he appraised the situation in an instant. Turning to Frank Loving, the dealer, he said, "Have you a six-shooter?" He handed his gun over to Holliday who sprang without hesitation through the doorway into the sidewalk, and throwing both guns down on the crowd, said, "throw up your hands!" This rather startled them and averted their attention. In an instant I had drawn my gun, and the arrest of the crowd followed. They were confined in Jail overnight and fined and released the following day. It was because of this episode that I became the friend of Doc Holliday ever after.[6]

Doc had finally made friends with the law, but it was time to move on. The Indian trouble made Kansas a less appealing country than it had once been, and the end of the cattle season meant fewer cowboys to play cards with. And the climate had not been good for his health—Dodge was a dusty city with all those cows tearing up the dirt, and his consumptive cough was troubling him. So, with Kate still along for the ride, Doc packed up and bought a pair of tickets on the Santa Fe Railroad, this time headed west to the clearer air of Colorado and the newest railroad boomtown of Trinidad.

The city lay in a narrow valley in the Sangre de Cristo Mountains of southeastern Colorado, where the Purgatoire River crossed the Santa Fe Trail. With the arrival of the Denver & Rio Grande Railroad in 1876 and the Atchison, Topeka & Santa Fe in 1878, Trinidad had become the major shipping point for most of New Mexico, Arizona, and west Texas. The town boasted a population of three thousand permanent residents, with eighty-three stores, three hotels, a daily newspaper and mail, and a red-light district that was the wonder of Colorado. Doc Holliday didn't wait long to add to the city's excitement.

According to Bat Masterson, who would later become marshal of Trinidad, soon after Doc's arrival he got into an altercation with a local sport by the name of Kid Colton, shooting and seriously wounding him. Although no legal record remains of either the incident or the victim, Bat claimed it was the Kid Colton shooting that made Doc move on again. Kate Elder, however, tells a much different story: "Doc was taken sick so we had to stay in Trinidad ten days. Then we had to hire an outfit to take us to Las Vegas, New Mexico. We traveled with a big freight outfit. The railroad was built only a few miles out from Trinidad. This was in November . . . and we arrived a few days before Christmas."[7]

Kate's spare writing doesn't do justice to the ordeal. With the railroad into New Mexico not yet complete, she and Doc traveled by covered wagon on the rutted Santa Fe Trail. South of Trinidad, the trail crossed over the treacherous Raton Pass, elevation 7,834 feet, with a grade so steep that wagons had to be tied down onto huge iron rings hammered into the mountainside to keep from careening out of control. The crossing averaged five days, the wagons crawling to the crest of the mountain and then crawling back down the other side. In the deep ravines below the road were the remnants of wagons that hadn't survived the crossing: wheels and axles and harness-trees smashed to pieces along Raton Creek. Beyond the pass, the road became easier, the mountain falling away into long plateaus with the green meadows of New Mexico lying ahead—except that Doc and Kate made the trip in the snowy late fall when the temperatures were frigid. Freight outfits stopped often to water and rest the horses, camping along the way, and the nights would have been cold and dangerous for a sick man. Doc and Kate surely welcomed one night of warmth in a real bed at Cimarron's St. James Hotel despite the noise from brawls and gunfights in the barroom below. And past Cimarron was the last landmark of the Santa Fe Trail, the massive stone uprising called Wagon Mound, looking like a carved prairie schooner with a canvas canopy blowing open in the wind. Then finally, the red adobe fortress of Fort Union, the end of the wagon train's trail.

As Kate's recollections don't give all the details of the journey, they also don't say why she chose to take Doc on such a harrowing adventure—the teamster who drove them remembered a man "in bad shape, and his 'woman friend,' who spoke with a 'German accent.'"[8] The answer lies in their final destination: not the old Spanish town of Las Vegas where the teamster delivered them, but the hot mineral springs up nearby Gallinas Canyon.

The Montezuma Hot Springs had been famous for a hundred years or more, named after the ancient Mexican king who supposedly took the healing waters there. The springs bubbled up out of the rocky bed of the Rio Gallinas, steaming and smelling of sulfur and drawing visitors from all over the country to come sit in the shallow pools carved by the water. *Milagro!* the Spanish-speaking locals called the miracle cures of the Montezuma Hot Springs, and the springs did seem to have worked a miracle for Doc Holliday. After taking sick in Trinidad, after traveling the Santa Fe Trail, after soaking and steaming and breathing in the sulfur and pine-scented air, he was finally well enough to start gambling and practicing dentistry again. And Kate Elder, at least for that part of their journey, was the heroine of the story. As for the unverifiable Kid Colton shooting back in Trinidad, Doc may have made up that story himself, preferring a reputation as a dangerous man to a dying one.

DEFENDER OF DODGE CITY

In 1907, lawman-turned-reporter Bat Masterson became Doc Holliday's first biographer when he wrote an article about the gambling dentist for *Human Life* magazine (later published as a chapter in Masterson's book *Famous Gunfighters of the Western Frontier*). Bat had known Holliday for most of his Western adventures, first meeting him when Doc arrived in Dodge City the summer of 1878. Bat was serving as sheriff of Ford County at the time, with headquarters in Dodge, a position he had won the year before in a hotly contested election. Bat's opponent in the race had been Dodge City's marshal, Larry Deger, with whom he'd previously had a contest of another sort. That match-up was reported in the *Dodge City Times* of June 9, 1877, describing how Bat tried to save a local sport named Robert Gilmore from being beaten and arrested:

> *This act was soon interrupted by Bat Masterson, who wound his arm affection-ately around the Marshal's neck and let the prisoner escape. Deger then grappled with Bat, at the same time calling upon the bystanders to take the offender's gun and assist in the arrest. . . . But Masterson would not surrender yet, and came near getting hold of a pistol from among several which were strewed around over the sidewalk, but half a dozen Texas men came to the Marshal's aid and gave him a chance to draw his gun and beat Bat over the head until the blood flew.*

Kansas peace officers Wyatt Earp and Bat Masterson, Dodge City, 1876. Wikipedia Commons. In the public domain.

It's interesting to note that Marshal Deger, around whom Bat wound his arm, was a rotund 315 pounds, and more than a match for Masterson. In the end, Bat was fined $25 for disturbing the peace—his reward for being the only man on the street brave enough to stand up to a bully.

Born Bartholomew William Barclay Masterson in Quebec, Canada, in 1853, Bat was the second of six children of a farming family that moved to New York, then Illinois, then Missouri before finally settling near Wichita, Kansas. When Bat was a teenager, he and his brothers Ed and Jim left home to hunt buffalo on the Great Plains and took short-term jobs grading a roadbed for the Santa Fe Railroad. When the railroad man who'd hired them wouldn't pay as promised, Bat chased him down and held him at gunpoint until the money was forthcoming—receiving applause from on-lookers.

In 1874, as a buffalo hunter in the Texas panhandle, Bat became an involuntary participant in the Battle of Adobe Walls, when Comanche leader Quanah Parker laid siege to the hunters' outpost. After five days of exchanging gunfire with casualties on both sides, the Comanche gave up the fight, and Bat gave up hunting to hire on as an Army Scout working out of Fort Dodge, helping rescue four little girls who'd been taken captive when their family was killed by Cheyenne. Two years later he was in Sweetwater, Texas, where he stood up to another bully and got involved in a deadly altercation—a story told by Doc's mistress, Kate Elder, who claimed to have been there when it happened:

> One night Sergeant King with several soldiers from Fort Clark came to town. Sergeant King got in a game of poker in Harry Fleming's saloon with Harry, Bat Masterson, and Jim Duffy. Late in the evening King went broke. . . . After the poker game broke up, Norton, Bat Masterson, and Mollie went into the dance hall and Norton struck a light back of the dance hall bar. Sergeant King came out of Fleming's saloon and saw them in the place. The door was not locked, so he walked in and accused Masterson of robbing him. Bat hotly denied it. After some words both of them drew their guns. As they did, Mollie jumped between them, just as King fired, his bullet striking Mollie in the abdomen. The shooting went on

with Mollie lying on the floor between them. Bat was shot in the groin and King was hit twice, fatally. It took quite some time for Bat to recover, and he was lame for the rest of his life.[9]

The wounded Bat Masterson went back to his family's farm in Wichita to recover, then set out again for Dodge City, aiming at a job in law enforcement. Since he kept having to handle bullies he might as well do it with a badge, and at the age of twenty-four he was hired as under-sheriff to Ford County sheriff Charlie Bassett. When Sheriff Bassett's term was up the next year, Bat ran for the office, beating out the rotund Larry Deger by three votes. A month later, Bat's brother Ed Masterson won Deger's Dodge City marshal position, and the young Masterson brothers became the law of Ford County, Kansas.

The Mastersons were a good law enforcement team, working together to capture the notorious train robber Dave Rudabaugh and his gang. But within months, City Marshal Ed Masterson was dead, killed by a drunken cowboy. Sheriff Bat Masterson was nearby when the accidental shooting happened and he fired on the cowboy, who died the next day. Two months later, Doc Holliday arrived in Dodge in company with Kate Elder. Bat was likely in no mood at the time to make a new friend, especially one who'd caused trouble for the law, and later claimed that he never liked Holliday. But he would also become Doc's staunchest supporter, defending him against the accusations of a lying bounty hunter and protecting him from a deadly return to Tombstone. Because standing up to bullies was, after all, what Bat Masterson did best.

THE DOCTOR WILL SEE YOU NOW

Doc Holliday arrived in Dodge City in the summer of 1878 and opened a dental office in the Dodge House Hotel, advertising his services in the *Dodge City Times*. To furnish his office, he arranged to have his portable dental chair and equipment sent up from Dallas and ordered some new dental tools in the form of a "Pocket Dentist Office," a small leather-covered box containing tiny dental tools that attached to an ivory handle. Engraved on the eagle-headed medallion on the lid of the box was "J.H. Holliday, 24 D.H., Dodge," along with a set of smiling teeth and the letters "Au," the chemical symbol for gold. Doc may have done the engraving himself, using one of the tools

Doc Holliday's Pocket Dentist Office, photograph by Rene Victor Bidez, Fayetteville, Georgia. Author's Collection.

Dodge House Hotel, c. 1874. Courtesy Kansas State Historical Society.

inside, showing a remarkably steady hand for a drinking man. The address carved onto the box may also have shown Doc's intention to make Dodge City his home for a while.

FAMOUS EDDY FOY

Born Edwin Fitzgerald in New York City, Eddie was six years old when his father died of syphilis-induced dementia and his widowed mother moved with her four small children to Chicago, where Eddie started performing in the streets and saloons to help support the family. At the age of fifteen, Eddie changed his last name to the less-Irish sounding Foy and headed west to spend years on the vaudeville circuit. With his partner Jim Thompson, Eddie Foy made appearances in most of the mining and cattle towns across Kansas and Colorado, including two summer seasons in Dodge City, where he met Doc Holliday, and two winters in Leadville, where he met and married Rose Howland of the Singing Howland Sisters, who were traveling the same circuit.

Three years later, the Foys left the vaudeville circuit and settled down in Philadelphia where Eddie joined a minstrel show. But a settled home life was not to be Eddie Foy's fate. Soon after moving to Philadelphia, Rose Foy died in childbirth along with the baby she was delivering. Eddie struggled through two years of mourning, then went back on the road, traveling all over the western United States.

Finally returning to the east in 1888 as a now-nationally popular entertainer, Eddie starred in variety shows in Chicago and became a musical comedy star on Broadway. In 1896 he married Madeline Morando, a dancer in his theater company, and the two had eleven children together, seven of the children surviving childhood to perform with their father as "Eddie Foy and the Seven Little Foys," and the act became a national sensation. After years of fame, Eddie Foy died of a heart attack at age seventy-one—appropriately while on the road, headlining at the Orpheum Theater in Kansas City, Missouri. In later years, Eddie's oldest son, Eddie Foy Jr., would portray his father in the film *Frontier Marshal*, based on the life of Wyatt Earp, with Doc Holliday defending Earp and Foy from a cowboy crowd.

THE LONGEST CATTLE DRIVE

The Cowboy Capital of Dodge City lay along the Great Western Cattle Trail that transported an estimated seven million head of cattle to ranches on the northern prairies or to rail cars for shipment to meat markets in the East. But though the great cattle drives started in Texas, the famous Texas Longhorn breed started out much farther away: in

A view of the Dodge City, Kansas business district in 1875. Courtesy Kansas State Historical Society.

Spain, having sailed to the New World with Christopher Columbus. The year was 1493, and Columbus was making his second voyage to the Western Hemisphere to establish a Spanish colony on the Caribbean island he named *La Isla Española*, "the island of Spain," now called Hispaniola and home to the two nations of Haiti and the Dominican Republic. The Admiral of the Ocean Sea had sailed from Cadiz, Spain, with seventeen ships and 1,200 men—and horses, sheep, and cattle for the new settlement.

Over the next two centuries, the Spanish colonists shipped their cattle north to the area that would eventually become Texas. Turned loose on the open range, the Spanish cattle evolved feed and drought-tolerant characteristics, and when early US settlers mixed them with their own Eastern cattle, the result was a hardy, rangy animal with long legs and long horns up to seven feet across: the now classic Texas Longhorn. But the longhorn were also lean and the cooked meat could be tough, a point played on in the classic 1957 film *Gunfight at the OK Corral*, where Wyatt Earp orders a meal at John Shanssey's Fort Griffin saloon but leaves it to find Doc Holliday:

> *"Keep that steak warm," Earp tells Shannsey, "I'll be right back."*
> *"You ain't missing much," the saloonkeeper replies wryly, "it's longhorn."*

The lean longhorn cattle were also unfavorable to the production of tallow, the rendered animal fat used for cooking and many other purposes. So, when the frontier gave way to settled farms and ranches, the open range Texas Longhorn fell from favor and were replaced with breeds that gained weight more easily and made for a better financial investment. By the early twentieth century the breed was facing extinction, until 1927, when the US Forest Service collected a small herd of breeding stock for the Wichita Mountains Wildlife Refuge in Oklahoma. Now protected in Texas state parks, the longhorn's intelligence and naturally gentle disposition have made them popular as riding steers—and as the mascot for the University of Texas at Austin, the Longhorns.

HOT SPRINGS HOTELS

When Doc Holliday and Kate Elder arrived in Las Vegas, New Mexico, in late 1878, there was one old hotel at the hot springs up Gallinas Canyon and another about to open, and Doc may have spent time at both while he recuperated from his health crisis in Trinidad.

The Old Adobe House had been constructed by the occupying US Army in 1846 as a resort for invalid soldiers. It was a utilitarian building: 125 feet by 30 feet, with a long front porch with rough timbers supporting the roof, two doors facing the Rio Gallinas and the natural hot springs, and a long boardwalk down to the riverbank and frame bathhouse. When the resort was abandoned by the army in 1862, the building was taken over by the ironically named Dr. Bloodworth, who advertised his health spa in the Las Vegas and Santa Fe papers, and then by retired railroad conductor W. Scott Moore, who made improvements and welcomed his old friend from Missouri, Jesse James.[10]

In early 1879, a second hotel opened at the springs on property adjoining the Old Adobe. The new Hot Springs Hotel was a stately three stories of native red sandstone with a square central tower and balustraded verandas overlooking the river and the two new bath houses below, one for mud baths and one for mineral water baths. With two hotels in operation, the springs along the Rio Gallinas were becoming a popular resort, and the next year the Santa Fe Railway bought the Hot Springs Hotel and surrounding property.

Although Doc Holliday left New Mexico for Arizona in 1880, he returned the next year to take care of some legal business and may have paid another visit to Gallinas Canyon and the Hot Springs Hotel, too. While there, he would have seen the Santa Fe's newest project under construction: the Montezuma Hotel, being built in Queen Anne style with long verandas and latticed balconies, stained glass windows and steeply gabled roofs, and 270 gaslit and steam-heated rooms for guests. Doc may have stayed at the newly finished Montezuma himself when he passed back through New Mexico in 1882, after his troubled time in Tombstone, taking the Santa Fe's new narrow-gauge spur up the canyon from the depot in Las Vegas.

Old Hot Springs Hotel, now part of the campus of World University, Las Vegas, New Mexico. Author's Collection.

But despite modern safety features like fireplugs, hose-reel attachments, and water piped to every floor, the wood frame Montezuma burned to the ground in 1884, less than two years after its grand opening. Almost immediately, plans were begun for another and even grander hotel to be built on the same site, and the second Montezuma Hotel opened in 1885, a supposedly fireproof fantasy of red sandstone, round turrets, and shingled towers. But less than four months after its opening, the second Montezuma also caught fire, with nothing left standing but the stone walls of the lower two stories. Challenging fate, the hotel was immediately rebuilt from the same plans and reopened in 1886 as the Phoenix Hotel, named for the legendary bird that rose from its own ashes, though the public preferred the now-sentimental name of Montezuma.[11]

Although the Old Adobe House is long gone, the Hot Springs Hotel of Doc Holliday's time and the third Montezuma Hotel are still standing, now part of the campus of World University, where they continue to welcome visitors to the pine-scented canyon and healing waters of the Rio Gallinas.

11

RAILROAD WARS

Las Vegas is Spanish for "the meadows," and the place was picturesque: set between the southern end of the Sangre de Cristo Mountains and the river called the Rio Gallinas, centered around a plaza with a windmill that doubled as a gallows for hangings, and watched over by the stately red-brick Catholic church called *Nuestra Señora de Dolores*, Our Lady of Sorrows. Las Vegas, New Mexico Territory was, most of the time, a peaceful pueblo and a good place for a sick man to rest and recuperate. But it was a bad place for a sporting man to ply his trade, and on March 8, 1879, Doc Holliday was caught by the territory's newly enacted gambling laws and fined $25 for keeping a monte table.[1] So he and Kate packed up again and took the Barlow & Sanderson stage north to the new town of Otero, recently raised to welcome the advancing tracks of the Atchison, Topeka & Santa Fe Railway.

Otero sat at the confluence of the Mora and Sapello rivers, at the northern edge of New Mexico and close to the Colorado border. Like all boomtowns, Otero had more saloons than any other kind of business, but it also boasted one good hotel, two restaurants, five stores, a schoolhouse, and an art gallery, so it seemed well on its way to becoming a real city. It even had a dental office, owned by a Dr. Fagaly, who was amenable to bringing in a new partner to share the office expenses, and John Henry Holliday, DDS, was back in business again. By the end of May, he was settled into the community enough to be mentioned in the second issue of the new *Otero Optic* newspaper:

> *A splendid violin was raffled off at Henry & Robinson's place, Saturday night. Ten chances were sold at five dollars each. Sam'l Burr was the lucky individual, he throwing higher dice than any of the others. The following gentlemen*

participated in the drawing: Sam'l Burr, Bob. Reagan, Wm. Martin, Frank White, Wm. Stokes, A. M. Blackwell, Henry Robinson, J. H. Holliday, D.D. Finch, and L.A Maden.[2]

Doc didn't win the raffle for the violin, but he soon found another diversion: answering an invitation from Bat Masterson to travel back to Dodge to help the Santa Fe in a dispute with the Denver & Rio Grande Railroad.

The cause of the trouble between the two railroads was the right-of-way through Colorado's Royal Gorge of the Arkansas River, a spectacular two-thousand-foot-deep, thirty-foot-wide slash through the mountains, and the shortest passage to the silver mines of Leadville and surrounding country. Both the Santa Fe and the Rio Grande wanted to run trains through the Gorge, carrying passengers and freight and precious metals, but there was only enough room for one set of tracks, and barely enough for that. When the railroads couldn't come to an agreement, the dispute went to the courts with a series of confusing decisions. In 1872, an Act of Congress gave the right-of-way to the Rio Grande; in 1878, a Circuit Court found in favor of the Santa Fe; in April 1879, a Supreme Court ruling gave the rights back to the Rio Grande, although by then the Santa Fe had already built most of the road. The legal debate turned physical when the Rio Grande sent in three hundred armed railroad workers to take back the Royal Gorge by force, and the Santa Fe sent to Dodge City for an army of its own, hiring Ford County sheriff Bat Masterson as acting general.

The Santa Fe was considered Dodge City's own railroad, the iron horse that carried beeves and buffalo hides from Western cattle trails to Eastern markets, and anyone with an interest in the business of Dodge wanted to see the Santa Fe succeed. So, Bat sent out an invitation to sixty or so of the best shooters he knew to defend the Santa Fe's claim—including Doc Holliday, who arrived back in Dodge in June 1879 to find the cowtown greatly changed from his last visit there. A season of drought had damaged the local grazing land, and half of the annual cattle drive was bypassing Dodge for greener pastures in Nebraska. With fewer herds came fewer cowboys, and less business for the saloons and sporting men.

Even the law was less busy than usual. Dodge City Assistant Marshal Wyatt Earp had made only nine arrests in three months and had so much free time on his hands that he agreed to collect ballots for a local beauty contest—the Ladies' Aid Society's "Beautiful Baby Contest" to raise money for a missionary fund. The ballots sold for $20 each, and the sporting community eagerly joined in the cause. But when the baby with the most votes was announced, it wasn't a baby at all, but the gambler's joke on the town: a prostitute from over the deadline, escorted to collect her title by Marshal Earp and Sheriff Masterson.

But Dodge was still entertaining, despite the slow cattle season, with traveling acts like the popular duo of Eddie Foy and Jim Thompson, back at the Comique for a second summer tour. This time the act included the three Singing Howland Sisters, one of whom had become Mrs. Eddie Foy in Leadville that spring. So, it may have been Eddie's newly married status that made him cautious of an offer from Doc Holliday to join in the expedition to defend the Santa Fe's claim to the Royal Gorge. As Eddie told it in his memoirs:

> *The Santa Fe, being "our own road," had Dodge's sympathy in the quarrel, and, besides, there was a promise of good pay for the fighters. Doc Holliday suggested that I join them.*
>
> *"But listen, Mr. Holliday," said I, "I'm no fighter. I couldn't hit a man if I shot at him."*
>
> *"Oh, that's all right," he replied easily. "The Santy Fee won't know the difference. You kin use a shot-gun if you want to. Dodge wants a good showin' in this business. You'll help swell the crowd, and you'll get your pay anyhow."*[3]

The pay Doc mentioned was $3 a day plus board, along with the possibility of doing some shooting, attractive terms for a bit of adventure. But Foy's reminiscence recorded more than just a recruitment speech—it captured the sound of Doc Holliday's Southern accent: not the melodious drawl of *Gone with the Wind*, but the nasal twang of country music. In Doc's rustic pronunciation, "Santa Fe" became "Santy Fee" and "you can" became "you kin." And ending a sentence with "anyhow" was classic piney-woods Georgia.

By mid-June, Bat Masterson's army of hired guns had gathered and Doc joined them on the Santa Fe special bound for Colorado. It was a long, hot ride—seven hours with the temperature hovering near one hundred degrees and the railcars crowded with some of the hottest tempers and quickest trigger-fingers in the West. Among them was gunfighter Ben Thompson, famous for his pistol skills and steely nerves, who would lead part of the men in defending the railroad roundhouse and the telegraph office at Pueblo, while Sheriff Masterson would take the rest of the men on to Cañon City, the entrance to the Royal Gorge.[4]

Pueblo had two roundhouses to turn trains, one built by the Rio Grande and the other by the Santa Fe, although the Santa Fe had control of both buildings as a result of a complicated lease arrangement. But having won the most recent court battle over the right-of-way through the canyon, the Rio Grande wanted its roundhouse back. The telegraph office was jointly owned, part of the Union Depot built and shared by both railroads when they had been on friendlier terms, and as the telegraph was the key to communication all up and down the rails, both companies wanted that, as well.

Stories say that Doc Holliday and Bat Masterson's deputy sheriff John Joshua Webb led the guard at the telegraph office, while at the nearby roundhouse Ben Thompson's men sighted their pistols and aimed a cannon stolen from the state armory.[5] And then, they waited. Although the Santa Fe may have lost the last court decision, it was betting on appeals to change the situation or at least to drag out the litigation.

The Rio Grande threw together its own fighting force under the direction of Chief Engineer James McMurtrie and Pueblo County Deputy Sheriff Pat Desmond, who armed a hundred miners and railroad workers with six-shooters and primed them with free whiskey. Deputy Desmond led the mob in a march on the roundhouse, demanding the Santa Fe men inside surrender, but Ben Thompson met them on the platform and refused the demand, saying that he'd been placed in charge of the Santa Fe's property and could not give it up without being authorized by proper authority.

The mob fell back, then rallied and moved to an easier target: the glass-windowed telegraph office. Deputy Desmond smashed the butt of his gun against the door, trying to break it open, then ordered his men to commence firing into the building. Inside, Doc Holliday and Josh Webb calculated their odds against an overwhelming force and decided to beat a hasty retreat, escaping out the back door of the office—though one of their men wasn't so lucky. Harry Jenkins, a Dodge City resident along for the adventure, fell as he ran for the back door and was shot in the back by the attackers as he lay on the floor.

It may have been the shooting of Jenkins that caused Ben Thompson to give up the roundhouse, not wanting to lose any more men in the service of the Santa Fe. The battle was, after all, mostly a legal fight between railroad companies, and not a real war—as Doc had told Eddie Foy, the Santa Fe just wanted to make a good showing. Or it may have been the legal papers delivered to Thompson that afternoon, by proper authority advising the Santa Fe to comply with the court order and turn over the rails and the roundhouse. Farther down the track at Cañon City, Bat Masterson was also served court papers and would surrender his position, as well. By the end of the day, the Battle for the Royal Gorge was over, although the two railroads would continue to battle in the courts for several more months.

The Dodge City expedition for the Santa Fe may have been brief but it wasn't bloodless: Harry Jenkins died of his wounds and Pueblo's Deputy Desmond was arrested and charged with murder. And there was one other casualty: Ford County Deputy Sheriff John Joshua Webb, who had helped to guard the telegraph office, lost a tooth in the melee. But Webb was lucky to know a good dentist—Doc Holliday—who fixed his smile with a shiny new gold tooth when they got back to Dodge.[6]

After the dust settled, rumors started swirling that Bat Masterson had taken a $20,000 bribe from the Rio Grande to give up the fight, money speaking even louder than court orders. If Bat actually received a bribe, perhaps he shared some of his riches with his comrade-in-arms, Doc Holliday, who seemed flush with cash on his return to New Mexico, buying new dental equipment and investing in real estate. But the land Doc bought wasn't in Otero—by the time he got back, the whole town had packed up and moved on to the newest end-of-track for the Atchison, Topeka & Santa Fe: the sleepy Spanish pueblo of Las Vegas.

Atchison, Topeka & Santa Fe Railroad.
TopsImages.com.

ON THE ATCHISON, TOPEKA & SANTA FE

In the 1946 movie musical *The Harvey Girls*, Judy Garland sings a love song about a train: the Atchison, Topeka & Santa Fe, which became a symbol of romance and adventure in the American West. And a love song seemed appropriate for a railroad that began as the dream of Pennsylvania lawyer Cyrus K. Holliday (perhaps distantly related to Doc Holliday) who moved to the new town of Topeka, Kansas, in 1854 and said glowingly of the possibilities of the place, "In a few years when civilization by its magic influence shall have transformed this glorious country from what it is now to the brilliant destiny awaiting it, the Sun in all his course will visit no land more truly lovely and desirable than this."[7]

But Kansas was still a frontier, and civilization could use some help getting there, so Cyrus began the task of organizing and building a railroad, first between Atchison on the Missouri River and Topeka, then across the territory to Colorado. It took a decade from the railroad's incorporation in 1859 to raise the capital and obtain rights-of-way before the first spade of prairie sod was turned for the Atchison & Topeka Railway, yet Cyrus Holliday boldly declared that his road would not end in Colorado as planned, but follow the old Santa Fe Trail into New Mexico and then all the way to the Pacific. The crowd at the ground-breaking ceremony laughed at his "lunatic" idea.

By the summer of 1870, the rails reached Emporia, Kansas, where the train took on traffic that would help to fuel its westward expansion: cattle. In May 1872, a branch line was opened to the Chisholm Cattle Trail town of Wichita, and in September the rails reached Dodge City, with the cattle shipping business turning Dodge into the Cowboy Capital. In 1875, the line added a connection to Kansas City, with the editor of the *Emporia Gazette* proclaiming, "The Santa Fe . . . is one of the best things that ever happened to Kansas."[8] The rail line wasn't just good for Kansas business—it was Kansas business, and wherever the rails went, new towns sprang up along the way.

But building toward New Mexico and into Colorado, the Santa Fe met its match in Colorado's own railroad, the Denver & Rio Grande, which laid rails through the Royal Gorge to the rich mining country of the Rockies. The Battle for the Royal Gorge ended the Santa Fe's hopes of adding mining to its cattle income, but the road kept building toward its goal, tunneling through the Raton Pass and paralleling the Santa Fe Trail on its way south and west. On February 16, 1880, the road reached its namesake city of Santa Fe in the New Mexico Territory, then continued on to Deming for a connection with the Central Pacific Railroad, giving the United States a second transcontinental line. But the Santa Fe wasn't content with just connecting to the Pacific, it wanted to reach the Pacific on its own track, and in 1883 it entered California at the desert town of Needles before pushing on to Los Angeles and San Francisco. In two decades from its beginnings as Cyrus Holliday's dream, the Atchison, Topeka & Santa Fe stretched from Chicago to the California coast, following and carrying the dreams of the American West.

HANGING BRIDGE

After years of legal battles and some armed skirmishes, the Denver & Rio Grande won the right to build through the Royal Gorge of the Arkansas River, but by then the Santa Fe had already laid miles of track. And it was the Santa Fe's engineer who figured out how to get through the most challenging part of the canyon, where the Royal Gorge was just two sheer cliff walls with a river between and no place at all for the rails.

President Roosevelt and his traveling companions at the Hanging Bridge, Royal Gorge, Colorado. Library of Congress.

The solution was to build an A-frame suspension bridge anchored to the cliff walls and hanging the rails in midair above the waters of the Arkansas River. Designed by Kansas engineer C. Shallor Smith and built by Santa Fe construction engineer A. A. Robinson for the impressive sum of $12,000, the bridge was hailed as an engineering marvel, and was one of the reasons the Denver & Rio Grande had to pay the Santa Fe $1.8 million, including a $400,000 bonus, to take over the rails. The bridge went into service in 1880, when the first Denver & Rio Grande train passed through the Royal Gorge on its way to the Colorado mining country. In later years, Doc Holliday would cross the Hanging Bridge many times during his travels between Pueblo and Leadville, and he surely enjoyed the view.

The famous Hanging Bridge is still in service nearly 140 years after its construction and is still a tourist site, with the Royal Gorge Route Railroad offering daily excursion trips from Cañon City to a terminus at Parkdale and stopping along the way for photo ops. But the bigger attraction now is another engineering marvel high above the Hanging Bridge: the Royal Gorge Suspension Bridge, spanning 1,260 feet across the gorge at a dizzying 995 feet above the river, the highest bridge in the United States.

BROTHERS IN ARMS

When Doc Holliday took the Santa Fe from Dodge City to Cañon City to join in the Battle for the Royal Gorge, he had good company: John Joshua "J. J." Webb, owner of the Lady Gay Saloon that housed Dodge's popular Comique Theater.[9] But the saloon business was just one of Webb's many occupations. Born along the Mississippi River in Keokuk, Iowa, and raised in Illinois, Nebraska, and Kansas, J. J. Webb had been a buffalo hunter, surveyor, and teamster before settling in Dodge and being deputized as a posse rider under Ford County Sheriffs Charlie Bassett and Bat Masterson. In 1878, as part of the posse that hunted down Dave Rudabaugh and his gang for robbing the westbound train at Kinsley, Kansas, it was Webb who talked Rudabaugh into surrendering, avoiding a deadly gun battle and earning the outlaw's later loyalty. When the Cheyenne rampaged southern Kansas that fall, J. J. Webb was one of the men selected by the commander at Fort Dodge to scout the area. So, in 1879, when Sheriff Bat Masterson asked for volunteers to help secure the Santa Fe's claim to the Royal Gorge, J. J. Webb was a welcome addition, having proven himself to be brave, skilled, and cool-headed in a hot situation. When he lost a tooth in the fight to hold the telegraph office at Pueblo, he had a good dentist with him to do the repair.

Alleged photograph of John Joshua Webb. Courtesy True West *Archives.*

Webb would later follow the Santa Fe's advance to Las Vegas, New Mexico, where he was employed as a police officer and where he got reacquainted with train robber Dave Rudabaugh. "Dirty Dave" had gone straight for a while after the Kinsley affair, turning informant on his partners in crime and winning himself a pardon, and even riding along as part of Bat Masterson's expedition to defend the Santa Fe's claim to the Royal Gorge. But he was back to his old habits in Las Vegas as part of the "Dodge City Gang" of shady characters masterminded by Hyman Neill, known as "Hoodoo Brown," the official coroner and unofficial mayor of the railroad community called New Town. Rumor had it that under Hoodoo's watch, the gang got away with stage hold-ups and train robberies and may have participated in a couple of lynchings, so J. J. Webb came under suspicion because of his previous association with Rudabaugh.

In March 1880, Hoodoo Brown learned that a freighter name Kelliher was carrying $1,900 in cash, and the Dodge City Gang supposedly decided to relieve him of it, with the result described in the *Las Vegas Daily Optic* and the *Ford County Globe*:

> *About four o'clock this morning, Michael Kelliher, in company with William Brickley and another man, entered Goodlet & Roberts' Saloon and called for drinks. Michael Kelliher appeared to be the leader of the party and he, in violation of the law, had a pistol on his person. This was noticed by the officers, who came through a rear door, and they requested that Kelliher lay aside his revolver. But he refused to do so, remarking, "I won't be disarmed—everything goes," immediately placing his hand on his pistol, no doubt intending to shoot.*

But officer Webb was too quick for him. The man was shot before he had time to use his weapon. He was shot three times—once in each breast and once in the head . . . Kelliher had $1,090 on his person when killed.[10]

If the shooting was, as it was rumored to be, an attempt to steal Kelliher's money, it's strange that no one took the loot. Instead, Officer Webb was charged with murder and sentenced to hang. But as he awaited his fate in the city jail, Dave Rudabaugh attempted to break him out. The escape plan failed, but J. J.'s sentence was commuted to life in prison. Rudabaugh fled Las Vegas and joined up with another New Mexico outlaw, Billy the Kid, then was arrested and sent back to Las Vegas where he joined J. J. Webb in jail. The two made another failed jailbreak attempt, then tried a third time, chipping out a 7" by 19" hole in the adobe brick and wriggling through to freedom.

"Dirty Dave" Rudabaugh was later killed in Texas, but the now-outlaw J. J. Webb went home to Kansas where he had once saved Rudabaugh's life by talking him into surrendering. All things considered, he may have regretted the effort.

JURASSIC PARK

While the Santa Fe and the Denver & Rio Grande were fighting over the Royal Gorge, another fight was going on in nearby Cañon City—part of the "Great Bone Wars" between rival paleontologists Othniel Marsh and Edward Cope. The men had started out as professional colleagues studying newly found fossils in the Western territories, but like miners competing for a rich silver lode, greed got in their way. The men sabotaged each other's archeological digs, paying workers to steal or destroy bones, and attacking each other in scientific journals. But despite the animosity, both men added much to the knowledge of the late

Othniel Marsh. Library of Congress.

Jurassic period, reconstructing fossilized skeletons of the Stegosaurus, Allosaurus, and Brontosaurus and naming dozens of others. In a gulch leading into Four Mile Creek near Cañon City, the sandstone yielded thirty-five boxes of dinosaur bones, including a nearly complete specimen of a Stegosaurus.

Reports of the dinosaur discoveries first appeared in the Colorado papers in 1877, explaining that the whole area had once been part of a great inland sea where sea-serpents and monsters roamed:

> *along the shores of this ancient sea squatted and leapt the Dinosaurs or terrible lizards . . . one of whom was perhaps twenty-four feet long . . . there was another, thirty-five feet long . . . in the air overhead huge bat-like creatures (Pterodactyls), combining a lizard, a crocodile, and a bat, flapped their leathery wings twenty-five feet from tip to tip over the sea.*[11]

Edward Cope. Library of Congress.

By the time Doc Holliday rode along with the Dodge City boys to Pueblo and Bat Masterson made his headquarters at Cañon City, the area was famous for its dinosaur bones. Colorado now has, in addition to a state flower and state bird, a state dinosaur: the Stegosaurus.

12

END OF TRACK

The tracks of the south-building Santa Fe arrived in Las Vegas, New Mexico, on July 1, 1879, and Doc Holliday arrived three days later, riding the inaugural train into town along with a crowd of celebrants. The Santa Fe had planned the train's arrival date of July 4 to take advantage of the Independence Day festivities, and the engine came dressed for the occasion in red, white, and blue bunting. Behind the engine came a string of platform cars with a caboose at the end to give the female riders some shade, and the spectacle was met with cheers and speeches and a brass band—and a new town going up all at once as old Otero was unpacked and rebuilt as the new end-of-track town of East Las Vegas. According to one of the riders on that first train, "We pulled into the yards of Las Vegas early in the afternoon and found the new town a busy place, indeed. Everywhere buildings were going up, while tents and hastily built shacks were being used as restaurants, saloons and living quarters."[1]

The new railroad town was a mile away from the old Spanish plaza, across the Gallinas River and away from the watchful eyes of the Nuestra Señora de Dolores. It was also just out of the legal jurisdiction of old town Las Vegas, so it had its own law in Hyman G. Neill, known as "Hoodoo Brown," a gambler who took over as unelected mayor and judge of the coroner's court.

Doc Holliday took a look at the two towns of Las Vegas and was pleased with the possibilities. In the old town, he opened a dental practice across from the plaza, buying expensive new equipment to furnish his office: a heavy iron-footed dental chair, a Morrison Dental Engine drill, a fancy case to hold his tools, and an ivory appointment book. In the new town, he opened a saloon on Center Street, close to the tracks and the depot on Railroad Street. So, he had a big investment in Las Vegas when trouble came to town less than a month later in the person of Mike Gordon, a former soldier in a squabble with his mistress. According to accounts in the July 26, 1879, *Las Vegas Gazette*:

> *Gordon tried to persuade her to accompany him to another hall on Railroad St. When she refused to go, he flew into a drunken rage and swore that he would kill someone or be killed himself before morning. Gordon was standing in the street to the right of the hall after some of his threats and drew a revolver and fired, the bullet passing through the pants leg of a Mexican and struck in the floor in line with the bartender who was standing at the rear of the bar. Other shots were fired immediately but it is difficult to tell how many or by whom. It is said that Gordon fired a second shot. Every person there says three shots were fired, while several maintain that five in all were fired.*
>
> *Gordon at once ceased firing and disappeared. An hour or two later a Mr. Kennedy went into his tent some thirty or forty yards away, to go to bed and hearing groans investigated and found Gordon laying on the ground outside. The news soon spread and his woman arriving on the ground had him taken to her room east of the Court house, where he died at 6 o'clock Sunday morning. In the afternoon the Coroner held an inquest and the jury returned a verdict of excusable homicide.*

Later news reports[2] claimed the gambling hall in question was Holliday's Saloon and that Doc himself was the shooter, a story also told by Bat Masterson:

> *Gordon came back and fired a shot from the sidewalk into the saloon. The bullet whizzed a couple of inches from Holliday's head and went crashing through a window at the rear of the room. Doc drew his gun and rushed to the front door and saw Gordon standing on the sidewalk with a revolver in hand. Gordon raised his revolver to fire a second time, but before he could pull the trigger, Doc had shot him dead.*

As the owner of a saloon charged with policing his place, Doc Holliday was lawfully defending his customers from a disorderly and dangerous drunk, hence the coroner's verdict of excusable homicide. But excused or not, the Mike Gordon story followed Doc and helped to build his reputation as a killer.

The day after the shooting, Doc made a payment for work done on his saloon, perhaps boarding up the tent sides to make a more secure structure.[3] And he may have entertained some other legendary Western characters in his saloon, as both Jesse James and Billy the Kid were in town that summer.

One thing Doc did remains a mystery. On July 30, he purchased the eight-foot-wide alley space next to his saloon and signed the deed for himself in his own name and for someone else by adding the initials *A. B. H.* The next day, the Justice of the Peace who recorded the transaction met with him again to make sure of his intent in adding a second deed holder. As the deed addendum states: "The said J. H. Holliday being first by me informed of the contents of the instrument did confess upon a separate examination independent and apart of his said wife that he executed the same voluntary and with[out] the compulsion or illicit influence of her said wife."[4]

In simpler terms, the Justice wanted to make sure that Doc was of his own free will adding his wife's initials, and therefore her ownership, to the property. The fact that Doc didn't have a legal wife wasn't really an issue—many Western mistresses were called wives and some actually fit the legal definition of a common-law wife. The historical issue is that Doc's mistress was Mary Katherine Harony, called Kate Elder, and the initials A. B. H. do not fit her. So, who was Doc Holliday's "said wife" in Las Vegas? Was she Kate, using yet another alias? Or another woman whose identity has been lost to history? And what was the purpose of adding eight feet to his property? Was it to build a new entrance to the saloon, or perhaps to open a small dental office? Whatever the purpose, why go to the trouble of adding a wife to the deed?

Doc had other, less puzzling, dealings in town, though they caused him more trouble. The day after signing the deed, he was a witness in a gambling case, then was arrested the same night for running a monte game for which he posted a $200 bond. Two weeks later he was indicted for carrying deadly weapons—clearly a necessary precaution in a town like East Las Vegas—and had to post a $100 bond for a later court appearance.[5] Life in Las Vegas was getting expensive, which may be why he decided to give up his saloon and let someone else pay the cost of hosting banking games.[6] But even that caused him trouble: When he turned over the saloon to the new owner he stopped making payments to his contractor for the work previously done, and the contractor filed a court action against him.[7]

So, when Wyatt Earp came through town that fall, traveling with his family by wagon from Dodge City to try their luck in the silver camp of Tombstone and invited Doc to ride along, it may have seemed an opportune time for leaving Las Vegas. And whoever A. B. H. was, Kate Elder was the woman who claimed to be his wife when he threw in with the Earp's wagon train, as she later recalled:

> *When we left Las Vegas, New Mexico our party consisted of Wyatt Earp and his wife Mattie, my husband and myself, Jim Earp and his step-daughter. Doc and I rode in Wyatt Earp's wagon. . . . It was during our trip from Las Vegas to Prescott [Arizona] that Doc and Wyatt became such good friends, which meant the end of the happiness we had enjoyed since our marriage.*[8]

For reasons she never explained, Kate disapproved of Doc's friendship with Wyatt Earp and did her best to separate them. Instead, the friendship separated Doc from Kate—after they arrived in Arizona, she left him and moved to the mining camp of Globe in the Pinal Mountains. When the 1880 Federal Census was taken in Prescott, Arizona, it listed J. H. Holliday as single and living with a new roommate: John Jay Gosper, the acting governor of the Arizona Territory, both of them residing on Montezuma Street in a house owned by mine superintendent Richard Elliott.[9]

Prescott, Doc's layover on arriving in Arizona, was the newly built territorial capital, situated in the cool pine-scented highlands of the central plateau, with stage transportation through Yuma to California and through Phoenix to the mining country along the Mexican border. But there was no railroad as yet, and no need for Doc to hurry along. Summers in Arizona were brutally hot and crossing the desert by stagecoach could be dangerous for a man in delicate health. So, when Wyatt and his family moved on to Tombstone, Doc stayed behind in his comfortable Montezuma Street lodgings and enjoyed the social life of the capital. Sharing a house with the acting governor put him in close contact with all sorts of influential people, and likely made for interesting discussions over poker hands. And unlike New Mexico, with its too-often enforced gambling laws, Arizona didn't mind a man's recreations, as long as he kept himself peaceful.

Another reason for him to linger in Prescott was that he still had business back in Las Vegas. His two arrests of the summer before had court dates to satisfy, so in March 1880 he took the stage back to New Mexico to make his appearance before the judge and to pay off the remaining debt to his contractor, ending that litigation, as well. But when he got back to Arizona and a pile of letters from Wyatt Earp, singing the praises of the mining camp on the Mexican border, he packed up again and headed to the silver promised land of Tombstone.

THE TWO TOWNS OF LAS VEGAS

Railroads didn't usually lay rail into towns; towns grew around the rails. In many places (Dallas, Denver, Tucson) the rail yards were on the outskirts of town and the town absorbed the area. In Las Vegas, New Mexico, where the rails were laid a mile away across the Gallinas River from the town proper, a separate town grew up around the rails. The original city centered around the old Spanish plaza became known as Old Town, and the new town was creatively called New Town before being unofficially named East Las Vegas, as it remains today. But since New Town was at the time outside the legal city limits of Old Town, it was also outside the city's law enforcement—which left an opening for the denizens of New Town to create their own police force, with Hoodoo Brown and the Dodge City Gang happy to take on the job. But just because the acting law enforcement was mostly gamblers and other shady characters didn't mean that New Town was wide open. There was plenty of real law in San Miguel County, and the county sheriff and his deputies kept a close eye on the happenings in New Town, making arrests and bringing charges, like those against

Bird's Eye View of Las Vegas, New Mexico, San Miguel County 1882. Library of Congress Geography and Map Division.

John Holliday for carrying deadly weapons and keeping a gaming table against state code. But Doc was a minor offender compared to others charged by the grand jury with rape, murder, and assault with intent to murder. And unlike others who skipped town before making a court date, Doc took care of his legal business, making his court appearances and paying his fines, and visiting the county courthouse to register the deed to his saloon property. He even returned from Arizona to pay his bills and finish his legal affairs before heading to Tombstone, and the fact that he held on to some of his property in New Mexico indicates that he may have hoped to return to do business there again.

DR. HOLLIDAY'S DENTAL CLINICS

When Doc Holliday settled in Las Vegas, New Mexico, he bought property near the railroad tracks and opened a saloon, and ordered new dental equipment for his new office on the plaza in Old Town: an oak and leather uphol-stered dental chair and a Morrison Dental Engine foot treadle drill. Years later his Las Vegas dental equipment was still in place when an agent for the Baker Gulch Mining Company moved into the space. As the agent explained in a 1908 affidavit:

Doc Holliday's dental chair from Las Vegas, New Mexico. Courtesy Dr. Richard Thomas Collection.

> *When I rented my office above the apothecary on the Plaza, I removed a dental chair to make room for my own furnishings. I later noticed the name John Holliday on this chair. I now have learned that this is the same John Holliday, the famous shootist of a few years prior. . . . I give this chair to the city free of charge in hope that a display of archives or a museum may use this infamous artifact.*

The identification the agent mentioned was found on the back of the chair, where two brass plaques are engraved: "John Holliday, D.D.S., made for dental practice, chair size Sm-Md," and "Dental Supply House, St. Joseph MO. 1877."

Name plate on dental chair. Courtesy Dr. Richard Thomas Collection.

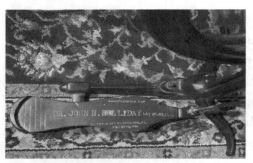

Morrison Dental Engine foot treadle. Courtesy Dr. Richard Thomas Collection.

The foot treadle for the drill is similarly marked: "Manufactured for Dr. John H. Holliday, Las Vegas, New Mexico by the Hisey Dental Manufacturing Co., St. Louis, Mo."

The Hisey Company was only in the dental equipment manufacturing business for a short time before turning their efforts to a more lucrative product: a proprietary local anesthetic mixture they called *Alvatunder*, a blend of phenol and cocaine they advertised as "A Practice Builder!" But the helpful product had not yet been invented in Doc's years of practice, so he had to rely on a more common form of anesthesia: alcohol.

But it's the fact that Doc ordered the new equipment and then left it there in Las Vegas that is most intriguing. Why didn't he just have his Dodge City equipment shipped to him at his new location, as he had done with his Dallas equipment when he moved to Dodge? Why leave behind two offices full of expensive dental equipment? Unless leaving the two offices intact was his plan: setting up dental offices along the Santa Fe rail line so that he could practice his profession wherever he happened to be, in Dodge City or Las Vegas or perhaps later in Albuquerque (where there is record of his owning some property). He was a sporting man, after all, working the circuit and traveling to wherever the money was flowing, but also a dentist, who could practice wherever he happened to be gambling. If a trip to Tombstone hadn't made him an outlaw and ruined his professional career, he may have returned to New Mexico and Kansas and continued to profit as John Henry Holliday, DDS.

YOURS TRULY, J. H. HOLLIDAY

One of the few authenticated photographs of Doc Holliday was made in Prescott, Arizona. It is also the only photograph of him known to bear his signature: *Yours Truly, J. H. Holliday*. The photo may have been made by early Prescott photographer

Daniel Frank Mitchell, who arrived in 1877 and owned the Capital Art Gallery into the 1880s, or by pioneer photographer George Rothrock, who briefly owned a studio on Montezuma Street close to Doc's boardinghouse. Whoever took the photo, it ended up with Doc's McKey relatives in Georgia, suggesting that he stayed in touch with his mother's family for years after he left home. Although some viewers see Doc wearing thin-rimmed wire-frame eyeglasses in this photograph, the lack of a glass reflection makes that unlikely. More importantly, he's wearing a dark double-breasted frock coat, fitting several later descriptions that said he dressed more like a preacher or a banker than a flamboyantly attired gambler. Appearances, however, could be deceiving.

Doc Holliday in Prescott, Arizona.
Courtesy True West *Archives.*

GOOD NEIGHBORS

Doc Holliday's landlord in Prescott was Richard Elliott, one of the owners of the Accidental Mine on Lynx Creek. The other occupant of the Elliott house was miner and stockman John J. Gosper, who also happened to be secretary of the Arizona Territory and acting governor during the extended absence of the great explorer-turned-politician John C. Frémont. Gosper had been an officer in the Illinois Cavalry, fighting in thirty battles during the Civil War and losing a leg at the Battle of Petersburg. Returning home after the war, he attended business school and was elected Secretary of the State of Nebraska (Gosper County, Nebraska, is named in his honor), and was then appointed secretary of the Arizona Territory by President Rutherford B. Hayes.[10]

Next door to the Elliott house was the home of William Mansfield Buffum and his family. Buffum was a California businessman who had come to Arizona in the early days of the territory, settling in Prescott and establishing a prosperous mercantile company. His wife, Rebecca Evans Buffum, was known for her dinner parties—her china is now on display at the Sharlot Hall Museum in Prescott.

John J. Gosper. Arizona State Library.

Some of those dinner parties were no doubt attended by Buffum's friend and former member of the Territorial Legislature, Thomas Fitch.

Fitch was one of the brightest legal minds in the Western territories—a lawyer, actor, orator, novelist, and newspaper editor who had worked with Mark Twain in Virginia City, Nevada. He had been a district attorney and a delegate to the Nevada State Constitutional Convention and helped draft the Utah state constitution. Although not a member of the Church of Jesus Christ of Latter-day Saints, he had served as general counsel to the Church and defended church leader Brigham Young during the polygamy trials. He witnessed the

William Mansfield Buffum. Press Reference Library (1915) Being the Portraits and Biographies of the Progressive Men of the West.

laying of the first rail at the western terminus of the Overland Route in Sacramento, California, and the last one at Promontory Summit in Utah.

Thomas Fitch. Arizona Historical Society, Portraits Collection.

Those were Doc Holliday's influential neighbors at a most interesting time in Arizona history. Down on the southern border of the territory, near the mining town of Tombstone, American cowboys were crossing the US-Mexico border into Sonora, stealing Mexican cattle and rebranding them to sell to US military bases, and sometimes killing Mexican citizens along the way. Mexico's government sent a series of angry communiqués to Washington, D.C., demanding an end to the depredations, but the federal government, operating under the Posse Comitatus Act of 1878, claimed the border was Arizona's problem and the Territorial Legislature should handle the trouble. The Territory disagreed, saying the federal border was Washington, D.C.'s responsibility, refusing to allocate funds for a police action and leaving the situation a stalemate. But when Mexico threatened a war over the border issues and Washington, D.C., ordered the Arizona Territory to quell the situation, Governor Frémont proposed a plan authorizing US Marshal Crawley P. Dake to appoint special deputies to hunt down the rustlers (Dake appointed Virgil Earp as one for Tombstone, in November 1879). Then the governor left Arizona, putting Acting Governor Gosper in charge of enforcing the plan.

So that was the lay of the land when Doc Holliday left Prescott for Tombstone in the late summer of 1880. Soon, he'd be personally involved in the border troubles—and may have been Governor Gosper's go-between in a dangerous solution to the depredations.

13

SOUTHERN PACIFIC

Doc Holliday left Prescott on the Arizona Stage Co. coach, riding 130 miles south past the desert town of Phoenix to the newly opened train depot at Maricopa Station, then boarding the Southern Pacific Railroad for another 130-mile ride to Tucson and on to Benson, thirty miles and another stage coach ride away from Tombstone. The Southern Pacific, laying rails from California to Texas to become the nation's second transcontinental line, swept that far south because Tombstone was the richest silver mining area in the Southwest and carrying out all that bullion could help to fund the railroad's expansion.

The town of Tombstone lay along a windswept ridge at the edge of the shallow San Pedro River Valley, thirty miles north of the Mexican border. To the west were the Whetstone and the Huachuca Mountains, to the east were the Dragoon Mountains, and farther to the east were the Chiricahua Mountains, home of the Apache—and it was the Apache threat that gave the town its name. When prospector Ed Schieffelin told soldiers at the nearby military post of Fort Huachuca that he planned to find ore in those desolate and dangerous mountains, they laughed and told him he'd likely only find his own grave. What he found, instead, were two rich silver strikes he named Tombstone and Graveyard in honor of the soldier's predictions.

Other prospectors, hearing of his luck, soon followed and found even richer veins—Lucky Cuss, Tough Nut, Grand Central, and Contention, assaying $15,000 and more to the ton—and the Tombstone silver rush was on. The mining country on the Mexican border was proving so rich that General William T. Sherman, who had once advised Congress to "get Mexico to take back" the Arizona Territory, now called Tombstone, "a permanent mine of silver to the United States."[1] In a matter of months, Tombstone's population had gone from one stubborn prospector to three thousand adventurers, including Wyatt Earp and his brothers, out to make their own profit off the silver boom.

But Tombstone was still more mining camp than city, its newly surveyed town blocks scattered with tents and lean-tos between adobe walls and board-sided buildings, and everything seeming to be under construction. Where only a year before a dirt-floored tent saloon had been the one watering hole, now there were thirty new saloons and three new hotels and enough gambling halls and bawdy houses to keep all of hell happily occupied.

Doc arrived in September 1880 and found a room at one of Tombstone's new hotels and scouted out the sporting scene. He also signed the Pima County voting register, though since he didn't order new dental equipment or open another office, as he had in other towns, he likely wasn't planning to stay around for too long.[2] The Earps, on the other hand, were settling in, buying land and becoming part of Tombstone's law and order: older brother Virgil had been appointed a Deputy US Marshal, younger brother Morgan was a stagecoach guard, and Wyatt had accepted an appointment as Pima County Sheriff's Deputy. The youngest Earp brother, Warren, would arrive a few months later, to join in their less orderly occupations of saloon life while looking for mining opportunities. And they'd already had run-ins with the other faction of Tombstone, the cattle ranchers and sometime rustlers called "cowboys" who didn't like the constraints of all that town and county law, men like the Clantons and the McLaurys. As Virgil Earp remembered the situation:

> The most of them are what we call "saddlers," living almost wholly in the saddle, and largely engaged in raiding into Sonora and adjacent country and stealing cattle, which they sell in Tombstone. . . . When cattle are not handy the cowboys rob stages and engage in similar enterprises to raise money. As soon as they are in funds they ride into town, drink, gamble, and fight. They spend their money as free as water in the saloons, dance houses, or faro banks, and this is one reason they have so many friends in town. All that large class of degraded characters who gather the crumbs of such carouses stand ready to assist them out of any trouble or into any paying rascality. The saloons and gambling houses into whose treasuries most of the money is ultimately turned receive them cordially and must be called warm friends of the cowboys. A good many of the merchants fear to express themselves against the criminal element, because they want to keep the patronage of the cowboys' friends.[3]

For Doc Holliday, not being a lawman, the cowboys were more nuisance than trouble, most of the time. He was happy to play cards with them and take their ill-gotten gains, as long as they behaved. His real trouble came from the other sporting men in town, in particular a California hustler named Johnny Tyler who made his home at the Oriental Saloon. On the evening of Sunday, October 10, Doc got into a heated argument with Tyler over a faro game and both men were disarmed and their pistols stashed behind the Oriental's bar, but the argument resumed when they both came back looking for their weapons. Bartender Milt Joyce ordered the men out of the saloon and Tyler left, but Doc refused to go and started up an argument with Joyce. But Milt Joyce was the wrong man to challenge, being a former blacksmith and more than a match for the consumptive dentist. He tossed Doc out into the street and refused to return his pistol to him. Humiliated by the rough treatment, Doc went to his room and came back with another pistol and "with a remark that would not look well in print, turned loose with a self-cocker. Joyce was not more ten feet away, and jumped for his assailant and struck him over the head with a six-shooters, felling him to the floor and lighting on top of him."[4]

As Doc went down, he fired and hit Joyce in the hand and another man in the foot. Then, bleeding badly from the head, he was arrested and carried away. Witnesses thought his wounds might be fatal, but he recovered enough to appear in court two days later, "in the custody of the town marshal, Fred White. None of the prosecution witnesses appeared in court. The defendant offered a plea of guilty to assault and battery. It was accepted and the charge of assault with a deadly weapon was dismissed. Holliday was fined $20 and costs of $11.25."[5] Doc Holliday had learned that Tombstone was going to be a tough town.

Trouble with the cowboys came soon after, when William "Curly Bill" Brocius and friends rode into town for a night of drinking and carousing and ended the evening "shooting at the moon" in front of the Alhambra Saloon, where Doc was banking a faro game. The shooting drew a crowd, including thirty-one-year-old Marshal Fred White, newly appointed Assistant Marshal Virgil Earp (who would later be appointed marshal) and Deputy County Sheriff Wyatt Earp. The marshal went into the street and ordered Curly Bill to give up his pistol, and when Curly Bill moved to pull his gun from the holster, Wyatt grabbed him from behind and the marshal jerked the pistol away. But Curly Bill's pistol had a hair-trigger, and spontaneously fired a slug into Marshal White's groin and intestines, igniting his clothing from the muzzle blast. According to Doc's later memory, he was also there on the night of the cowboy disturbance:

"Trouble first arose with them by the killing of Marshal White by Curly Bill. Marshal White fell into my arms when he was shot."[6] The marshal died of his wounds two days later, leaving a wife and two small children, and Curly Bill was arrested and charged with murder, though the shooting was later ruled accidental. Marshal White's funeral at Tombstone's Boot Hill Cemetery was held on an appropriately ghoulish day: October 31, Halloween.

Curly Bill wasn't the only cowboy leader causing trouble in the border country. Johnny Ringo, who'd been part of the rustler gang in Fort Griffin, Texas, had moved on to Arizona to continue his illegal occupation. According to Wyatt Earp biographer Casey Tefertiller, "His activities in Arizona will never be certain—rustlers did not keep records. He stole cattle, almost certainly participated in the raids and murders against the Mexicans, and may well have taken a hand in a stage robbery."[7]

But the town of Tombstone was generally peaceful for a few months, until a young gambler nicknamed "Johnny-Behind-the-Deuce" shot and killed a local mining man over a game of cards. The gambler was arrested and on his way to court in Tucson when an angry mob gathered to give him quicker justice, and Wyatt Earp had to take over the transfer to keep the prisoner from being lynched. Doc Holliday was one of the pistoleers who backed up Wyatt against the mob, once again putting Doc on the side of law and order.

He also joined Wyatt in less dramatic, but potentially more lucrative pursuits. In February 1881, he added his name to the Wyatt Earp Water Right Deed in Hayes and Turner Canyon, the Clark Water Right Deed in Mormon Canyon, and the Holliday Water Right Deed in Ramsey Canyon. The water rights meant that Doc and Wyatt were going into the mining business, water being essential to the process of ore extraction—the mine being The Last Decision, which they owned together with four other investors. After the dark days of his troubled past, Doc's future looked to have a silver lining.

According to one story, he also had a chance to play Southern gentleman to a lady in distress: Josephine Sarah Marcus, who was living with her boyfriend, Johnny Behan, sheriff of the newly created Cochise County. "Sadie," as she was called, had a quarrel with Behan and ordered him out of the house her parents had paid for. But Behan had paid for the lot the house had been built on and threatened to have her house moved out from under her. Sadie asked Doc Holliday for help, and he gave her the money to put the lot in her own name, which may have been the situation he described in a later newspaper interview:

A word further about this man Behan. . . . He first ran against me when I was running a faro bank, when he started a quarrel in my house, and I stopped him and refused to let him play anymore. We were enemies after that. In that quarrel I told him in the presence of a crowd that he was gambling with money I had given his woman. The story got out and caused him trouble. He always hated me after that, and would spend money to have me killed.[8]

Then an old friend came to Tombstone, and things got even more complicated. Billy Leonard, who'd been a jeweler by trade when Doc had made his acquaintance in Otero and Las Vegas, had since turned his skills to melting down stolen bullion and retooling Winchester rifles into carbines for saddle guns—work that made him useful to Luther King, Harry Head, and Jim Crane, cowboy confederates who were looking for a stagecoach to rob. On the night of March 15, Billy Leonard joined the robbers in a botched attempt to hold up the stage from Tombstone to Benson, killing the driver and a passenger but not getting away with any treasure. And while two posses rode out in pursuit of the robbers, rumors flew around Tombstone: Doc Holliday was known to have been friendly with Billy Leonard and had gone out riding on the same night as the stage holdup occurred, making him seem somehow complicit. Doc responded to the rumors with derision, saying, "If I had pulled that job, I'd have got the $80,000. . . . Whoever shot Philpot was a rank amateur. If he had downed a horse, he'd have got the bullion."[9]

The rumors persisted, perhaps urged on by Milt Joyce of the Oriental Saloon who was still recovering from the gunshot wound to his hand from the previous fall. When Doc walked into the Oriental, Joyce announced, "Well, here comes the stage robber."[10] Doc's unrecorded response got him a day in the Justice Court and a charge of Threats Against Life. But Joyce wasn't done with him yet. On May 30, the *Tombstone Epitaph* reported, "Doc Holliday has been indicted by the Grand Jury on account of participation in a shooting affray some time since." The case was continued until October, but Milt Joyce seemed determined to get his revenge, one way or another.

Doc had enough trouble already, between his friendship with a road agent and his wars with a barkeeper and the county sheriff, when Kate Elder came to town for a visit, hoping for a reconciliation and getting drunk and angry instead. On July 5, Kate signed an affidavit accusing Doc Holliday of complicity in the attempted robbery of the Benson Stage and the murders of driver Bud Philpot and passenger Peter Roerig. Doc was arrested by Sheriff Behan and taken before Judge Wells Spicer, then released on a $5,000 bond backed by Wyatt Earp and the owners of the Alhambra Saloon, where Doc had his faro game. Later that day, Kate was arrested by Virgil Earp for being drunk and disorderly, and spent the night locked in a hotel room until she cooled off. She was released the next morning, then arrested again for Threats Against Life. As the *Tombstone Nugget* reported, "Such is the result of a warrant sworn out by an enraged and intoxicated woman."[11] Kate later said of the situation:

> *I became desperate and in a vain hope of breaking up their [the Earps] association with Doc, whom I loved, I swore out a warrant charging him with the murder of Philpott and Roerig and was arrested by Sheriff Behan. But Wyatt Earp and others of his gang of legalized outlaws furnished $5,000 bail to get him out. It took all of the persecution of the Earps and other law officers aligned with them to make me quit. In doing it I had known I was taking a desperate chance and I was not astonished when I lost out.*[12]

Kate clearly did not like Doc's friends and perhaps hoped that getting him arrested for murder would show him that he needed to keep better company. If so, her plan backfired. When the case came before Judge Spicer on July 9, the District Attorney said that he had examined all the witnesses and was satisfied that there was not the slightest evidence to show the guilt of the defendant and asked that the case be dismissed. Having failed to separate Doc from the Earps, Kate left town and went back to Globe. Wyatt's comment on Doc's guilt was simple: "Doc was not in on the Benson stage holdup. [He] never did such a thing as holdups in his life."[13]

But the story of the Benson Stage holdup wasn't over yet. Wyatt had been one of the posse members searching for the robbers and, hoping to get a lead on their trail, he'd cut a secret deal with ranchers Ike Clanton and Frank McLaury. In exchange for information, he would give Clanton and McLaury his share of the reward money when the robbers were captured, dead or alive. Ike and Frank, with their questionable connections to rustlers and robbers, were logical informants-for-hire, but Wyatt's purpose wasn't strictly law enforcement. He was planning to run for Cochise County sheriff in the next election, challenging Johnny Behan, and he hoped a notable arrest would earn him votes. But the deal went bad when Billy Leonard and Harry Head were shot to death in another altercation, Luther King was killed by his own cowboy partners, and Jim Crane got away. Which left Wyatt Earp, Ike Clanton, and Frank McLaury in an uncomfortable situation: Wyatt had promised payback for the capture of Doc Holliday's friend, and Ike and Frank had cut a deal to double-cross their cowboy friends. It was a dangerous secret they shared, one that could get them all killed.

If Wyatt needed more proof that the cowboys were murderous men, it came on July 27 in *El Cajon del Sarampion*, the Canyon of the Scorpion, a rugged mountain pass that had long been a smugglers' route from Sonora to Tucson. The Americans called it Skeleton Canyon, a name that became more appropriate when a Mexican pack train was attacked by a gang of fifty cowboys. The surprised Mexicans never had a chance to fight back and were left with four dead and thousands in goods and gold stolen. Even their mules were slaughtered, and the narrow canyon walls were covered with blood.

Vengeance came swiftly. On August 13, a patrol of Mexican Federales discovered cowboys herding stolen cattle through Guadalupe Canyon. The pre-dawn attack killed nine cowboys, including "Old Man" Clanton, patriarch of the Clanton family. The "Guadalupe Canyon Massacre," as the papers quickly named it, seemed to prove that the Clantons weren't just friendly with the rustlers—they were in on the operation. But the incident also implicated Doc Holliday in an unexpected way: one of the rustlers killed in the attack was Jim Crane, the last of the suspects in the Benson Stage holdup, giving rise to the rumor that Doc and the Earps were somehow behind the attack, targeted to kill Crane so he couldn't give away Doc's supposed part in the botched stagecoach robbery.

The accusation was glaringly inaccurate in the details—the two survivors of the Guadalupe Canyon Massacre both claimed the attackers were Mexicans, not the Earps and Doc Holliday—but it wasn't entirely groundless. Doc did have cause to want the story of the Benson stage robbery laid to rest, and Wyatt and his brothers likely were trailing the rustlers and hoping to make a capture, if not a killing, and that was enough to give the grieving Ike Clanton one more reason to hate the Earps and Doc Holliday.

As for Frank McLaury, the other informant in Wyatt's secret deal, he had his own reasons to hate the Earps, as revealed in a conversation that followed another crime. On the night of September 8, robbers stopped a stage on the way to the mining town of Bisbee, south of Tombstone, taking $2,500 from the treasure box and $600 and a gold watch from the passengers. Two posses went after the robbers: one made up of Sheriff Behan's deputies, another of the Earp brothers. Three days later, the Earp posse brought in the surprising suspects: Pete Spence and Frank Stillwell, two of Behan's deputies. Both men were later released on lack of evidence, but the Earps had uncovered the corruption of Sheriff Behan's office and its connection to local outlawry, with the sheriff hand-in-glove with the rustlers, the robbers, and whoever else had money to share. And soon after, Frank McLaury stopped Virgil Earp on the streets of Tombstone, incensed about the arrests of his friends, Spence and Stillwell. As Virgil remembered Frank's ominous words: "I understand you are raising a vigilance committee to hang us boys . . . I'll tell you, it makes no difference what I do, I never will surrender my arms to you . . . I'd rather die fighting than be strangled."[14]

Having come to Tombstone for the games and the silver, Doc Holliday instead found himself at the center of a game of life and death.

CAN YOU HEAR ME NOW?

The Tombstone silver rush would likely not have happened at all without the Southern Pacific Railroad, which arrived in Arizona just as the mines were opening and carried out hundreds of millions of dollars in bullion to banks across the country. Without the rails, the riches of remote Southern Arizona may have remained just a prospector's dream.

Southern Pacific steam locomotive. Courtesy History San Jose, Ernie Kissel Southern Pacific Railroad Collection, Catalog #1978-152-248.

The Southern Pacific began in 1865 with a plan to lay rails from San Francisco south along the Pacific Coast to Los Angeles. By 1870 it had merged with the Central Pacific with a much grander goal: building east across the country to become part of the nation's second transcontinental railroad. After the first train pulled into the small city of Los Angeles in 1876, the company kept building south and east, crossing into Arizona Territory at Fort Yuma on the Colorado River in 1877 and reaching Tucson in March 1880, where it was met with a thirty-two-gun salute and a military band playing patriotic tunes. But when the railroad built on from Tucson, a military escort accompanied the construction forces as the Apaches were on the warpath.

In June 1880, the Southern Pacific reached Benson, twenty-five miles north of Tombstone, and two months later Doc Holliday made his first trip down from Prescott, taking the stage to the Maricopa depot and riding the train from there to Benson before boarding the Kinnear Co. stage the rest of the way to the silver boomtown. By

1881, the Southern Pacific reached to New Mexico and El Paso, Texas, and arrived in New Orleans in 1883 on the newly christened "Sunset Route"—and the era of stage travel was near its end.

Wherever the Southern Pacific laid rails and strung telegraph wires, new towns sprang up and small towns became cities. The health of those communities was important to the railroad's business, so like other large railroad companies it founded hospitals along its routes, such as in San Francisco and Tucson, where at one time it maintained a tuberculosis sanitarium in a converted freight station. In the 1970s, it also founded a telecommunications network with state-of-the-art microwave and fiber optics that evolved into Sprint—the Southern Pacific Railroad Internal Networking Telephony, taking communications across the country as it had taken passengers in the days of Doc Holliday.

GOVERNOR GOSPER'S BOUNTY

In January 1881, Doc Holliday's housemate from Prescott, Acting Governor of the Arizona Territory John Gosper, joined US Marshal Crawley P. Dake on a trip to Tombstone to evaluate the situation on the border. The cowboy trouble was continuing, with American cattle rustlers crossing over into the Mexican State of Sonora to steal Mexican cattle and kill any Mexicans who happened to get in the way. The federal government had ordered the Arizona Legislature to take measures to stop the depredations, and Governor Frémont had authorized Marshall Dake to hire deputies to corral the rustlers but had left the territory for the calmer life of Washington, D.C., without funding the police action. Secretary Gosper, now left with the task of finding the money and stopping the rustling and murders before Mexico declared war on the United States, asked that the absent Frémont be removed from office so that he, Gosper, could have full authority to act. Washington was slow to respond.

While Gosper waited for the government's answer, the depredations continued. In May, the cowboys massacred Mexicans near Fronteras in the state of Sonora. In July, they massacred more Mexicans at Skeleton Canyon. Finally, Gosper decided to "take action," and although his private correspondence does not specifically state what that action was, within weeks the bloody Guadalupe Canyon Massacre occurred in which several cowboys were killed—including rustler boss Old Man Clanton. The rumors at the time suggested that Doc Holliday and Wyatt Earp had somehow been involved—were they part of Gosper's plan of action, a private police force to protect the border country? As Holliday later said of the reasons behind the O.K. Corral gunfight, "we hunted the rustlers, and they all hate us."[15]

Secretary Gosper was no stranger to employing such vigilantism under the legal power afforded him, as shown in an 1879 directive from his office in Prescott: "I, John J. Gosper, Acting Governor of the Territory of Arizona, do hereby authorize the payment out of the Territorial Treasury, the sum of $500 to any individual who shall kill, by means of fire arms, or otherwise, the highway robber while in the act or attempt of robbing the mail or express, or search of the passengers."

Perhaps Gosper tried the same tactic to rid the country of cowboys, as well, which would explain much about the trouble in Tombstone. It also might explain a surprising addition to the Holliday-Earp defense team at the later O.K. Corral hearing—attorney Thomas Fitch from the territorial capital in Prescott, bringing a $10,000 bond along with him.

THE LAST DECISION MINE

When Doc Holliday arrived in the silver mining camp of Tombstone, Arizona, he opened a gambling game at the Alhambra Saloon and became a partner in another kind of gamble: a silver mine called the Last Decision, co-owned with Wyatt Earp and two other investors. The mine claim was a vein of precious ore running through twelve-hundred feet of quartz rock that shared a section of another claim called the Intervenor, owned by a Philadelphia mining syndicate. Some folks might have called the new mine filing "claim jumping," but as the two veins ran at different angles after their shared section, the Mining Act called the filing a relocation, and perfectly legal.

But owning a mine was only profitable on paper. To make any real money on the claim, the mine had to be worked, with the raw ore crushed in a steam-powered mill and washed to extract the silver. So, the owners of the Last Decision mine also filed deeds for water claims in Hayes, Turner, Ramsey, and Mormon

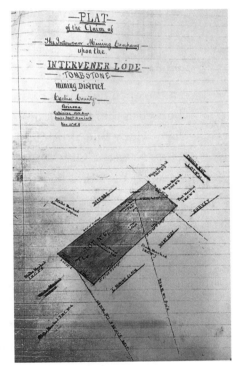

Plat map of the Intervenor Mine showing crosscut of Last Decision claim. Author's Collection.

Canyons. It seemed that Doc and Wyatt were on their way to a lucrative career as silver mine owners.

But in June 1881, they sold their shares in the Last Decision mine to Tombstone attorney Marcus Smith for the paltry price of $1.00. It seems a surprisingly bad business deal for Doc and Wyatt to have made, giving Smith a share in what could have become a silver fortune for such a small buy-in, and one has to wonder what else Marcus Smith may have given in exchange for a partnership in the mine. The answer may lie in Smith's other business associates: his clients, Frank and Tom McLaury, who owned a ranch near Tombstone and were friends of the cowboys suspected of stealing Mexican cattle—the Clantons, Curly Bill Brocius, and Johnny Ringo. The McLaurys were said to have had a part in the rustling business, too, allowing the cowboys to use their ranch for the stolen stock. Perhaps the sale of those shares in the Last Decision mine was a payoff to the McLaurys' attorney in exchange for information about the rustlers. If so, that would explain why, weeks before the O.K. Corral gunfight, Frank McLaury told Virgil Earp he'd "rather die fighting than be strangled."[16] "Strangling" was another term for hanging, the punishment for cattle rustling.

FOUNDER OF THE FEAST

In the opening scenes of the 1993 movie *Tombstone*, Curly Bill Brocious introduces himself as the "founder of the feast" and the boss of the cowboys. But in real life, William "Curly Bill" Brocious was a more minor character, a hireling of the real cowboy boss, Newton "Old Man" Clanton. In the original screenplay for *Tombstone*, "Old Man" Clanton is, as he was historically, the head of the cowboy consortium, a rancher who enlarged his own herd with stolen cattle rustled through the mountain passes between Mexico and Southern Arizona. But as filming began, famed actor Robert Mitchum, who was set to play Clanton, was injured and unable to fill the role. Rather than recast the film, the director opted to just rewrite the script, promoting Curly Bill to the leader of the cowboys and splitting Old Man Clanton's lines between him and other characters.

There was some poetic justice to the last-minute change. Wyatt Earp really did kill Curly Bill Brocius in a dramatic showdown at Iron Springs (Doc Holliday called it "miraculous"), so now the death of Curly Bill, the leader of the evil cowboys, became the theatrical finale of Wyatt's Vendetta Ride. Real life, however, is rarely so neat. After the death of "Old Man" Clanton, it was his son Isaac "Ike" Clanton who took over the operations of the ranch and rustling business, and who was Wyatt Earp's worst foe, bringing charges against him for the murder of younger brother Billy Clanton at the O.K. Corral and more charges at Charleston (a popular cowboy hangout nine miles southwest of Tombstone) when the first charges didn't stick. Through all the legal tangle Curly Bill was just a sidebar. But Wyatt Earp didn't kill Ike Clanton, his biggest adversary, he killed Curly Bill—so for the sake of the movie Curly Bill Brocious made a better antagonist.

And because Wyatt Earp kills Curly Bill in the film, Doc Holliday must kill Johnny Ringo, each man having his final showdown with his worst enemy. But that, too, was poetic justice and literary drama—when the real Johnny Ringo died, Doc Holliday was hundreds of miles away from Tombstone and glad to be gone.

Isaac "Ike" Clanton in Tombstone, 1881; photo by Camillus Fly. Arizona State Library.

14

BENSON FREIGHT

It was a good time, all things considered, for Doc Holliday to get out of Tombstone. He might have chosen to get out of Arizona entirely and found a place with a more hospitable climate, but he still had one legal matter to settle: his trial for the Oriental Saloon shooting of the previous fall, with a court date postponed until the coming October. So, his getaway would have to be a short excursion, consisting of a train ride on the Southern Pacific Railroad to Tucson to visit the fiesta.

Before the coming of the rails, San Augustin del Tucson had been little more than a collection of adobe houses along the Santa Cruz River. The Old Pueblo, the locals called it, was known for its hundred-year-old walled Presidio and bell-towered cathedral, its flat-roofed barrios and chicken fights in the streets. But when the Southern Pacific Railroad built a Tucson depot on the new line crossing Arizona Territory, the pueblo became a boomtown, growing to a population of eight thousand in a year's time and becoming the biggest city between San Diego and San Antonio. The railroad also made the city's annual religious celebration into a tourist attraction, bringing visitors and sporting men from all over the territory.

La Fiesta de San Agustin del Tucson began as a Catholic festival honoring the city's patron, Saint Augustine, with all the customary pageantry: a street procession of children carrying a statue of the saint, a vespers service and ringing of bells, a High Mass and an evening rosary, a benediction and recessional. Then a German Jewish brewer named Alexander Levin saw a way to profit off the Catholic celebration, opening his brewery grounds as a "pleasure park" for two months following the festival. Soon, Levin's Park was being advertised as the finest resort in Arizona Territory, with shade trees and an open-air ramada for dancing, croquet grounds, a bowling alley, skating rink, shooting gallery, gambling hall, and, of course, a beer garden—especially appropriate, since Augustine was also the patron saint of brewers.

But Doc Holliday had come to Tucson mostly for the games, as Levin's Pleasure Park hosted every form of gambling known on both sides of the border—from poker, roulette and faro to Chusa, Malilla and Lotería. And he wasn't planning to be alone at the party, having invited Kate Elder to go along. He may have been hoping for a reconciliation, despite Kate's efforts to get him hung, or he may have just wanted some company. But once he had her there, he couldn't get loose of her. As Kate remembered things:

> *One evening at the Fiesta, Doc was bucking at Faro. I was standing behind him, when Morgan Earp came and tapped Doc on the shoulder and said, "Doc, we want you in Tombstone tomorrow. Better come up this evening." Doc said, "All right." He cashed in his chips. Morgan Earp did not want Doc to take me back with them . . . Doc said to me, "You had better stay here. I will come after you tomorrow or in a day or two." I said, "No, I am going back with you." Then he said, "We are going back on a freight train." I said, "If you can go on a freight, so can I." Then he said, "We are going to Benson on a freight. Then we have to ride on an open buckboard." I said, "If you can ride on an open buckboard, so can I." They saw that there was no way of getting rid of me, so the three of us went back to Tombstone.[1]*

The fact that they rode the freight train back to Benson rather than waiting for the regularly scheduled passenger train, then took a buckboard to Tombstone instead of waiting for the regular stage, was a sign of the seriousness of the situation. According to Wyatt's later testimony, a skittish Ike Clanton was worried that his secret deal with Wyatt Earp had been discovered and was blaming Doc Holliday for giving him away. Ike had reason to be nervous, knowing how his cowboy associates would deal with disloyalty, but Wyatt assured him that Doc knew nothing of the deal and would prove it as soon as he returned from Tucson. Then Wyatt sent Morgan Earp to bring Doc back on the Benson freight.

Doc likely *didn't* know about the deal when it was first made, as it was designed to capture one of his friends, but he surely knew about it by the time Ike started talking. But if Wyatt thought Doc could calm Ike's fears about the story spreading to the cowboys, he'd bet on the wrong players. When Ike ran into Doc at the Alhambra Saloon back in Tombstone, the cowboy was drunk and Doc was indignant, and their conversation only made matters worse. "I understand that you say the Earp brothers have given you away to me," Doc said, "and that you have been talking about me?" Then he called Ike a damned liar if he had said such things. According to Wyatt's later testimony:

> They quarreled for three or four minutes . . . Morgan Earp was standing at the Alhambra bar talking with the bartender. I called him over to where I was sitting, knowing that he was an officer and told him that Holliday and Clanton were quarreling in the lunch room and for him to go in and stop it. He climbed over the lunch room counter from the Alhambra bar and went into the room, took Holliday by the arm and led him into the street. Ike Clanton in a few seconds followed them out. I got through eating and walked out of the bar. As I stopped at the door of the bar, they were still quarreling. Just then Virgil Earp came up . . . and told them, Holliday and Clanton, if they don't stop their quarreling he would have to arrest them.[2]

Not wanting to risk another arrest, Doc went back to finish his faro game at the Alhambra, but Ike was still fuming, telling Wyatt that when he had met Holliday he wasn't "fixed just right," but that in the morning he would "have man-for-man." Ike's bravado was likely just liquor talking, but when Wyatt and Doc both finished work later that night they took the precaution of walking together down Allen Street to their homes—Wyatt to his rented house on Fremont Street, and Doc to his boardinghouse room at Fly's Photography Gallery, next to the O.K. Corral.

If Ike Clanton had gone to get some sleep, as well, the Tombstone story might have turned out very differently. Instead, he kept drinking and joined in an all-night poker game, and sometime after daybreak stopped Marshal Virgil Earp with a message for Doc Holliday: "The damned son of a bitch has got to fight." When Virgil declined to carry such a message, the cowboy said angrily, "You may have to fight before you know it."[3] Then, drunk and sleep-deprived, Ike wandered through town telling anyone who would listen that as soon as the Earps and Doc Holliday showed themselves on the street, they would have to fight. By noon he was tired of waiting for a confrontation and decided to make the first move. As Kate recalled that deadly day:

"In the morning Ike Clanton came to Fly's photograph gallery with a Winchester rifle. Mrs. Fly told him that Doc was not there. Doc was not up yet. I went to our room and told Doc that Ike Clanton was outside looking for him, and that he was armed. Doc said, "If God lets me live long enough to get my clothes on, he shall see me."[4]

While Doc was getting ready for another tense day in Tombstone, the Earp brothers were trying to get Ike under control. According to Virgil's later testimony:

I found Ike Clanton on Fourth Street between Fremont and Allen with a Winchester rifle in his hand and a six-shooter stuck down in his breeches. I walked up and grabbed the rifle in my left hand. He let loose and started to draw his six-shooter. I hit him over the head with mine and knocked him to his knees and took his six-shooter from him. I ask [sic] him if he was hunting for me. He said he was, and if he had seen me a second sooner he would have killed me. I arrested Ike for carrying firearms, I believe was the charge, inside the city limits.[5]

But instead of putting Ike in a cell to cool off and dry out, Virgil hauled him into court where he was fined $25 and released, with his weapons stashed behind the bar at the Grand Hotel. And Ike wasn't the only angry cowboy in town—his friend Tom McLaury was in Tombstone, too, and went to see what trouble Ike was into. Instead, he ran into Wyatt Earp.

"If you want to fight," McLaury told him, "I will fight you anywhere."

"Right here, right now!" Wyatt said, having grown tired of the constant threats from Ike and his gang. Then he pulled his pistol and hit McLaury on the side of his head, knocking him to the ground. Tom struggled to his feet as Wyatt walked away, then went to the Capitol Saloon to deposit his gun.[6]

While Ike and Tom were having their run-ins with the law, Doc had taken his time to dress in his usual dapper fashion: gray suit and pastel shirt, stiff paper collar and slouch hat, long gray overcoat and gold-headed cane. He must have assumed that the Earps by now had the Ike Clanton situation under control, for when he happened onto Ike's younger brother Billy, newly arrived in town together with Frank McLaury, he gave him a cordial greeting: "How are you?"[7] he said, offering his hand to Billy in proper Southern manner before continuing on his way.

But the situation was far from settled, and once Billy and Frank learned of their brothers' head injuries from the Earps' pistols, tensions escalated. Although some later reports said that Billy and Frank determined to take their brothers home, they all first stopped together into Spagenberg's gun shop—which looked like they were preparing for a battle, not a retreat.

By the time Doc arrived at the Alhambra Saloon to check on his faro game, the cowboys had moved from the gun shop to the O.K. Corral, and the Earps were headed that way to discover their intentions. If the Clantons and McLaurys were truly leaving town, they would be allowed to keep their guns. If their plan were something more sinister, they would have to be disarmed before being allowed back on the streets. And it may have been the cowboy's location that caused Doc's comments:

"You're not going to leave me out, are you?" he said to Wyatt.

"This is none of your affair," Wyatt replied.

"That is a hell of a thing for you to say to me!"[8]

As Doc saw things, the affair had everything to do with him. Ike Clanton's threats had been especially aimed at him; Ike had come looking for him at his boardinghouse with a rifle in hand; now Ike and the other cowboys were armed and waiting at the O.K. Corral next to his boardinghouse. If there were to be a fight, it was as much his as the Earps'. Virgil, perhaps agreeing, took Doc's cane and gave him a shotgun, telling him to hide it under his long overcoat to avoid exciting the town, in essence deputizing him.

But the town was already excited, with crowds gathering to watch what would happen next as the cowboys moved out of the corral and onto Fremont Street, still armed. Court testimony recalled the next tense minutes:

"They have horses," Morgan said as the Earps and Doc Holliday began their walk down Allen Street toward a certain confrontation. "Had we not better get some horses ourselves, so that if they make a running fight we can catch them?"

"If they try to make a running fight," said Wyatt, "we can kill their horses and then capture them."

There wasn't much more conversation between them, and Doc whistled quietly and nodded to the people they passed. In the cold October wind, his overcoat blew open to reveal the shotgun, and a witness heard someone say, "Let them have it," and Doc replied, "All right."

Ahead of them, Cochise County Sheriff Johnny Behan had made a futile attempt at disarming the cowboys, and stopped Virgil with his hands outstretched:

"Hold up boys! Don't go down there or there will be trouble."

"Johnny, I am going down to disarm them," Virgil said.

"I have been down there to disarm them," Behan replied.

Misunderstanding the sheriff to mean that the cowboys were now disarmed, the Earps and Doc Holliday relaxed a little, but continued their walk toward Fremont Street, while the cowboys backed away from the street into the vacant lot between the O.K. Corral and Fly's Boarding House.

Doc knew his place as backup to the real law, and stayed out in the street while Virgil, Wyatt, and Morgan faced off with the cowboys in the narrow empty lot. Billy Clanton and Frank McLaury had their pistols in plain view, with Winchester rifles stuck into saddle boots on their horses.

"Throw up your hands, boys!" Virgil ordered, raising Doc's cane over his head. "I intend to disarm you!"

"We will!" Frank said as he and Billy Clanton reached for their pistols and Tom McLaury opened his coat as if going for a weapon.

"Hold!" Virgil shouted, "I don't mean that!"

But it was past time for talking. According to Wyatt's later testimony:

> When I saw Billy Clanton and Frank McLaury draw their pistols, I drew my pistol. Billy Clanton leveled his pistol at me, but I did not aim at him. I knew that Frank McLaury had the reputation of being a good shot and a dangerous man, and I aimed at Frank McLaury. The first two shots were fired by Billy Clanton and myself, he shooting at me, and I shooting at Frank McLaury. I don't know which was fired first. We fired almost together. The fight then became general.
>
> After about four shots were fired, Ike Clanton ran up and grabbed my left arm. I could see no weapon in his hand, and thought at the time he had none, and so I said to him, "The fight has commenced. Go to fighting or get away," at the same time pushing him off with my left hand.... He started and ran down the side of the building and disappeared between the lodging house and photograph gallery. My first shot struck Frank McLaury in the belly. He staggered off on the sidewalk but fired one shot at me.

Frank and Billy kept firing, hitting Virgil in the calf and Morgan Earp in the back. "I'm hit!" Morgan cried as he stumbled to the ground, while the Earps' return fire struck Billy Clanton in the chest and the wrist. Doc Holliday, waiting in the street with the shotgun, saw Tom McLaury reach across a horse, likely going for a rifle in the saddle boot, and fired a double load of buckshot into Tom's right arm and side. The shotgun spent, he threw it down and pulled his nickel-plated revolver, then looked up to see Frank McLaury staggering toward him into the street.

"I've got you now!" Frank said.

"Blaze away!" Doc said. "You're a daisy if you have."

Their shots rang out together, with Doc's bullet striking Frank in the chest and Frank's tearing through Doc's coat and grazing his hip. "I'm shot right through!" Doc said, but before he could fire another round, the wounded Morgan Earp raised up and took one last shot, putting a bullet into Frank McLaury's head.[9]

The affray that would come to be known as the Gunfight at the O.K. Corral lasted less than three minutes, with three men dead or dying, three men wounded, and only Wyatt Earp and Ike Clanton, who'd started the war, left unscathed. Kate Elder remembered Doc's reaction:

> *After the fight was over, Doc came in, and sat on the side of the bed and cried and said, "Oh, this is just awful—awful." I asked, "Are you hurt?" He said, "No, I am not." He pulled up his shirt. There was just a pale red streak about two inches long across his hip where the bullet had grazed him. Then he went out to see what had become of the two Earps that were wounded; they were afraid to leave them for fear that the cow rustlers would take them in the night.*[10]

But it was the law, not the outlaws, that Doc and the Earp brothers would have to battle next. When the coroner's report came back the next morning, it found that the cowboys had died "from the effects of gunshot wounds by Virgil Earp, Morgan Earp, Wyatt Earp, and one Holliday—commonly called Doc Holliday."[11] What the report did not say was that the shootings were done in the line of duty. The next day, Ike Clanton swore out a complaint of murder against the Earps and Doc Holliday and warrants were issued for their arrest, though only Doc and Wyatt were jailed, as Virgil and Morgan were in bed healing from their wounds.

On October 31—one year to the day since the Halloween funeral of Tombstone Marshal Fred White—a hearing began to determine if the case against the Earps and Doc Holliday should be sent to the grand jury. The proceedings would go on for nearly a month, with testimony for both sides from dozens of witnesses, a rambling tirade from Ike Clanton, a bedside deposition from the wounded Virgil Earp, and a long written statement from Wyatt Earp. But neither defense nor prosecution would call Doc Holliday to testify, though he was central to the trouble—which meant that his version of events was never recorded, and the truth about Tombstone will never be fully known.

Kate Elder didn't wait around to learn the disposition of the case. Midway through the proceedings, she took a friend's advice to leave town and move back to the safety of Globe. It was good advice, though the source was surprising:

> I kept close to my room at Mrs. Fly's during the Earp-Holliday trial. . . . Ringo had come to town and visited me at Fly's twice. The second time he advised me to return to Globe, but I told him I did not have enough money to do so as Doc had lost all my money, about $75.00, playing faro while we were at the Tucson Fiesta. He said the Clantons were watching for Doc to come to the room and intended to get him there. "If you haven't enough money to go," he said, "here is fifty dollars." So, I left that evening.

Kate always remembered Johnny Ringo fondly, saying of him, "whenever I think of him, my eyes fill with tears."[12]

Though the curious relationship between Johnny Ringo and Doc Holliday's woman added to the tensions of Tombstone, Kate was long gone when the hearing concluded and Judge Spicer wrote his opinion of the case:

> In view of these controversies between Wyatt Earp and Isaac Clanton and Thomas McLaury, and in further view of this quarrel the night before between Isaac Clanton and J. H. Holliday, I am of the opinion that the defendant, Virgil Earp, as chief of police, subsequently calling upon Wyatt Earp, and J. H. Holliday to assist him in arresting and disarming the Clanton and McLaurys—committed an injudicious and censurable act . . . yet when we consider the conditions of affairs incident to a frontier country; the lawlessness and disregard for human life; the existence of a law-defying element in [our] midst; the fear and feeling of insecurity that has existed; the supposed prevalence of bad, desperate and reckless men who have been a terror to the country and kept away capital and enterprise; and consider the many threats that have been made against the Earps, I can attach no criminality to this unwise act. In fact, as the result plainly proves, he needed the assistance and support of staunch and true friends, upon whose

courage, coolness and fidelity he could depend, in case of an emergency.... There being no sufficient cause to believe the within named Wyatt S. Earp and John H. Holliday guilty of the offense mentioned within, I order them to be released.[13]

But not all of Tombstone agreed with Judge Spicer's opinion, and Doc and the Earps would need all the courage they could muster to face the coming storm of the cowboys' revenge.

PLEASURE PARK

When the Southern Pacific Railroad first reached Tucson in March 1880, the welcoming banquet was held at Levin's Pleasure Park, the center of entertainment in the newly made railroad town. Thousands gathered to watch the train steam into town, the Sixth Cavalry Band played, and Southern Pacific Railroad President Charles Crocker was presented with a silver spike from the Toughnut Mine in Tombstone, signifying the economic tie between the railroad and the boomtown. As the *Arizona Daily Star* extolled on the day before the celebration:

Levin's Park Advertisement, Tucson–Tombstone Directory 1883–1884, page 66. Arizona Historical Society.

> *Go on brave toiler for the benefit of mankind. Open our opulent mountains until treasures stream down their sides; gladden the valleys with the harvest and the vine; make the cattle on a thousand hills skip for joy; span the Rio Grande; stretch over the plains of Texas and rest your head by the waves of an "American lake" called the Gulf of Mexico.*[14]

When Levin's Park wasn't welcoming railroad officials, it entertained one and all with its three acres of shade trees, shooting gallery, archery range, skating rink, bowling alley, and croquet grounds and eventually a dance hall, restaurant, and two-thousand seat opera house—and Levin's own Tucson brewed beer.

"YOU'RE NO GOOD, BABY, YOU'RE NO GOOD"

The 1970s hit by Tucson-born singer Linda Ronstadt might have been Kate Elder and Doc Holliday's theme song, as both of them caused trouble in their troubled relationship. And the singer herself has a connection to Doc and Kate, through Levin's Pleasure Park in Tucson.

In 1890, Alexander Levin's daughter Sara married Federico José María "Fred" Ronstadt. The couple had four children together, but Sara died while expecting her fifth child, becoming a casualty of a scarlet fever epidemic.

Lupe Dalton, Bookkeeper. Courtesy University of Arizona Libraries Special Collections, Fred Ronstadt Album, no. 3.

The next year, twenty-one-year-old Guadalupe "Lupe" Dalton applied for a job as a bookkeeper at Fred Ronstadt's company, and the two fell in love, marrying on Valentine's Day of 1904. Fred had four more children with Lupe, raising them in a Tucson home now on the National Register of Historic Places. Lupe's look-alike granddaughter is singer Linda Ronstadt.

But Linda is actually the second Ronstadt girl to become a music star. Her great-aunt Luisa, Fred's daughter with first wife Sara Levin, had a long and successful career as the internationally known singer Luisa Espinal, spending time in Spain and weaving the music, acting, and dance of the Spanish culture into her popular shows across America.

The Ronstadts have one more interesting connection to Doc Holliday, through his friend Wyatt Earp. When Lupe's English grandfather first arrived in the United States, he settled in California and bought a rancho at Santa Anita, land which was eventually purchased by real estate speculator Elias Jackson "Lucky" Baldwin, who later owned a yacht where Wyatt Earp and Josephine Sarah Marcus were reportedly married.

Luisa Ronstadt Espinal. Arizona Historical Society, Portrait Collection (69493).

ALL RIGHT CORRAL

It's the most famous horse lot in American history, but where did the name of the legendary O.K. Corral come from—and what does it mean?

According to author Alan Metcalf (*OK: The Improbable Story of America's Greatest Word*), the term "O.K." began with an 1830s fad for abbreviating misspelled words: K.C. ("knuff ced"), O.W. ("oll wright"). It was just fun word play and forgotten now, except for one term that lingered on: O.K. for "oll korrect," a playful misspelling of

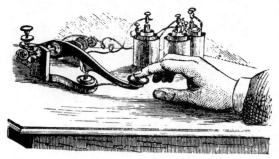

Telegraph operator. iStock by Getty Images #182778767.

the common phrase "all correct," meaning that everything was in order. The abbreviation "O.K." first appeared in print in the *Boston Post* of March 23, 1839, and the term went from there to other newspapers across the country, first explaining the meaning ("O.K.—means all correct"), then leaving out the definition as "O.K." moved into the vernacular. With the invention of the telegraph in 1844, the letters "OK" became the fast way to say, "message received" by operators on the railroads. In spoken language, okay (as it is often spelled) has become a "neutral affirmative": It conveys no feelings, just acknowledges and accepts information. Most of us say it dozens of times a day without even thinking about it. So, the O.K. Corral was all right, not great, but acceptable. How different might the legend have been if the cowboys had chosen to make their stand at the Dexter Stables down the street, or at Dunbar Brothers livery, where Sheriff Behan had his office? Would "gunfight in the street behind Dexters" or "gunfight in the alley beside the Dunbar Brothers" have had the same ring as "Gunfight at the O.K. Corral?" Like the names Wyatt Earp and Doc Holliday, the name O.K. Corral just sounded good—and likely helped to propel the Tombstone street fight into legend.

CAMILLUS FLY, FRONTIER PHOTOGRAPHER

Camillus Sydney Fly was born to the frontier—within weeks of his birth in May 1849, his family set out in a wagon train from Missouri to California, where he grew up on a farm in Napa County. But "Buck" Fly, as he preferred to be called, did not want to spend his days farming, so he moved to San Francisco and became a photographer, marrying divorcee and fellow photographer Mollie McKie Goodrich, with whom he opened a photographic studio. When the Flys heard of the silver rush in Southern Arizona, they packed up their equipment and moved to the boomtown of Tombstone, arriving in December of 1879, the same month the Earp family wagon train arrived from Prescott.

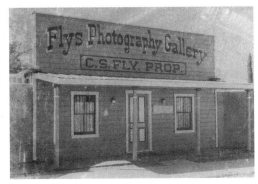

C.S. Fly Photography Gallery, Tombstone. Courtesy Mike Mihaljevich.

The Flys made their first home in Tombstone in a canvas tent before building a twelve-room boardinghouse on Fremont Street with a photography studio at the back. Mollie managed the boardinghouse and the photography business and did indoor sittings for a charge of thirty-five cents, while Buck took his camera on the road for outdoor images of mills, mountains, cavalry troops, cowboys, Indians, townspeople, and schoolchildren. As their photographic collection grew, the Flys built display cases in the hallway beside their studio and the public was welcome to come enjoy the "Fly Gallery." The mayor of Tucson, C. M. Strauss, would later remember Fly's photographic technique: "Fly is an excellent artist and he was not a respector of persons or circumstances, and even in the midst of the most serious interviews with the Indians, he would step up to an officer and say, 'just put your hat a little more on this side, General. No Geronimo, your right foot must rest on that stone,' etc., so wrapped was he in the artistic effect of his views."

In 1881, Doc Holliday and Kate Elder rented a room in the Fly's boardinghouse—where a drunk and armed Ike Clanton came the morning of the O.K. Corral gunfight, looking for Doc. Later that day, Buck Fly heard gunshots outside his studio and grabbed an unloaded gun used as a photo prop, running into the alley beside the boardinghouse in time to take away the dying Billy Clanton's empty Colt revolver. Although Fly did not photograph the immediate aftermath of the gunfight, he documented the event with an iconic image: the dead Tom and Frank McLaury and Billy Clanton in their ornate open caskets.

Tom McLaury, Frank McLaury, and Billy Clanton in their caskets, Tombstone 1881; photo by Camillus Fly. Courtesy Western History Collections, University of Oklahoma Library, Rose 1820.

MISSING PERSON

By the morning after the O.K. Corral gunfight, the story published in the *Tombstone Epitaph* and *Tombstone Nugget* had gone by telegraph wire to newspapers all over the country, including the *Atlanta Constitution* in Doc Holliday's home state of Georgia. But the story printed by the *Constitution* differed slightly from most other accounts: It was missing the name of John Henry Holliday as a participant in the affray.

The omission was likely more purposeful than bad proofreading. The Exchange Editor of the *Atlanta Constitution* in 1881 was Pascal Moran, whose wife Roberta Holliday was sister to Mattie Holliday—and Doc Holliday's cousin. Pascal Moran's daily work was to edit articles taken over the wire from other papers, and his editorial discretion determined which wire stories made the paper and which did not. There were at least three versions of the Tombstone story sent over the wire, so Moran picked the one that did not include the Holliday name, saving the family some embarrassment. The Atlanta Hollidays were respected members of the community—Dr. John Stiles Holliday a city councilman, Dr. Robert Holliday a dentist, George Henry Holliday a business owner—and having a shootist in the family would not be good for their reputations. In addition to being edited, the item was also buried on page eight of the October 27 edition of the paper, behind all the other news.

In comparison, the *Oil City Derrick* of Oil City, Pennsylvania, the *Ogden Herald* of Ogden, Utah, and several other papers ran a version that not only included the names of all the combatants, but gave Doc Holliday a more prominent position in Tombstone than he really had:

> *Four cowboys, Ike and Billy Clanton and Frank and Tom McLowery [sic], have been parading the town several days drinking heavily and making themselves*

Reprint of the O.K. Corral shooting story from the San Francisco papers in the Atlanta Constitution, *Atlanta, Georgia, October 27, 1881, page 8. Author's Collection.*

obnoxious. The city marshal arrested Ike Clanton. Soon after his release, the four met the marshal, his brothers Morgan and Wyatt Earp, and City Marshal J.H. Holliday. The marshal ordered them to give up their weapons when a fight commenced. About thirty shots were fired rapidly. Both the McLowery boys were killed, Bill Clanton mortally wounded, dying soon after, Ike slightly wounded in the shoulder. Wyatt is slightly wounded, the others were unhurt.

In weeks to come the story dubbed the Gunfight at the O.K. Corral would become widely known and discussed as the name Doc Holliday gained national notoriety, but for a few days, at least, the Atlanta Hollidays were spared the shame of their celebrity relation, thanks to a little editorial discretion.

15

CONTENTION CITY

The cowboys were more a loose confederation of outlaws than an organized crime syndicate, but they all had reasons to be rid of the Earps and Doc Holliday and anyone who sided with them. There was even a rumored Death List, signed in blood in a midnight ceremony in one of the cowboy's mountain hideaways, which named everyone from Judge Spicer to the defense attorneys to Mayor Clum—whose newspaper, the *Tombstone Epitaph*, had come out in support of the Earps. But rumor or not, the truth was that Tombstone had turned into an even more dangerous place than it had been before the O.K. Corral shootings, with fighting in the streets and the saloons, and the crack of pistol shots echoing through the dark December nights.

For safety's sake, the Earps had moved out of their neighboring cottages on the outskirts of town and into adjoining rooms on the second floor of the Cosmopolitan Hotel where they could be better guarded. But they had just gotten settled when the cowboys took a suite of rooms at the Grand Hotel across the street from the Cosmopolitan, with the shutters closed and one slat missing as though to allow the barrel of a pistol to peek through, and things didn't seem any safer than they'd been before.

Mayor Clum's response to the situation was to send a wire to Governor Gosper in Prescott, asking for the protection of additional arms, and Gosper wired back that he would ask President Chester A. Arthur to allow for martial law in Tombstone. But while Washington discussed and deliberated, the rumors and the tensions mounted, and Wyatt and Doc went about their business heavily armed and wary. But it was Mayor Clum who took the first fire, when he left town for a trip to Washington, and ran into road agents halfway to the railhead in Benson. He was one of five passengers on a coach with no treasure box and no shotgun guard and knew at once what the shooters wanted as they fired a volley that killed a horse and wounded the driver. And not wanting to put the other travelers into more danger, Clum grabbed for his six-guns and jumped from the stage, running across the lots and into the darkness. It took him all night to walk back to Tombstone, where he learned that after he'd left the stage the robbers had disappeared without taking so much as a pocket watch from the other passengers. And what kind of stage robbers held up a stage without robbing it? Their intent, he was sure, was nothing less than his own murder.

The two local papers battled out the holdup in fiery editorials, with the cowboy-friendly *Nugget* calling Mayor Clum a paranoid coward who saw outlaws at every turn, and Clum's *Epitaph* calling for better policing of the roads in this time of local trouble. But, other than that one attack, the roads were safe enough and the rumored Death List seemed to have been just a rumor, after all.

Then, three days after Christmas, Tombstone erupted again. As Virgil Earp walked the one block from the Occidental Saloon to his rented room at the Cosmopolitan Hotel, a volley of shotgun blasts rang out. Virgil was struck and knocked to the ground, the buckshot shattering his left arm and striking near his spinal column. Other shots crashed through the windows of the Eagle Brewery and lodged in the outside wall and awning posts. Virgil dragged himself to his feet and staggered back to the Occidental and was carried from there to the hotel where attending doctors removed five inches of bone from his mangled arm. "Never mind," he told his wife Allie, "I've still got one good arm to hug you with."[1] But Virgil was just trying to solace his wife—the doctor thought he would die of his wounds, and Wyatt sent a telegram to US Marshal Crawley Dake at Tucson: "Virgil was shot by concealed assailants last night. His wounds are fatal. Telegraph me appointment with power to appoint deputies. Local authorities are doing nothing. The lives of other citizens are threatened."[2]

Marshal Dake wired back the appointment, and Wyatt assembled a posse that included Doc Holliday—now deputized as a duly appointed federal lawman. But the posse would not be put to work for another ten days, while Virgil hovered near death and Wyatt stayed close to guard him. (Virgil survived, although it took him two years to recover and he never regained full use of his injured arm.) It was during that tense period that Doc came close to another street fight, this time with cowboy Johnny Ringo, as reported in the January 18, 1882, *Tombstone Nugget*:

> *A difficulty occurred yesterday afternoon in front of the Occidental Saloon, Allen Street, between John Ringo and Doc Holliday, that very nearly terminated in bloodshed. The parties had been on bad terms for some time past, and meeting*

yesterday morning words were exchanged and both parties stepped back, plac-
ing their hands on their weapons with the intention of drawing and using them.
Fortunately, Chief of Police Flynn was at hand and placed both parties under
arrest. They were taken to Judge Wallace's court and fined $32 each for carrying
deadly weapons.

No report remains of the cause of the fight, but it was likely of a purely personal nature. Johnny Ringo had shown favors to Doc Holliday's woman, reason enough for a Southern gentleman to engage in a duel. One story has Ringo offering his hand-kerchief to Holliday to measure the distance between them—a nineteenth-century dueling tradition, to which Holliday responded, "All I want of you is ten paces out in the street."[3] In the 1927 novel, *Tombstone: An Iliad of the Southwest*, author Walter Noble Burns gives Holliday a more colorful reply: "I'm your Huckleberry. That's just my game."

Ringo was troublesome, but the more immediate threat was the gang that had tried to assassinate Virgil Earp. On January 23, Wyatt's federal posse finally rode out, armed with arrest warrants for the suspects: Ike Clanton (whose hat was found behind the saloon the night of the shooting), his brother Phin Clanton, and their associate Pony Deahl. Along the way, the posse was joined by another thirty volunteers from Tomb-stone who wanted the cowboy situation settled. The posse's destination was the mill town (and known cowboy resort) of Charleston, nine miles southwest of Tombstone. But by the time they arrived, Johnny Ringo had ridden ahead of them to warn of the posse's arrival, so there were no cowboys around to be served. The next day, Sheriff Behan received a wire from cowboy sympathizers in Charleston:

Doc Holliday, the Earps, and about forty or fifty more of the filth of Tombstone
are here armed with Winchester rifles and revolvers, and patrolling our streets, as
we believe, for no good purpose. Last night and to-day they have been stopping
good, peaceable citizens on all the roads leading to our town, nearly paralyzing
the business of our place. We know of no authority under which they are acting.
Some of them, we have reason to believe, are thieves, robbers, and murderers.
Please come here and take them where they belong.

Although the federal posse wasn't successful in making an arrest, the show of force convinced Ike and Phin Clanton to surrender to another posse a week later and take their chances with the judge. The charge was "assault with intent to commit murder, the specific offense being the waylaying and shooting of Virgil Earp some weeks ago."[4] A trial in Tombstone followed soon after, with cowboy friends swearing Ike had been in Charleston the night of the shooting, and the jury returning an acquittal. A frustrated Wyatt was told by the judge, "You'll never clean up this crowd this way; next time you'd better leave your prisoners out in the brush where alibies don't count."[5]

Perhaps preparing to take the judge's advice and handle the cowboys in a less lawful manner, Wyatt and Virgil publicly resigned their federal deputy marshal badges on February 2, although Marshal Dake refused at the time to honor their resignations. Which meant that Doc Holliday, as their special deputy, still had his federal authority, as well. But that didn't stop Ike Clanton from turning to the law again for another try at avenging his dead father and brother.

Although the O.K. Corral hearing had censured Doc and the Earps, the grand jury of Cochise County could still call for a trial if it found cause, so Ike swore out another warrant in a new venue. Sheriff Behan again made the arrests, and a dozen armed riders accompanied the prisoners to court in the mill town of Contention City, ten miles northwest of Tombstone on the San Pedro River. According to Tombstone diarist George Parsons:

> *Earps were taken to Contention to be tried for the killing of Clanton. Quite a posse went out. Many of Earp's friends armed to the teeth. They came back later in the day, the good people below beseeching them to leave and try the case here. A bad time is expected again in town at any time. Earps on one side of the street with their friends and Ike Clanton and John Ringo with theirs on the other side—watching each other. Blood will surely come.*[6]

Parsons' prediction was right, for when the second judge also declined to recommend a trial, saying that without any new information a new examination would only duplicate the first hearing, the legal solutions had come to an end and justice would have to be found outside of the law. So, the dangerous game between the lawmen and the outlaws had come to a draw, with both sides waiting for the next card to turn—as it did on the stormy night of March 18.

Doc and Morgan Earp had been to see the show at Schieffelin Hall that evening—a touring group of the popular comedy, *Stolen Kisses*, which surely seemed like a good relief from the stressful times they'd all been enduring. But as they walked into the theater, a local lawyer cautioned them, "You fellows will catch it tonight if you don't look out."[7] So after the show, Doc heeded the lawyer's advice and went back down the street to his room at Fly's Boarding House. But Morgan wasn't done yet for the night and set out to find a game at Campbell & Hatch's Saloon and Billiard Parlor on Allen Street. On the way, he met his brother Wyatt who was also concerned about rumors of trouble that night and cautioned him to go on home, then agreed to let him have a game or two and stayed to keep an eye on things. Around 11:00 pm, as Wyatt sat watching his brother play billiards, a sudden gust of wind blew out the glass in the backdoor of the saloon, or so it seemed until two gunshots smashed through the broken glass. The first bullet hit Morgan in the back, slamming him against the table before he slumped to the ground in a pool of blood. The second bullet drove into the wall just above Wyatt's head.

While witnesses ran out the backdoor looking for the shooter, Wyatt and others lifted Morgan from the floor. "Don't, boys, don't!" he said, when they tried to put him on his feet, "I can't stand it! I have played my last game of pool."[8]

Morgan was laid in the card room, where the doctor examined him and found that a bullet had entered just left of his spinal column, passed through a kidney, and come out through his groin. It was too much damage to be repaired, and before midnight Morgan Earp was gone.

At his side at the end were his brothers and their wives and Doc Holliday, who'd been called from his room to join them. The next day, the men escorted Morgan's casket to the new spur train depot at Contention City for the long ride to his parents' home in Colton, California. It was Wyatt Earp's thirty-fourth birthday.

FAMOUS LAST WORDS

In the last moments before Morgan Earp died, shot to death while he played billiards at Campbell & Hatch's Saloon in Tombstone, he whispered something in the ear of his older brother Wyatt, as reported in the *Tombstone Epitaph* of March 20, 1882.

Two months after the Tombstone tragedy, Wyatt said of his brother's last words, "When they shot him he said the only thing he regretted was that he wouldn't have a chance to get even. I told him I'd attend to it for him."[9]

Wyatt may have been giving justification for his Vendetta Ride, when he hunted down and killed Morgan's murderers. In later years, author Stuart Lake's 1931 novelized biography *Wyatt Earp: Frontier Marshal* has Wyatt explaining things differently:

Morg got me to read one of his books [about life after death experiences]. I told him I thought the yarns were overdrawn, but at his suggestion we promised each other that, when the time came for one of us to go, that one would try to leave for the other some actual line on the truth of the book. . . . He was sensitive to the fun others might poke at such notions, so, in the last few seconds of his life, when he knew he was going, he asked me to bend close. "I guess you were right, Wyatt," he whispered. "I can't see a damn thing."

Lake's likely imagined scene is repeated in the movie *Tombstone*, with Morgan whispering to his brother: "Remember what I said about people seein' a bright light before they die? It ain't true. I can't see a damn thing."

Rancher Henry Hooker's daughter Forrestine (who grew up during the Tombstone trouble and wrote *Tombstone Vendetta: The Truth about Wyatt Earp*), records a scene similar to what Wyatt said those first months after his brother's death:

"Do you know who did it?" Morgan said.

"Yes, and I'll get even."

"That's all I ask. But Wyatt, be careful."

Wyatt's later wife Josephine Sarah Marcus echoed the Hooker manuscript: "They got me, Wyatt, you be careful, don't let them get you. Father, mother . . . "

According to the memoirs of Kate Elder, who would have heard it from Doc, Morgan's last words were, "Oh, if only I could get even before I die." Wyatt vowed, "Never mind, Morg; we will get even for you."

Morgan Seth Earp, Tombstone 1881, by Camillus Fly. Courtesy Arizona Historical Society, Portrait Collection #1442.

GHOST TOWN

The story of Contention City, Arizona Territory, starts with a couple of thirsty mules and two lucky prospectors. Ed Williams and Jack Friday were camped one night near the Whetstone Mountains when their mules wandered away looking for water, dragging their chains behind them. Come daylight, the men were able to track the mules by following the trail left by the chains—and noticed that where the chains

Recreated Contention Depot at Old Tucson Studios.
Flickr.com/Marv Hanson.

had scraped away the topsoil there was a gleam of metal, the outcropping of a silver lode. They found the mules in the camp of fellow prospector Ed Schieffelin, who had already staked his Tombstone claims and wasn't happy to hear that Williams and Friday had found another silver lode on land he considered his territory. Schieffelin disputed the men's claim, which was eventually split in two, with the upper end going to Williams and Friday and named the Grand Central Mine, and the lower end going to Schieffelin, who named it the Contention Mine in honor of the dispute.

Contention City, named for the mine, was founded in 1879 ten miles northwest of Tombstone on the banks of the San Pedro River as a milling site for the Contention, Grand Central, and other mines in the area. In a few months the town had a population of over one hundred, and within a year Contention City had a post office, saloon, hotel, blacksmith, butcher shop, general stores, and a Chinese laundry. Two stages stopped in Contention, connecting it to Tombstone and Tucson, and in March 1882 the New Mexico & Arizona Railroad arrived from Nogales with a connection to the Southern Pacific Railroad at Benson. On March 19, the new Contention City depot gained a morbid fame as the departure point for Morgan Earp's last train ride, when his casket was placed on the train to be taken to his family's home in Colton, California, for burial.

Like Morgan Earp, Contention City was gone too soon, living a short energetic life and passing away with the end of the silver boom, leaving little more than stone foundations along the muddy banks of the San Pedro River. Even the railroad tracks were taken up.

DRAG QUEEN

When Doc Holliday and Morgan Earp went to see the show *Stolen Kisses* at Schieffelin Hall, they knew they'd be getting the promised "2½ hours of incessant laughter." The star, Englishman William Horace Lingard, was one of the greatest showmen of the day, famous as a comic singer, quick change artist—and female impersonator.

Lingard based *Stolen Kisses*, his new vaudeville review, on the popular French play, *Bébé*, a farce of mistaken identities and double entendre, and it had already been a hit on the London stage before enjoying a whirlwind tour across the United States. The Tombstone audience surely appreciated the show's risqué jokes and references to gambling games and illicit romances.

After two nights of performances in Tombstone March 18 and 19, 1882, the Lingard troupe took the train to New Mexico, where the *Santa Fe Daily New Mexican* of October 22 reported, "The largest audience that ever assembled to see a theatrical company in Santa Fe assembled last night at the Alhambra to see the Lingard company. . . . The burlesque comedy of 'Stolen Kisses' . . . is brimful of fun and kept the audience in a roar of laughter from the time the curtain rose until it fell upon the last scene." The *Pueblo Colorado Daily Chieftan* called the show, "ravishing, coquettish, melodious" and "intensely amusing."

"Stolen Kisses" advertisement in the Tombstone Daily Nugget, *March 15, 1881. Author's Collection.*

Horace Lingard, J. Gurney & Son CDV. Courtesy Terry Alphonse Collection.

After a long career on the vaudeville circuit that took Lingard and his wife, theater actress Alice Dunning Lingard, as far abroad as Australia and New Zealand, they settled in New York City where Horace became manager of the popular Woods Theater. Sheet music from his productions continued to sell, showing Lingard dressed in his trademark female fashion for popular songs like "The Grecian Bend" and "The Gay Masque Ball."

DAISIES AND HUCKLEBERRIES

In the 1993 film *Tombstone*, Doc Holliday challenges his nemesis Johnny Ringo with the words, "I'm your huckleberry," a phrase that has become the film Doc's signature line, repeated by millions of fans around the world and used on all kinds of promotional media, from t-shirts to tattoos. But what does the phrase actually mean?

Val Kilmer as Doc Holliday in the 1993 film Tombstone. *© 1993 Hollywood Pictures.*

Huckleberries have long been a part of American slang. The tiny size of the berries led to their use as a way of referring to something small, often affectionately, as in the lyrics of "Moon River": "my huckleberry friend." In the early nineteenth century, the phrase "a huckleberry over my persimmon" was used to mean "a little beyond my abilities." By the 1870s the phrase became, "I'm your huckleberry," meaning "I have the right abilities; I'm the right one for the job." So essentially, Doc is telling Ringo, "I'm up to the challenge; I'm your man."

But did the real Doc Holliday really say those words to Johnny Ringo, or anyone else? There is no contemporary evidence that he did, though the phrase was popular in his day, as in this report from the *Galveston Daily News* of December 7, 1875, when Doc was living in Texas:

> *The street corners about the Opera House Saturday night were made lively with discussions of the "speck of war" rising, and some men wanted to know who to go to in order to offer their services to the greatest government the world ever saw. Said one enthusiastic man, "If there is any fighting on the Mexican border, I'm your huckleberry." This speech was well received by all.*

So, Doc Holliday certainly *could* have said those words somewhere to someone. But the first time they are attributed to him in print is in the 1927 novel *Tombstone: An Illiad of the Southwest* by Walter Noble Burns:

> *Doc Holliday, second only to Wyatt Earp in the affairs of the Earp faction, remained standing in the door, a cold little smile on his cadaverous face. Ringo drew a handkerchief from the breast pocket of his coat and flipped a corner of it toward Holliday.*

"They say you're the gamest man in the Earp crowd, Doc," Ringo said. "I don't need but three feet to do my fighting. Here's my handkerchief. Take hold."

Holliday took a quick step toward him.

"I'm your huckleberry, Ringo," replied the cheerful doctor. "That's just my game."

Had Burns found some forgotten and unfootnoted old-timer who remembered that Doc said it just that way? Or was he himself inspired by another writer—best-selling turn-of-the-century novelist Edward Stratemeyer, whose 1900 novel *True to Himself* has farm boy Roger Strong having a Doc Holliday-esque conversation:

"I will pay you for whatever you do for me."

"Then I'm your huckleberry. Who are you and what do you want to know?"

Stratemeyer is better known by his many pen names under which he wrote more than 1,300 adventure books for teens, including the Rover Boys, the Bobbsey Twins, Tom Swift, the Hardy Boys and even Nancy Drew—eventually employing a stable full of ghost writers to turn his detailed outlines into finished books. In an era when novels could sell for fifty cents a copy, Stratemeyer became a millionaire, with his action-filled plots and snappy dialogue beloved by a generation of adolescent Americans—including, no doubt, a young Walter Noble Burns, who grew up loving adventure stories before becoming a journalist and best-selling author himself.

So it's not surprising to find the phrase "I'm your huckleberry" repeated in Burns's 1927 novel in the dramatized version of the Holliday-Ringo confrontation, and then to find it again in screenwriter Kevin Jarre's script for the movie *Tombstone*, with scenes and dialogue inspired by Burns's novel, introducing the archaic phrase to a whole new generation of Tombstone fans. If Doc Holliday didn't say "I'm your huckleberry," he should have.

As for Doc's other iconic phrase, "You're a daisy if you do," there is evidence that he may have said something sort of like that. On the morning after the O.K. Corral gunfight, both Tombstone newspapers printed reports of the shootings, with mostly the same eyewitness accounts but with some difference in style and direct quotes. While the *Tombstone Nugget* quoted Frank McLaury as telling Doc, "I've got you now," with Doc replying, "Blaze away! You're a daisy if you have," the competing *Tombstone Epitaph* recorded Doc's words as a less dramatic, "You're a good one if you have." The meaning of both sentences was essentially the same, so for Doc's intent it hardly mattered whether he said "daisy" or "good one." And when Morgan Earp came to Doc's aid, raising a pistol and putting a bullet through Frank's brain, Doc's final words to him made no difference at all.

16

TUCSON TRAIN YARD

The day after sending his brother Morgan's body home to California for a proper burial, Wyatt packed up Virgil and Allie Earp and put them on the train back to California, as well. But getting them safely away from Tombstone wouldn't be easy, with too many places along the road where the cowboys could make them target practice: from the depot at Contention City to the railhead at Benson, from a change of trains at Benson to a layover in Tucson before the Southern Pacific finally headed west. So, Wyatt and Doc Holliday went along as armed bodyguards, with Wyatt's younger brother Warren and two members of the federal posse, Sherman McMaster and Jack Johnson, as backup.

When the train pulled into Tucson, Doc was first off the car, greeting the local US Deputy Marshal and stashing two shotguns in the depot. Though the layover would only be long enough for the train to take on water and coal and the passengers to get supper at the station restaurant, it was too long for comfort, with evening coming on and darkness falling over the tracks. So, Virgil and Allie were escorted by their armed guard to the restaurant, then escorted back to the train again when they'd finished eating—and it seemed that the trip had been safely accomplished, after all.

Then another passenger pointed out two men with shotguns lying on a flatcar near the locomotive, and Wyatt thought he recognized them as Frank Stillwell and Ike Clanton. But as he pulled up his shotgun and moved toward them, they saw him and started running, and he was only able to apprehend Stillwell. As the story is told in *Wyatt Earp: Frontier Marshal*:

> *What a coward he was. He couldn't shoot when I came near him. He stood there helpless and trembling for his life. As I rushed upon him he put out his hands and clutched at my shotgun. I let go both barrels, and he tumbled down dead and*

mangled at my feet. I started for Clanton then, but he escaped behind a moving train of cars. When the train had passed I could not find him.[1]

As the westbound Southern Pacific pulled away from the station, Wyatt raised one finger toward Virgil's shaded window and mouthed the words, "One for Morgan."[2]

Although Wyatt's dramatic account gives him both the credit and the blame for the killing of Frank Stillwell, the man he suspected of murdering his brother Morgan, the truth is something more democratic. After the first shotgun volley, Doc Holliday and the others caught up with Wyatt and emptied their own guns into the wounded Stillwell, making them all suspects in his killing. Which may have been their purpose, giving all of them a plausible deniability—when a firing squad takes aim, whose gun fires the fatal bullet? Or as Doc would say for years after, "I know that Stillwell was a stage robber and a murderer, but I do not know that I had anything to do with his death."[3] He never said he didn't shoot Stillwell, only that he didn't know if he had killed him.

Wyatt's posse didn't wait around to see what would happen next. With Virgil's westbound train safely away from the station, they started walking the other way, covering nine miles in the desert darkness until they caught an eastbound freight at the Papago water station. They were in Benson by the time Stillwell's body was found in the Tucson train yard the next morning, and in Tombstone by the time an arrest warrant had been wired to Sheriff Behan.

It hadn't taken the Tucson coroner's jury long to name the suspects after Frank Stillwell's mangled corpse was found alongside the tracks. He was "the worst shot up man I ever saw,"[4] according to one witness, with shotgun blasts through his belly and liver and left leg, bullet holes in his right leg, his arm, and his lungs, and his left hand singed by gunpowder from catching hold of the muzzle of a shotgun. Although no witness to the actual shooting came forward, the newspapers were full of the story of the feud between the cowboys and the Earps, and plenty of people had seen the heavily armed posse in the train yard that night—including the local US Deputy Marshal who had watched Doc Holliday carry two shotguns onto the platform. So, it was clear who had done the shooting, and why. As for the sound of gunfire that should have alerted someone to the shooting sooner—that had been mistaken for a celebratory salute to Tucson's first gaslights, lit that very night on the streets surrounding the courthouse, a blazing tribute to law and order.

Back in Tombstone, Doc and Wyatt and the posse gathered at the Cosmopolitan Hotel and made plans. They had brought their own kind of justice to Frank Stillwell, but he hadn't worked alone, and the others involved in maiming Virgil and murdering Morgan were still roaming free. So, there was more work to do in cleaning up the cowboy menace before the cowboys murdered them all. They knew the names of the men behind the attacks: Pete Spence, Fritz Bode, Hank Swilling, and Florentino "Indian Charlie" Cruz. And they knew who was behind the attackers: Ike Clanton, who had still not found satisfaction for the deaths of his father and brother, along with his cowboy associates Curly Bill Brocious and Johnny Ringo. But there was one enemy who could prove the most dangerous of them all: Sheriff Johnny Behan, who sided with the outlaws but had the law on his side, and held an arrest warrant for the Earp posse for the murder of Frank Stillwell in the Tucson train yard. The March 22, 1882, *Tombstone Epitaph* described the confrontation:

> *Last evening Wyatt Earp, Doc Holliday, Sherman McMaster, Texas Jack and Mysterious Johnson came into town and at once went to the hotel. About eight o'clock they were joined by Charley Smith and Tipton. They at once left the hotel and got on their horses that were tied in front of it. Sheriff Behan stepped up to them and said, "Wyatt, I want to see you for a moment." Earp replied, "I have seen you once too often," and they rode quickly out of town.*

Wyatt later recalled that as they rode away, a local banker stopped them to ask if they needed anything. "Doc Holliday has no gun," Wyatt replied, and the banker went into the bank and returned with his own Winchester rifle.[5] This isn't to say that Doc was unarmed. He was known for owning several handguns, including a family heirloom Colt Navy Revolver and a fancy nickel-plated Colt Peacemaker rumored to be a gift from Bat Masterson. But not being a man who had regular work on horseback, he likely didn't own a saddle gun like a rifle. Even the shotgun he used in the Tombstone street fight wasn't his own, but Virgil Earp's, traded for his gold-headed cane as they walked down Allen Street to the O.K. Corral.

Riding away from the unserved arrest warrant, Wyatt's posse camped that night near Watervale, three miles north of Tombstone, and close enough for Sheriff Behan to ride after them if he had wanted to. But Behan was waiting for Sheriff Bob Paul of Tucson to join him the next day and assist in the arrest, and by then the posse had moved on to the South Pass of the Dragoon Mountains, where Pete Spence had a wood-cutting operation. Spence had been Frank Stillwell's partner in various enterprises, including at least one stagecoach holdup, and was the suspected trigger man in Morgan Earp's murder. Perhaps knowing he was next on Wyatt's agenda, Spence had decided to leave the wood camp early and travel back to Tombstone to turn himself in, taking his chances with Sheriff Behan's easy law instead of Wyatt Earp's revenge. But Florentino "Indian Charlie" Cruz, who'd been lookout the night of Morgan's murder, was still at the camp when the posse arrived. Various versions of the story exist, but all end the same way: Indian Charlie was shot four times and left for dead in the middle of the Chiricahua Road.

A coroner's jury quickly charged Doc Holliday and the Earp party as Cruz's killers, though no one could tell who really did the shooting. Nor did everyone in Tombstone fault them for it. As diarist George Parsons wrote, "More killing by the Earp party. Hope they'll keep it up."[6] And when Sheriff Bob Paul of Tucson arrived in town, Parsons observed, "Paul is here but will not take a hand. He is a true, brave man himself, and will not join [Sheriff Behan's] murderous posse here. If the truth were known, he would be glad to see the Earp party get away with all these murderous outfits."[7]

In fact, there were two posses now hunting the Earps, one led by Sheriff Behan and the other led by his newly assigned deputy, Johnny Ringo. And it was a lucky break for suspects Hank Swilling and Fritz Bode to be arrested by their own associates and returned to the safety of the Tombstone jail, rather than face the surer justice of the Earps and Doc Holliday.

While the sheriff's two posses were searching for them in the Dragoons, Wyatt's posse had quietly returned to Watervale, where they stopped for provisions and news before heading west toward the Whetstone Mountains. The foothills of the Whetstones were covered with mesquite and scrub plants, the narrow canyons filled with hackberry and walnut trees, the few watering holes shaded by cottonwoods and sycamores and wild grape vines. There were also enough caves and caverns to shelter most of the outlawry of the Arizona Territory. But while the Whetstones were a good place to go hiding, they were a bad place to go seeking, the narrow canyons too narrow, the watering holes too scarce. And without knowing every cave and cavern, a posse could get turned around or trapped and never make it out again. Going into the Whetstones with a posse on their trail, especially one led by Johnny Ringo who'd spent his share of time in those same mountains, might have seemed like a bad bet—except for a bit of news that Wyatt had gleaned in Watervale: Curly Bill Brocious was in those mountains, too, and tracking him down was worth the gamble.

As Doc Holliday later told the story:

> *We were out one day after a party of outlaws, and about 3 o'clock on a warm day after a long and dry ride from the San Pedro River, we approached a spring which was situated in a hollow. As we did so eight rustlers rose up from behind the bank and poured from thirty-five to forty shots into us. Our escape was miraculous. The shots cut our clothes and saddles and killed one horse, but did not hit us. I think we would have been all killed if God Almighty wasn't on our side. Wyatt Earp turned loose with a shot-gun and killed Curly Bill. The eight men in the gang which attacked us were all outlaws, for each of whom a big reward has been offered.*[8]

But Doc left out the most famous part of the story: when Wyatt Earp shot Curly Bill, he was standing alone against the cowboys, the other men having remounted their horses for a hasty retreat to the safety of the trees. They weren't leaving him behind on purpose—they thought Wyatt was riding off with them—but he'd gotten tangled up in his gun belt and couldn't get back on his horse, giving him no option but to stand his ground and shoot. When he got himself mounted and returned to his men, Doc gently took hold of his arm and said, "You must be shot all to pieces," and offered to go back against the cowboys himself. But though bullets had torn through Wyatt's clothes and boots and sheared through his saddle horn, he was, as Doc put it, miraculously unwounded—and done fighting for the day. "If you fellows are hungry for a fight you can go on and get your fill," Wyatt said and turned his horse in the other direction.[9]

The Vendetta Ride, as it would come to be known, had lasted only five days, from the March 20 shooting of Frank Stillwell in the train yard in Tucson to the March 24 killing of Curly Bill. But it was enough to launch the Earps and Doc Holliday into Western history as avenging angels and bring the whole of Arizona law against them, and it was time for them to leave the territory and seek sanctuary elsewhere.

GUN SHOTS AND GASLIGHTS

In her later memoirs, Kate Elder said of the killing of Frank Stillwell: "This happened when Tucson was first lighted with gas. Everybody thought the shooting was in honor of the City being lighted."[10] It's a historical detail not mentioned by early writers about the Tombstone saga, and that lends credence to Kates's story—only someone who had been in Southern Arizona at the time would have known about the gas lights and the months of anticipation leading up to an evening of celebration. Almost every edition of the *Arizona Daily Star* in 1882 carried a story about the gas: the plans and the streets that would be serviced, the pipes arriving by rail car, the "stringing of lines" on Main and Pennington and Sixth and Stone, the gas fixtures for sale at the offices of the Tucson Gas Company. And for residences and businesses that applied for gas service before the official first lighting, the gas meters would be set up *free of charge*, as M. G. Elmore, Superintendent of the Tucson Gas Co., promised in a series of advertisements.

Finally, the evening for the lighting arrived, and the *Arizona Daily Star* reported on the festivities in the March 21, 1882, edition. As the gas was turned on, cheers went up on the streets around the Pima County Courthouse—a celebratory noise that conveniently covered the sounds of gunshots in the nearby train yard, where Wyatt Earp and his posse were filling Frank Stillwell full of lead.

> life.
> ### Lighting Up.
> Last night the streets were thronged with our citizens taking a look at the illumination by gas, the principal attraction being the fine new store of L. Zeckendorf & Co., with its hundred jets enclosed in globes and attached to costly fixtures.
> Among the other places lighted up we observed the Palace Hotel, Cosmopolitan Hotel, J. S. Mansfeld's, the "Elite" the "Standard," the "Fashion"— including the keno room, Stevens' stove store, W. C. Davis', H. Horton's, F. Burns', Alex. Levin's and the STAR office, which had a dozen jets throwing light upon the busy fingers of the compositors.
> Over the door of the gas company's office were the words "Gas Company," blazing in jets of gas.
> As our people used the article for the first time last night, it is presumable that many of them blew out the lights instead of turning off the gas, and so indulged in all the luxuries of the occasion.

"Lighting Up" in Arizona Daily Star, *Tucson, Arizona, March 21, 1882, page 4. Author's Collection.*

But not everyone in Tucson was enthusiastic about the new lights. As an editorial in the paper on the day before the lighting cautioned: "There is no calculating where this light business will end. If invention continues perfecting its discoveries we may require legislation to prevent too much light, as a certain degree of darkness is as necessary to life and health as is light."[11]

It was a surprisingly prophetic statement. Twentieth-century Tucsonites discovered that "light pollution" obscured the dark skies necessary to view stars at the area's observatories, and in 1972 Pima County and the City of Tucson adopted the nation's first Dark Sky ordinances. Amended in 2012 to add LED lights to electric and neon offenders, the ordinances establish maximum illumination levels, shielding requirements, and limits on signage "while not compromising the safety, security, and well-being of persons engaged in outdoor nighttime activities." Tucson, the city that once celebrated the end of dark desert nights, is now one of the darkest cities in the country, where residents can still see the Milky Way overhead.

MEN IN BRONZE

The Southern Pacific Railroad arrived in Tucson in 1880, and the next year the city's first railroad depot was opened: a two-story wood frame building with long windows and wide shady eaves extending from each floor. The railroad had business offices on the second floor, with the passenger waiting room, baggage room, agent's office, and Wells Fargo Express office filling the first floor. In later months, a freight depot

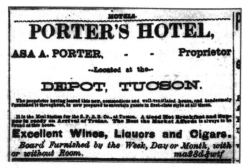

Porter's House Hotel advertisement in the Arizona Daily Star, *Tucson, Arizona, March 5, 1882, page 4. Author's Collection.*

would be added adjacent to the passenger depot. Two hotels were conveniently close to the depot: The San Xavier and the popular Porter Hotel, which in 1882 was in the midst of remodeling to add sixteen new guest rooms. Porter's, as it was usually called, had a "broad and breezy piazza" with comfortable chairs, a saloon, and a dining room that had passenger meals ready whenever the train pulled into town.

When Wyatt Earp and his posse gunned down Frank Stillwell in the train yard close to Porter's Hotel, the commotion was at first ignored. As the *Arizona Weekly Citizen* reported on March 26:

> *There were many who heard the shooting and some even saw the flash of the guns, but thought it to be no more than the reckless firing of some over jubilant citizen on account of the illumination [the first gas lighting of the city that evening]. Daylight this morning however, revealed the dead body of Stilwell lying [sic] near the railroad crossing a short distance west of Porter's Hotel. He was buried this afternoon, the coffin being conveyed to the grave in an express wagon unfollowed by a single mourner.*

The city reacted with understandable disgust to the affray, as editorialized in the pages of the March 22, 1882, *Arizona Sun* with a column headlined "The Shadow of Tombstone's Bloody Feud Reaches Tucson": "The boldness of the act, right at the depot in a peaceable city, around and amid the bustle of visitors at the train, only adds to the offense, and the effrontery of these desperados . . . is as provoking and outrageous to our citizens as it is damned in the sight of heaven."

Yet over the years, as the first depot was replaced with an elegant Spanish-style station and the Porter's Hotel was torn down to make way for the new station's parking lot, the affront to the community faded and the bloody event became just an interesting anecdote from Tucson's Wild West days, dramatized in books and movies and TV shows. So, in 2005 when the city celebrated the 125th anniversary of the coming of the railroads with a renovation of the 1907 station, it seemed appropriate to add a monument to the train yard's most dramatic event: the shooting of Frank Stillwell by Wyatt Earp and Doc Holliday.

The life-size bronze statues of Earp and Holliday stand behind the restored Southern Pacific station on Toole Avenue, near the Southern Arizona Transportation Museum. Funding for the $41,000 pair of figures came mostly from private donations, with City Councilman Fred Ronstadt heading up the project—Ronstadt being kin to the owner of the 1880's Levin's Pleasure Park in Tucson, where Doc Holliday played cards in the last weeks before the O.K. Corral gunfight.

Tucson area sculptor Dan Bates, who spent much of his childhood on a ranch in the Chiricahua Mountains close to Tombstone, chose to show the men not in the act of the shooting itself, but standing with guns loaded, watching for danger. It's the noble part of an ignoble episode: Wyatt Earp and Doc Holliday standing together to protect family and friends. And thanks to Dan Bates's men in bronze, if the ghost of the murderous Frank Stillwell ever visits from the old cemetery nearby, he'll find Wyatt and Doc still standing guard in the Tucson train yard, waiting for him.

Doc Holliday and Wyatt Earp Statues, Tucson Amtrak station. 1907-1922-2.jpeg., Marine 69-71 at English Wikipedia, CC BY-SA 3.0 (edited with vignette).

VENDETTA RIDES

When Wyatt Earp led his posse to hunt down the cowboys who had murdered his younger brother Morgan, he was nominally acting as a duly authorized federal officer. Wyatt had been made a Deputy US Marshal in December 1881 after his brother, US Deputy Marshal Virgil Earp, was attacked and maimed on the streets of Tombstone.

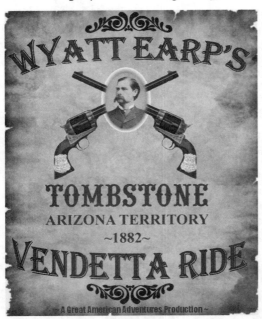

But in January 1882, after failing to make hoped-for arrests, Wyatt wrote to US Marshal Crawley P. Dake, offering to resign the Earp brothers' commissions. Marshal Dake did not accept the offer, leaving both Virgil and Wyatt as his official deputies with the authority to appoint their own deputies as needed. So, in March, when Wyatt took along his brother Warren Earp, with Doc Holliday, Dan Tipton, Sherman McMaster, and Jack Johnson to track down Morgan's killers, he was essentially making them deputy marshals for the duration of the hunt. They may not have worn badges, but they had authority to find and arrest the suspected killers. But authority to arrest the suspects did not make them judges and executioners, hence their own arrest warrants after the killings of Frank Stillwell and Florentino Cruz.

Wyatt Earp's Vendetta Ride poster. Courtesy Great American Adventures.

The quasi-legal actions of the Earp posse made it controversial then and a compelling story now, with Wyatt portrayed as the epitome of manly courage and filial loyalty—if the law wouldn't protect his family, he would become the law himself. As he said dramatically in the movie *Tombstone*: "Hell's coming and I'm coming with it!" Now modern men and women can follow Wyatt's trail by joining a "Vendetta Ride" excursion offering five days in the saddle, a full day ride into the Dragoon Mountains, a ride to Iron Springs in the Whetstone Mountains where Curly Bill was killed, and a visit to Johnny Ringo's gravesite in the Chiricahua Mountains. Where Wyatt Earp once drew pay for expenses of the ride, now Tombstone fans pay to recreate the experience.

COWBOYS AND ALIENS

Wyatt Earp's Vendetta Ride lasted less than a week, from the murder of Morgan Earp to the murder of Curly Bill Brocious, and then things in Tombstone quieted down—and kept getting quieter. The Earps and Doc Holliday left the Territory in March 1882, and two months later a fire that started in a Chinese laundry engulfed the cowboy's favored Grand Hotel, then jumped Fremont Street and destroyed most of the business district—including the O.K. Corral. It almost seemed the town was trying to burn away the memory of its worst days. And while the fires burned above, most of the water in Tombstone was underground slowly flooding the mines. The owners of the Grand Central Mine bought a special pump to clear out the water, but in 1886 a fire at the mine burned the hoist and pumping plant, and sections of the mine caved in. The price of silver fell, mine workers were laid off, and an earthquake in the Sonoran Desert seemed to portend doom to the whole area. By 1890 the US Census reported that the population of Tombstone had declined from more than ten thousand residents to a mere 1,900.

Then the *Tombstone Epitaph* of April 26, 1890, printed a story that would surely bring attention back to the dying town:

Tombstone Fire, 1882. Courtesy Mike Mihaljevich.

FOUND ON THE DESERT

A Strange Winged Monster Discovered and Killed on the Huachuca Desert

A winged monster, resembling a huge alligator, with an extremely elongated tail and an immense pair of wings, was found on the desert between the Whetstone and Huachuca Mountains last Sunday by two ranchers who were returning home from the Huachucas. The creature was evidently greatly exhausted by a long flight and when discovered was able to fly but a short distance at a time. After the first shock of wild amazement had passed, the two men who were on horseback and armed with Winchester rifles, regained sufficient courage to pursue the monster and after an exciting chase of several miles succeeded in getting near enough to open fire with their rifles and wounding it. The creature then turned on the men, but owing to its exhausted condition they were able to keep out of its way and after a few well directed shots the monster partly rolled over and remained motionless. The men cautiously approached, their horses snorting with terror, and found that the creature was dead. They then proceeded to make an examination and found that it measured about ninety-two feet in length and the greatest diameter was about fifty inches. The monster had only two feet, these being situated a short distance in front of where the wings were joined to the body. The head, as near as they could judge, was about eight feet long, the jaws being set with strong, sharp teeth. Its eyes were as large as a dinner plate and protruded about halfway from the head. They had some difficulty in measuring the wings as they were partly folded under the body, but finally got one straightened out sufficiently to get a measurement of seventy-eight feet, making the total length from tip to tip about 160 feet. The wings were composed of a thick and nearly transparent membrane and were devoid of feathers or hair, as was the entire body. The skin of the body was comparatively smooth and easily penetrated by a bullet. The men cut off a small portion of the tip of one wing and took it home with them. Late last night one of them arrived in this city for supplies and to make the necessary preparations to skin the creature, when the hide will be sent east for examination by the eminent scientists of the day. The finder returned early this morning accompanied by several prominent men who will endeavor to bring the strange creature to this city before it is mutilated.

The story never mentioned the names of the monster-fighting ranchers, nor the "prominent men" who had gone to bring back the creature, nor even the name of "this city," making it hard to either defend or deny—the perfect kind of light reading for page three, where it was printed. And the fact that the *Epitaph* never printed a follow-up gives an idea of how seriously they took the report. The editor may even have invented the story himself to fill a little extra space in the paper, or perhaps to generate some interest in a dying town.

But Tombstone didn't die, saved not by flying monsters but by the silver screen. In the twentieth century as the story of the O.K. Corral inspired novels and movies and TV shows, tourists gambled on a road trip to the Southern Arizona desert and the town started to boom again. Property owners restored or recreated the Tombstone of the 1880s, taking up the modern asphalt streets and turning the saloons and stores into restaurants and gift shops and bed and breakfast hotels. Now annual events like Helldorado Days (named after a book by Sheriff Behan's deputy Billy Breckenridge), Wyatt Earp Days, and Doc Holli-Days (with guests Doc actors Val Kilmer and Dennis Quaid) bring thousands of visitors to make the legendary walk down Allen Street and belly up to the bars on Fremont Street. As Tombstone used to ship out millions of dollars in silver on the Southern Pacific railroad, now the "town too tough to die" rakes in the tourist dollars. As for the winged creature of the Huachucas, it was never seen again.

17

SUMMIT STATION

By the time word reached Tombstone of the killing of Curly Bill Brocious, the warm spring days had turned chill again and a cold wind was blowing clouds of dust across the desert. It was a bad time for a man with lung problems to be traveling the open road, but there was no time to wait around in town until the weather improved. Sheriff Behan's two posses were still out searching the countryside and would soon follow their trail back to Tombstone. So, Doc and Wyatt's posse stopped in town just long enough to resupply, then rode northeast for a rendezvous with the Southern Pacific Railroad.

They weren't making an escape by train—that would be too obvious and too easily foiled—but meeting with a messenger, likely from the Wells Fargo Co. The express company had an interest in keeping the roads safe from stage robbers and other outlaws and approved of the results of the vendetta, and the Southern Pacific owned a one-third interest in Wells Fargo and wanted to keep it profitable. So, the railroad was transporting the messenger, and the messenger likely had money for Wyatt as payment for services rendered. As recorded in an entry in the Wells Fargo Cash Book for April 1882: "paid Earp & posse a/c Stillwell & Curly Bill $150."[1]

The meeting point was Summit Station in the foothills of the Dragoon Mountains, a rail stop with a post office and telegraph office and not much else, making it a convenient place for a clandestine meeting. The riders arrived around mid-day, the train pulled in at 1:00 pm, and Doc and Wyatt went aboard to find their messenger. The *Los Angeles Daily Times* of March 27 reported that "after passing through the cars [the men] mounted their horses and started in the direction of the mountains."

The best description of the posse's movements comes from Doc Holliday himself, in a letter to the editor of the *Epitaph* written from the trail. Although he signs himself cryptically as *One of Them*, the language and style reflect a man of education, and the sarcasm is surely Doc's caustic sense of humor:

> *In Camp, April 4, 1882*
>
> *Editor Epitaph: In reply to the article in the Nugget of March 31, relating to the Earp party and some of the citizens of Graham and Cochise counties, I would like to give you the facts in this case during our trip to Cochise and Graham counties. Leaving Tombstone Saturday evening, March 25, we went into camp six miles north of town. Next morning we were overtaken by three prospectors on the road from Tombstone to Winchester district, who asked us to partake of a frugal meal, which we ate with relish, after which we traveled in company with them on the main road to Summit station where we had dinner and awaited the arrival of the passenger train from the west expecting a friendly messenger.*
>
> *From here we continued our journey on the wagon road to Henderson's ranch where we had refreshments for ourselves and horses. Here we were informed that a gentlemanly deputy sheriff of Cochise county, Mr. Frank Hereford (for whom we have the greatest respect as a gentleman and an officer) was at the ranch at the time of our arrival and departure, and have since learned the reason for not presenting himself, was fears for his safety, which we assure him were groundless. Leaving this ranch we went into camp on good grass one mile north. At seven next morning we saddled and went north to Mr. H. C. Hooker's ranch in Graham country, where we met Mr. Hooker, and asked for refreshments for ourselves and stock, which he kindly granted us with the same hospitality that was tendered us by the ranchers of Cochise County.*
>
> *As regards to Mr. Hooker outfitting us with supplies and fresh horses, as mentioned in the Nugget, it is false and without foundation as we are riding the same horses we left Tombstone on, with the exception of Texas Jack's horse, which was killed in the fight with Curly Bill and posse, which we replaced by hiring a horse on the San Pedro river. In relation to the reward offered by the Stock Association, which the Nugget claims Mr. Hooker paid to Wyatt Earp for the killing of Curly Bill, it is also false, as no reward has been asked for or tendered.*
>
> *Leaving Hooker's ranch on the evening of that day, we journeyed north to within five miles of Eureka Springs. There we camped with a freighter and was cheerfully furnished the best his camp afforded. Next morning, not being in a hurry to break camp, our stay was long enough to notice the movements of Sheriff*

Behan and his posse of honest ranchers, with whom, had they possessed the trail-
ing ability of the average Arizona ranchman, we might have had trouble, which
we are not seeking. Neither are we avoiding these honest ranchers as we thor-
oughly understand their designs.

At Cottonwood we remained overnight, and here picked up the trail of the
lost Charlie Ross, "and a hot one." We are confident that our trailing abilities will
soon enable us to turn over to the "gentlemen" the fruits of our efforts, so they may
not again return to Tombstone empty-handed.

Yours respectfully, One of Them[2]

In mentioning the "lost Charlie Ross," the letter throws ridicule on those who
claim to seek, but never find, their prey—like Sheriff Behan, whose posses purportedly chased outlaws, but were mostly made up of outlaws. The then-famous Charlie
Ross case concerned a four-year-old boy who was stolen from in front of his Philadelphia home in 1874 and became the subject of America's first kidnap-for-ransom.
Little Charlie's parents received a demand for $20,000 for his safe return, and law-
men and fortune hunters from across the country started searching for him, and the
press often reported that another lead, "and a hot one" had been found. By 1882,
when Doc and Wyatt were ranging around southern Arizona, Charlie Ross was still
missing and still being hunted with great public attention, a situation that the writer
of the letter turns into something of a joke. But what follows is serious: the promise
that their own search will be more successful and deliver more dead cowboys to
Tombstone.

Hooker's Ranch, where Doc and Wyatt and the posse stopped to rest, was the
Sierra Bonita, owned by Colonel Henry Clay Hooker, a massive cattle operation that
spread over three hundred thousand acres of the Sulphur Springs Valley in southeastern Arizona. Hooker had come to the Territory from New Hampshire by way of the
California gold fields, and now owned the biggest cattle ranch in Arizona, his property so vast that it took ranch hands four days to ride clear around it. He had thirty-
thousand head of prime beef, hundreds of award-winning riding horses, and a cordial
relationship with both the army and the Apaches. But like the rest of the members of
the Cattleman's Association, which he headed, he had trouble with cattle rustlers and
was willing to pay to put a stop to it. In response to the killing of Curly Bill, Hooker
was quoted as saying, "Good work, Wyatt! Keep it up, and when you have finished I'll
get you pardoned."[3]

Hooker's ranch house was a sprawling adobe hacienda with walls twenty inches thick and windows all facing toward an inner courtyard, making it both impregnable in case of an Indian attack and a safe haven for Wyatt's posse in case Sheriff Behan decided to make a stand. But when the Sheriff's posse was spotted in the distance, Wyatt decided to move his men to a position three miles north of the ranch, near the Galiuro Mountains, and by the time the sheriff arrived, Colonel Hooker's welcome had cooled. When Behan asked for directions to find Earps' new refuge, Hooker told the sheriff, "Damn you, and damn your posse; they are a set of horse thieves and outlaws."[4]

Hooker's words were bold, but the truth was that the Cochise County sheriff had no authority in Graham County, where the Sierra Bonita was located, so there was nothing much Behan could do but ride away empty-handed. As Doc and the Earps waited in their camp near the mountains, Behan rode on to the army post of Camp Grant at the northern end of the valley, where he asked the commander for Indian scouts to help in his search. But when he told the commander that Hooker had said he did not know where the Earps were and would not tell him if he did, the commander replied, "Hooker said that did he? Well, if he did, you can't get any scouts here."[5]

Sheriff Behan was running out of patience and out of money. His expenses in trailing Doc Holliday and Wyatt Earp had amounted to $13,000 and he was no closer to finding them than when he first set out, so he finally gave up the chase and went back to Tombstone to reconsider the situation. Some accused him of simply being afraid of a confrontation with men well-armed and willing to fight.

With the law off their trail for the time being, Doc and Wyatt's men returned to the Sierra Bonita and stayed for several more days, and more financial support was delivered to them there: $1,000 from a prominent Tombstone mine owner, and another $1,000 from Wells Fargo. While their work against the cowboys had been partly revenge and mostly outside of their legal commissions, they had gained the backing of many of the better people of the country.

Leaving Hooker's ranch, Wyatt's posse rode north to Camp Grant, where they found a much warmer welcome than Sheriff Behan had. According to an Earp relative, the commander cautioned, "Wyatt, I'm going to have to hold you here. They're looking for you and there are warrants out for your arrest. We're going to have to hold you. But come in and have something to eat first."[6] When the dinner was over, the commander excused himself from the room and the Earp posse found he'd left them fresh horses and an open gate for their escape. It was a kindness that may have saved their lives: back in Tombstone, a new posse had been formed headed by the dead Frank Stillwell's brother Jack, accompanied by Johnny Ringo, Ike Clanton, Pete Spence, and thirty other cowboys ready for revenge.

But Doc and Wyatt and their men were safely out of Arizona Territory, reaching Silver City, New Mexico, by mid-April. Their arrival was noted in the *New Southwest and Grant County Herald* of April 22, 1882:

> *Last Saturday evening at about 10 o'clock the Earp boys' party and Doc Holliday arrived in Silver City. They went at once to the Exchange Hotel to find the stage agent to make arrangements to leave the next morning on the Deming coach. They slept in some private house up town and took breakfast that morning at the Broadway restaurant, and as they had not registered at any hotel it was not known they were in town until after their departure. The party came on horseback, and put up at the Elephant corral. They were all well mounted and armed to the teeth. One of the men, when asked his name, answered John Smith, and another Bill Snooks. This excited the suspicion of Mr. White, the owner of the corral, and the next morning when they offered to sell him their horses, he refused to buy them, fearing to get himself in to trouble. They offered six of their horses for $300, but as the horses were worth much more than that, this offer was also looked upon as unfavorable to them. They finally sold the six horses to Mr. Miller, who is about to start a livery stable here. This done they spoke to Mr. White about hiring a team to take them to Fort Cummings, but he advised them to go by stage, which they decided to do. The saddles and two horses they failed to sell were left here with Charley Bagsby.*

From Silver City, they took the stage south to Deming to catch the Atlantic & Pacific Railroad north to Albuquerque, where they laid over for two weeks. And sometime during those weeks, Doc and Wyatt had a quarrel. According to the May 13, 1882, *Albuquerque Evening Review*, Doc "became intoxicated and indiscreet in his remarks, which offended Wyatt and caused the party to break up." The split was so surprising that it made the papers, and the cause of the quarrel was even more of a surprise. As described in a letter written by the son of the governor of New Mexico, who knew both men: "Earp and Holliday had a falling out at Fat Charlie's one night. They were eating when Holliday said something about Earp being a Jew boy. Something like Wyatt are you becoming a damn Jew boy. Earp became angry and left. Charlie said that Holliday knew he had said it wrong, he never saw them together again."[7]

If authentic, Doc's seemingly anti-Semitic comments likely had more to do with romance than religion. Josephine Sarah Marcus, the actress who had once kept company with Johnny Behan, was Jewish—and had turned her attentions to Wyatt. Doc may have disapproved of Josephine herself, or of Wyatt's interest when he already had a common law wife, or he may have just been jealous. Whatever the cause of the quarrel, Doc left Wyatt Earp behind in Albuquerque, and took the northbound Santa Fe Railroad, heading back to Colorado.

CANDY FROM STRANGERS

> At Cottonwood we remained overnight, and here picked up the trail of the lost Charlie Ross, "and a hot one." We are confident that our trailing abilities will soon enable us to turn over to the "gentlemen" the fruits of our efforts, so they may not again return to Tombstone empty-handed.
> Yours respectfully,
> One of Them

Thus, ended a taunting letter written by a member of Wyatt's posse from the trail back to Tombstone—most likely written by Doc Holliday himself, the most literate of the posse members. In addition to displaying wit, the letter showed knowledge of a story that started in Philadelphia, where Doc had spent his two years of dental school: the kidnapping case of young Charles Brewster Ross.

In the summer of 1874, four-year-old Charley and his five-year-old brother Walter were playing in front of the Ross family home in the Germantown neighborhood of Philadelphia when two men in a carriage pulled to a stop. The men offered the boys candy and fireworks if they would go along with them for a ride, and the boys climbed into the carriage. After a drive through Philadelphia, the carriage stopped at a store and Walter was given twenty-five cents and told to go buy the promised fireworks. When he came back out of the store, the carriage and his little brother Charley were gone.

Over the next four months, the abductors sent the Ross family twenty-three ransom letters mailed from post offices in and around Philadelphia, demanding $20,000 for the return of the little boy and threatening Charley's life if the police were involved.

Although the Ross family lived in a mansion, they were not wealthy, having suffered financial setbacks in the Panic of 1873, and without money to pay the ransom they had no choice but to go to the police. Hoping for a lead, the police sent the story to the press and enlisted the help of the Pinkerton's Detective Agency, which sent out millions of posters with Charley's likeness, making the story a media sensation, the first kidnap-for-ransom case to become nationally known. The case even inspired two popular songs, "Bring Back Our Darling" and "I Want to See Mama Once More."

Lester S. Levy Collection of Sheet Music, Sheridan Libraries, Johns Hopkins University.

The Charley Ross case was still ongoing in November when two men were shot while trying to burglarize a home on Long Island in New York. Both men died that night, but one first confessed to police that he and his partner were the kidnappers of Charley Ross—though the dead partner was the only one who knew where Charley had been taken. Five-year-old Walter Ross was taken to the city morgue to see if he could identify the dead men as the same ones who had abducted him that summer, and he said they were—one man had a deformed nose that Walter had earlier described as a "monkey nose." But Charley was still missing.

In 1876, Charley's father published a book on the case, *The Father's Story of Charley Ross, the Kidnapped Child*, to raise money to continue the search for his son. When interest in the case began to wane, the determined father reprinted the book and began giving lectures and the search went on, with newspapers often reporting a new lead, "and a hot one." The story still filled the papers in the 1880s with ongoing reports of Charley Ross sightings.

Little Charley Ross was never found, though over the years hundreds of boys and eventually grown men claimed to be him. In 1924, newspapers honored the fiftieth anniversary of the nation's first kidnap-for-ransom case by interviewing Walter Ross, by then a stockbroker, and his three sisters, who said they still received letters from men claiming to be their missing brother. The case was still in the national consciousness in 1936, when newspaper columnist H. L. Mencken played a prank at the Democratic National Convention before President Franklin D. Roosevelt was to appear, having the announcer summon a "Charles Ross" to the press area over and over again.

> Chicago detectives claim that they have discovered the whereabouts of Charley Ross. We don't believe they have, for it appears that there is now living in the Navajo Indian country, with the Indians, a white man and boy who have been there since the time Charley Ross was abducted. From inquiring of those who have once or twice caught a glimpse of the man and boy, the description of the latter answers to that of Charley, while the man is said to be a foreigner. The most reasonable conclusion to be arrived at is, that Charley Ross is with the Navajo Indians.

This notice—one of many alleging a sighting of the missing Charley Ross—reports that the boy had been seen living with the Navajo Indians. The Weekly Arizona Miner, Prescott, Arizona, May 26, 1882, page 4. Author's Collection.

The tragic Charley Ross kidnapping case also coined a phrase that has become a classic in American culture: the warning to children, "Don't take candy from strangers."

LOTTIE DENO'S PLACE

When Doc Holliday and Wyatt Earp arrived in Silver City, New Mexico, after their hard Vendetta Ride, the papers noted that they spent the night at "some private house up town" then took breakfast at the Broadway Restaurant. But it's what the papers don't say that's more interesting. The owner of the Broadway Restaurant was Mrs. Frank Thurmond—known in her earlier

Broadway Street in Silver City, New Mexico, site of the Broadway Hotel and Lottie Deno's restaurant, c. 1882. Courtesy Silver City Historical Museum (Broadway St. 1902 #00182)

days as Lottie Deno, the Lady Gambler of Fort Griffin, Texas. Lottie and Frank had left Texas for a new life in New Mexico, where they established themselves in both

Silver City and Deming. Frank owned saloons and became manager of a bank, and Lottie managed their restaurant and spent her later years as a bastion of St. Luke's Episcopal Church of Deming. Doc had known Lottie when they were both living in Fort Griffin and there had been rumors that the two were involved in more than just card play together. Stories from Fort Griffin linked them romantically, and Kate Elder's later memoirs describe a time when she found Doc with "another woman" and used a knife to convince him to go back home. So it's not surprising that Doc chose to have breakfast in Silver City at Lottie's place where he could catch up on old times, and it's possible that the "private" house where he and Wyatt and the men spent the night was Lottie and Frank's home—a good hideout for men who were running from the law.

ALIAS SMITH & SNOOKS

"Cocking a Snook," Punch Magazine, *July 17, 1874. Gutenberg.org.*

On April 22, 1882, the Silver City *New Southwest and Grant County Herald* wrote of the Earp posse arriving in town: "They were all well mounted and armed to the teeth. One of the men, when asked his name, answered John Smith, and another Bill Snooks. This excited the suspicion of Mr. White, the owner of the corral."

It wasn't just the use of aliases that aroused the corral owner's suspicions, but the particular aliases being used. John Smith was, as it is now, the most common of American names, like giving one's name as John Doe. And the name Bill Snooks was even more suspicious, as the word *snook* meant to put a thumb to one's nose, a universal sign of disrespect. The word was popular in the 1870s to 1880s in the idiom to *cock a snook*, such as in the phrase, "a painter who cocks a snook at traditional techniques." So, Mr. Bill Snooks was clearly thumbing his nose at authority when he gave his alias—which sounds very much like something Doc Holliday would be clever enough, and defiant enough, to do.

HENRY HOOKER'S FIRST HERD

Between the Dragoon Mountains east of Tombstone and the Chiricahuas east of the Dragoons lies the hundred-mile-long Sulfur Springs Valley, where Henry Clay Hooker established his Sierra Bonita ranch, turning one homestead into a ranch of three hundred thousand acres—the largest spread in Arizona.

But Hooker hadn't started out as a rich man, or even as a cattleman, with his first herd being more of a flock. Hooker began his career as a merchant in the California gold mining town of Placerville, nicknamed Hangtown for its wild ways. And if it hadn't been for a fire that swept through Hangtown and destroyed his store along with most of Main Street, he might have stayed in the mercantile business. But with no goods left to sell and only a few hundred dollars to his name, Henry Hooker was forced to make a fast career change. So, he bought a flock of five hundred turkeys for $1.50 a head and proposed to drive them like cattle over the mountains and sell them for a profit to the hungry miners of the Nevada silver fields.

Henry Hooker at the Sierra Bonita Ranch, Arizona, 1872. Courtesy Arizona Historical Society, Portrait Collection, Ranches–Cochise & Graham (#15993).

But turkeys don't herd like cattle, as Hooker soon discovered, even with a hired drover and two shepherd dogs worrying at them, so the men spent more time chasing the big birds around than leading them to market. And when something spooked the flock and they all took off running and disappeared over a ridge, Hooker figured he'd lost his investment for good. Then he and the drover crested the height and found the turkeys flocked together down below in a stand of aspen trees, contentedly pecking for food. So, although the whole adventure had seemed absurd at the outset, Hooker got the birds all the way to Carson City and sold them for a neat profit of $5 a head.

Having made one successful drive, Henry Hooker decided to try his hand at another, and invested his turkey profits in a business supplying beef to the military posts and Indian agencies of the Arizona Territory. Along the way, he learned how to appease the Apache, made friends with Chief Cochise, and became so expert in the cattle trade that he eventually bought out his partners and took over the business for himself, becoming the richest rancher in Arizona.

Henry Clay Hooker's ranch and adobe home are now the Sierra Bonita National Historic Landmark and are still managed by the Hooker family.

MEZUZAH

Several sources claim that Doc and Wyatt had a falling out in Albuquerque, but only one gives details about the time, the place, and the cause. According to a letter supposedly written by future New Mexico governor Miguel Otero, who knew both men:

> *Earp and Holliday had a falling out at Fat Charlie's one night. They were eating when Holliday said something about Earp being a Jew boy. Something like Wyatt are you becoming a damn Jew boy? Earp became angry and left. Charlie said that Holliday knew he had said it wrong, he never saw them together again. Jaffa told me later that Earp's woman was a Jewess. Earp did mu–[illegible/ mezuzah?] when entering his house.*[8]

The Jaffa mentioned was Henry Jaffa, an Albuquerque businessman and head of the Albuquerque Board of Trade, who was evidently helping the Earp posse as they passed through New Mexico on their way to sanctuary in Colorado. After revealing that Wyatt's woman Josephine Sarah Marcus was Jewish, the last sentence of the letter describes Wyatt doing something—the word is illegible and cannot be clearly read—when entering the Jewish Jaffa family's home. The supposition is that Wyatt, in a relationship with a Jewish woman, honored the ancient Jewish custom of touching the mezuzah case at the door.

Mezuzah. Sepavane/Depositphotos.com, Image #5764686.

Mezuzah means "doorpost" in Hebrew, but the name actually refers to a small handwritten scroll with the words of the Shema, rolled into a protective case and affixed to the doorposts of Jewish homes. The Shema is a prayer taken from two sections of the Book of Deuteronomy, which start: "Hear, O Israel, the Lord is our God, the Lord is one," continuing with the commandment to love God with all one's heart and a direction to write these things "on the doorposts of your house and on your gates."

On the reverse of the scroll is written one of the names of God, which in Hebrew has just three letters that form an acronym meaning "Guardian of the doorways of Israel." When passing through the doorway where a mezuzah has been affixed, the observant glance at it or touch it, and some then kiss their fingertips. The custom both honors God and is a reminder throughout the day that God is always present and protecting, inside or outside the home.

Wyatt's honoring the mezuzah demonstrated both an understanding of Jewish custom and a thoughtful cordiality to his hosts—and perhaps an intent to spend more time with Josephine Marcus.

18

UNION DEPOT

Doc Holliday was in familiar territory again, back in Colorado and seeking sanctuary. But after stops in Trinidad and Pueblo, he arrived in Denver to find a city he hardly recognized. From the Gothic grandeur of the new Union Depot, built to replace the separate and smaller train depots of the four connecting Denver railroads, to the soaring new Tabor Grand Opera House, Denver was a city transformed by silver.

Horace Tabor was the Silver King of Colorado, making millions from his Leadville mines and using the money to tear down whole blocks of frontier Denver and replace them with Victorian splendors like the Tabor Block of business buildings, the Tabor Telephone Company, and the Tabor Grand Opera with its own dance troupe, "The Taborettes." Horace Tabor even made over his marriage, divorcing his first wife and replacing her with the stunning Elizabeth Bonduel McCort Doe, nicknamed "Baby Doe," and causing a scandal that derailed his goal of winning the presidency of the United States. So he settled for Lieutenant Governor of Colorado instead, and settled Baby Doe into the most luxurious suite of the most luxurious hotel west of the Mississippi: the Windsor, modeled after England's Windsor Castle and featuring French diamond-dust mirrors, marble fireplace mantels, hot and cold running water, a full mile of Brussel's carpeting, and a basement saloon that boasted three-thousand silver dollars embedded in the floor. Horace Tabor, of course, was the hotel's major investor.

For Doc Holliday, weary from the Wild West troubles of Tombstone, Denver must have seemed like a civilized world away and a safe haven once again. He got off the Denver & Western Railroad at Union Depot and took a horse-drawn trolley into town, then registered for a hotel room and spent the rest of the afternoon watching the sulky races on the grounds of the new National Mining and Industrial

Exposition—another of Horace Tabor's projects—then headed back to the Windsor for a planned meeting with an executive from a Leadville mining company who had offered to fund his next travels.

He was only a block or so from his hotel, passing the glass storefront of Daniels & Fishers Department Store, when a man stepped out of the shadows and pointed two pistols him. "Throw up your hands. Doc Holliday, I have you now!" When Doc raised his hands in surprise, a deputy clapped handcuffs on him.

By the time Doc and his arresters arrived at the nearby office of the Arapahoe County Sheriff, the press was in attendance, as well, and the whole drama played out in the Colorado papers. The *Denver Tribune* of May 16, 1882, was the first to break the story:

> *The prisoner's name was John H., alias Doc, Holliday, a man very much hated in Arizona by the cowboys, and who was recently compelled to leave there through fear of being assassinated, as two of his friends and brother officers have been. The man who arrested him on the street gave his name as Perry Mallan and claimed to be a Deputy Sheriff from Los Angeles, California. To the officers here he gave Doc Holliday the record which the cow-boys give him in the South, charging him with every conceivable crime and exhibiting telegrams ordering Holliday's arrest as an accessory in the murder of Frank Stilwell [sic] at Tucson, the murder of a railroad conductor on the Southern Pacific road, the murder of a ranchman named Clanton near Tombstone, and attempted murder of his brother, the murder of Curley Bill the noted cow-boy and half a dozen other crimes. Just what part Holliday had in these affairs is not known. He is represented by one side as a desperado and on the other side a well-known officer told a reporter last night that Holliday had been a United States Marshall in the employ of the government for years and stood well wherever he was known. The record of Holliday, as given by his enemies, however, has attained wide celebrity, and this was what Mallan claimed for him last night.*
>
> *Following close upon the capture a Tribune reporter was in the Sheriff's office, where a curious scene was witnessed.*
>
> *Behind the railing and partially screened by the desk stood a man demanding to know why he had been arrested. Deputy Linton was telephoning frantically for a hack. Just on the other side of the desk from Holliday, stood a young thick-set man, with a short-cropped reddish moustache, his foot resting on the seat of a*

chair. A second glance showed that he held a revolver partially concealed behind his back.

"Oh, you can drop that," said the first man, who proved to be Holliday, "I am not going to try to get away from you. I have no weapons."

"No, you won't get away from me again," exclaimed Mallan, still holding his pistol in his hand. "You killed my partner, you blood-thirsty coward, and I would have taken you in Pueblo if the men I had with me had stood by me."

"I did not come here to be abused," said Holliday, looking toward the deputy for protection.

Just then a crowd of rough looking fellows filed into the Sheriff's office. To them Holliday appealed that he wanted to make a statement.

"This is not a court or jury," said Deputy Linton.

"But I want to set myself right," said the prisoner. "Is it customary in this country to deny a citizen the right of speech? Is it right? Is it justice?"

No answer.

It was evident that the whole spirit of the Sheriff was with Mallan, and as he still grasped the revolver, he held the winning hand.

"I can show who that man is," said Holliday, vehemently, like a man at bay, but a threatening movement from the man with the pistol checked his speech for a moment. "I can prove that he is not the Sheriff, and, in fact, no officer from Cochise county," he continued boldly. "I can show you his reasons for bringing me here. I can show—" but Mallan and the Deputy Sheriff alike cut short his speech. He desired to make a statement, but they said it was no place for it. . . . The prisoner was taken in a hack and hurried to the county jail.

The statement Doc wanted to make was that Perry Mallon (whose name was misspelled in the article) was no kind of lawman, but a con artist turned bounty hunter hoping to collect a $500 reward offered by Sheriff Johnny Behan of Tombstone. Mallon had no proper warrant with him nor any authority to make an arrest, so he'd made up an elaborate story about being a Deputy Sheriff from Los Angeles whose partner had been murdered by Doc Holliday in a St. George, Utah saloon. According to the tale, he'd been following Doc for seven years, engaging in bloody gun battles with him all over the Southwest, then finally apprehending him on the city streets of Denver. The story was sensational and filled several editions of the local papers, until it was discredited by the fact that Doc had never been to Utah and Mallon said that he may have been mistaken in identifying him as the killer. But the false story had served its purpose: keeping Doc Holliday in jail while a real warrant was sent charging him with the killing of Frank Stillwell in the Tucson train yard.

Doc was in a dangerous situation, but he wasn't alone. He had a lawman friend in Denver—not Wyatt Earp, but Bat Masterson, the former sheriff of Ford County, Kansas, and recently appointed City Marshal of Trinidad, who was in town on business. Bat visited Doc at the Arapahoe County Jail and arranged for the best lawyers in the city to handle the case. Then he accompanied Doc to a hearing before the judge, who found no good grounds for holding the prisoner and released him from custody—only to see him immediately rearrested on another charge brought by Bat himself, accusing Doc of swindling a Pueblo gambler out of $400.

Bat Masterson wasn't being disloyal, just using the legal system on Doc's behalf. He knew that the Arizona arrest warrant would be arriving soon, and that the Colorado courts could not honor a warrant from another state or territory while a local prosecution was in process. So, he threw together a reasonable accusation in a local venue—Doc Holliday as a shifty gambler—and used it to keep him from being sent back to Arizona to stand trial there. As he and Doc both knew, if Holliday went back to cowboy country, he wouldn't last long enough to make a court date. Bat later explained: "The charge . . . made against Holliday, at this time, was nothing more than a subterfuge on my part to prevent him being taken out of state by the Arizona authorities."[1]

Then the Arizona warrant arrived, carried by Pima County Sheriff Bob Paul of Tucson. Although a friend of the Earps, Sheriff Paul was a man of duty who intended to take the prisoner back to face charges for the murder of Frank Stillwell. So, Doc had one charge dismissed and two more charges keeping him in jail—and an extradition order on its way from Arizona. And while he waited for the final draw of the game, he gave an interview to a reporter from the *Denver Republican* and used it to tell the story his own way. The reporter, happy to have an exclusive, wisely let him talk. It was the longest, and most important, interview of Doc Holliday's life:

> *The visitor was very much surprised at Holliday's appearance, which is as different as could be from the generally conceived idea of a killer. Holliday is a slender man, not more than five feet six inches tall, and would weigh perhaps 150 pounds. His face is thin and his hair sprinkled heavily with gray. His features are well formed and there is nothing remarkable in them save a well denned look of determination from his eyes. . . . His hands are small and soft like a woman's,*

but the work they have done is anything but womanly. . . . Holliday was dressed neatly in black, with a colored linen shirt. The first thing noticeable about him in opening the conversation was his soft voice and modest manners. He explained the case as follows:

"The men known as cow-boys are not really cow-boys. In the early days the real cow-boys, who were wild and reckless, gained a great deal of notoriety. After they passed out their places were taken by a gang of murderers, stage robbers and thieves, who were refugees from justice from the Eastern States. The proper name for them is Rustlers. They ran the country down there and so terrorized the country that no man dared say anything against them."

"Do you apprehend trouble when you are taken back?" asked the visitor.

Holliday paused for a minute and gazed earnestly out of the window of Jailor Lambert's room into the rain outside and then said slowly, "If I am taken back to Arizona, that is the last of Holliday." After a pause he explained this by saying, "We hunted the rustlers, and they all hate us. John Behan, Sheriff of Cochise county, is one of the gang, and a deadly enemy of mine, who would give any money to have me killed. It is almost certain that he instigated the assassination of Morgan Earp. Should he get me in his power my life would not be worth much."

"But Sheriff Paul, of Tucson, will take you to that place, will he not?"

"Yes, and there lies my only chance for safety. I would never go to Tombstone. I'd make an attempt to escape right outside this jail and get killed by a decent man. I would rather do that than be hung by those robbers there."

"Cannot Paul protect you?"

"I am afraid not. He is a good man, but I am afraid he cannot protect me. The jail is a little tumble down affair, which a few men can push over, and a few cans of oil thrown upon it would cause it to burn up in a flash, and either burn a prisoner to death or drive him out to be shot down. That will be my fate."

"Haven't you friends there who would rally to your assistance?"

"Yes, the respectable element will stand by me, but they are all intimidated and unorganized. They will never do anything until some respectable citizen is shot down, when the people will rise and clean them out, as they did at Fort Griffin, where twenty-four men were hung on the tree when I was there. The Tombstone Rustlers are part of this Fort Griffin gang."

"*You were charged with killing Frank Stillwell. What do you know about that affair?*"

"*I know that Stillwell was a stage robber and one of Morgan Earp's assassins, and that he was killed near Tucson, but I do not know that I am in any way responsible for his death. I know that he robbed a stage, from the fact that he gave the money to a friend of mine to keep, and I know that he helped in the assassination of Morgan Earp, as he was seen running from the spot by several responsible citizens. Pete Spence was with him, and I am morally certain that Sheriff Behan instigated the assassination. He did it for two reasons. One was that he was the officer elected by the Rustlers and the other was that he was afraid of and hated Morgan Earp, who had quarreled with and insulted him several times. He feared Earp and had every inducement to kill him. . . . He has always stood in with the Rustlers and taken his share of their plunder, and in consequence he is in their power and must do as they say. This is shown by the fact that he has two Rustlers under him as deputies. One of these men is John Ringo, who jumped on the stage of the variety theater in Tombstone one night about three weeks ago and took all the jewels from the proprietor's wife in full view of the audience. These are the men who want me and that is the kind of country I am going back to for my health.*"

"*It's a nice, sociable country,*" I must admit, responded the visitor, who ran over mentally all the terrible outrages which had been committed of late by the noted Rustlers, including a train robbery or two and several stage robberies. Holliday, in response to a question, then turned his attention to Mallon, the officer who followed him and caused his arrest here.

"*The first time I met him,*" said Holliday, "*was in Pueblo before I came to Denver. He approached me in a variety theater and introducing himself said he wanted to do me a favor in return for saving his life in Santa Fe once. I told him I would be very thankful for any favor he wanted to show me, but he must be mistaken about my saving his life in Santa Fe, as I had never been there. He did not reply to this, but told me that he had just come up on the train with Josh Stillwell, a brother of Frank Stillwell whom I was supposed to have killed, and that he had threatened to shoot me on sight. I thanked him for his information, and he replied, 'If you give me away I will kill you.' I told him I wasn't traveling around the country giving men away, and he left me. I met him in a saloon a few days afterwards, and asked the barkeeper who he was. He told me that Mallon represented that he was a ranchman, who had sold out in the lower country,*" *and was looking for a location, upon which he borrowed $8 at one time and $2 at another. I met the barkeeper several times afterwards, and told me that the money had never been paid. I then considered that there was no truth in his story which he told to me. The next time I met him was in Denver, when he cropped his guns on me and caused my arrest. Paul does not know him, and I believe he is a crank. He acted like one at Pueblo, when he took down his clothes and showed a mark which he said was a bullet wound, but which was the mark of disease. I laughed in his face, the thing being so funny that I couldn't help it. One thing which Mallon tells gives him away bad. He told in your paper that he was stand-ing alongside Curly Bill when the latter was killed. . . . If Mallon was alongside of Curly Bill when he was killed, he was with one of the worst gang of murderers and robbers in the country."[2]*

On May 25, ten days after Doc Holliday had been arrested and jailed on false charges, the extradition order was delivered to Colorado Governor Frederick Pit-kin, demanding the prisoner be sent back to Arizona to stand trial for murder. While the governor studied the papers, Bat Masterson left Denver and headed south amid rumors "that he is organizing a party to guard the train upon which Holliday will be taken back."[3] Doc would need all the guarding he could get, as the May 27 *Albuquerque Review* reported: "Cowboys have all left Tombstone, and it is thought that they have gone out in order to intercept Sheriff Paul as he returns from Denver with Doc Hol-liday, and assassinate his prisoner. They have threatened that Holliday will never again enter Tombstone alive." A story in the May 26 *Rocky Mountain News* called Holliday, "completely broken up by the arrival of the requisition."

But Doc wasn't leaving Denver just yet, being locked in jail for another five days while Governor Pitkin considered the options. Doc had claimed in more than one interview that he had already been pardoned by the governor of Arizona, or at least been promised a pardon. So it's possible that the governors of Arizona and Colorado had already come to a gentleman's agreement granting sanctuary to the fugitives— until Holliday's very public arrest and the plethora of press that accompanied it had made the secret deal difficult and forced a legal process. Should Governor Pitkin honor the extradition order or honor the original agreement?

In the end, the governor of Colorado returned the extradition papers to the gover-nor of Arizona, citing a missing signature, as indeed there may have been, and perhaps purposely so. As the May 31 *Tucson Daily Star* commented, "Of course the papers were defective. It was the easiest way out of the difficulty." But even if the papers had been flawless, Holliday still had the Pueblo swindle case to settle before he could be released to another jurisdiction. Which meant that he would have to stay in Colorado for the foreseeable future, giving him sanctuary, after all, and adding a new term to the legal lexicon, *Hollidaying*: the use of one legal charge to avoid answering for another.[4]

UNION STATION

On Doc Holliday's first trip to Denver in 1876, there were five railroads and four train depots in different parts of the city. The first depot was built in 1868 at Wazee and Twenty-First Streets by the Denver Pacific Railroad, sharing space with the Kansas Pacific and the Colorado Central Railroads. In 1872, a second depot was built at Wynkoop and Nineteenth Streets by the Denver & Rio Grande Railroad because right-of-way conflicts kept it from reaching the existing depot. In 1874, a third depot was built at Walnut and Sixth Streets by the Denver, South Park & Pacific Railroad, and in 1875, when the first depot got overcrowded, a fourth depot was built at Delgany and Sixteenth Streets by the Colorado Central Railroad. So, Denver was crisscrossed by rail lines, and passengers with transfers had to haul their luggage through crowded city streets from one depot to the next to catch another train.

The solution was simple, but expensive. Denver's four railroads organized a joint company to build a new depot big enough for all of them, creating Union Station—a Romanesque cathedral of transportation 503 feet long with a great central passenger waiting room, two massive wings for baggage and business offices, and a clock tower soaring 128 feet above the city. The building materials came from quarries all over Colorado, with sandstone from Manitou Springs, stone from Castle Rock, and a rose-colored volcanic rock called rhyolite from Colorado Springs. In July 1881, when Union Station celebrated its grand opening with a crowd of twenty thousand eager spectators, it was the largest building

Old Union Station, photo by Louis Charles McClure. Courtesy Denver Public Library, Western History Collection #MCC-3281.

west of the Mississippi at a final cost of $525,000, far exceeding the city's next most expensive property, the fabulous Windsor Hotel, built at a cost of $400,000, including all of its elegant furnishings.

Doc Holliday was surely impressed by the grand new Union Station when he arrived in May 1882 after his troubled adventures in Arizona and hoping for the start of a better chapter in his life. And he surely had no idea that the next time he entered the building, he'd be in handcuffs.

THE SILVER KING

The money man behind the Gilded Age transformation of Denver was Horace Tabor, a Kansas farmer who'd found a fortune in the dirt around the mountain town of Leadville. Horace and his wife Augusta had arrived with their young son in the Rocky Mountain reaches of the old Kansas Territory in 1859, joining the "Fifty-Niners" in the territory's first gold rush. They tried prospecting in Colorado City and Buckskin Joe (a ghost town near present-day Fairplay) and set up a store in Oro City before settling in the new town of Leadville in the newly made state of Colorado.

Horace Tabor by Mathew Brady.
Library of Congress, Brady–Handy
Photograph Collection.

It was a lucky day in May 1878 when two German immigrants came into the Tabors' general store in Leadville and asked Horace to grubstake them in their silver prospecting, giving supplies in exchange for a share in whatever mining opportunities they found. A month later, the group knew they had a bonanza on their hands: the Little Pittsburg Mine. By the end of the summer the mine had paid out a $10,000 dividend to its three owners. Horace went on to buy, among others, the famous Matchless Mine and became a millionaire. With his new wealth, Tabor established newspapers, a bank, the Tabor Opera House in Leadville, and the Tabor Grand Opera House in Denver. With his new notoriety, he was elected lieutenant governor of Colorado. And by his side through it all was his wife Augusta, who had followed him from Kansas to a hard, but beautiful life in the Colorado mountains. As she later wrote of those early days in the mining camps, "I shall never forget my first vision of the park. I can only describe it

Elizabeth McCourt Doe Tabor. Credit: Courtesy Colorado Mountain History Collection 01241CC 1873.

by saying it was one of Colorado's sunsets. Those who have seen them know how glorious they are."

But Augusta's beautiful life came to an end when another beauty came into Horace Tabor's life: a young divorcee named Elizabeth Bonduel McCourt Doe, nicknamed "Baby Doe." Horace was a silver king, Baby Doe was an available young beauty, and the two soon started a scandalous affair. Horace moved out of his family's home in Leadville and begged Augusta for a divorce, but she refused. So, Horace arranged for a secret divorce in Durango, and though that turned out to be not legal, he set up residence with Baby Doe at the Windsor Hotel in Denver—where they were living in silver rush luxury when Doc Holliday arrived in town.

THE WINDSOR HOTEL

The Windsor Hotel, opened in 1880 as Denver's first true luxury hotel, was modeled after a section of England's Windsor Castle and the newly opened Windsor Hotel in Montreal. Local papers called it the "largest and most complete hotel between Chicago and San Francisco." Like the new Union Station, the building used sandstone and rose rhyolite from local quarries, brought in on Denver based railroads.

The Windsor had two entrances: a main lobby on Larimer Street and a "Ladies' Entrance" on 18th Avenue, both with an iron porte-cochere and elegant lamp posts. The hotel's restaurant was supplied with food from its own farm and game delivered by its own hunter, and the wine cellar was fully stocked. Sporting men could enjoy the games in the Cattleman's Room or have a drink at the Bonanza Bar where the floor was inlaid with thousands of silver

The Windsor Hotel by W. H. Jackson. Courtesy Denver Public Library, Western History Collection #WHJ-1574.

dollars. The "floating floor" in the ballroom cost $50,000 and was suspended by cables that allowed it to give slightly under the weight of dancers, making them feel lighter on their feet. And after an evening of dinner and dancing, guests were pampered at the underground spa with its Turkish (hot air), Russian (steam), and Roman (hot water) baths fed by artesian wells. A podiatrist, barber, and ladies' hairdresser were always available.

The most elegant rooms of the Windsor were those occupied by one of the owners, Silver King Horace Tabor, and his mistress, Baby Doe. The Tabor suite was comprised of a bedroom and living room with marble fireplaces, a bathroom with a gold leaf bathtub, and hand-carved walnut furnishings including a 1,500-pound bed and matching dressers. While Horace and Baby Doe's scandalous love affair had a luxurious setting, more ordinary guests of the hotel—like Doc Holliday—could choose a bedroom on the American Plan (with a shared bath) for $2.00 a night, or with a private bath for $2.50 a night.

THE MYSTERIOUS PERRY MALLON

When Doc Holliday's 1882 Denver arrest made the papers and wire reports, another character jumped into the national news: Perry Mallon, the California sheriff who spent years trailing the deadly dentist who'd killed his partner, but who finally got his man. Except that Mallon was neither from California nor a sheriff, and had never had a partner who'd been killed by Doc Holliday.

Perry Mallon was a con man, born in 1855 in Akron, Ohio, where as a youth he spent two years in the Ohio Reform School for Boys before heading west to a life of violence and crime. In 1879, he was in the railroad town of Ogden, Utah, where he met and married a young woman named Rozina and fathered a child—then deserted wife and child and took the train to Nebraska. In Omaha, he pretended to be the owner of a patent on a reaping machine and sold an elderly man a share in the nonexistent business. Taking the man for $50, Mallon headed back to Ogden, where his wife was suing him for divorce due to desertion. Her petition to the court described him as a "man of indolent habits" whose treatment of her had been "unkind, harsh and cruel and caused her bodily harm and great mental distress"—including a threat to "mash her brains in with a board."

Despite his violent portrayal, Mallon quickly found another woman who fancied him: his divorce lawyer's wife, Virginia Shannon, with whom he had a brief affair while moving from one boardinghouse to another in the spring and summer of 1881. At each stop, he conned his hosts into giving him horses, wagons, clothing, and credit while he traveled on supposed business. Locals described him as "a man about 40 years of age, five feet five or six inches high, light complexion, short red mustache, blue eyes, straight nose, light curly hair and the little finger off his left hand."5 The papers also noted that Virginia had taken her two-year-old daughter along with her, and Mallon was seen kicking and beating the child. But though arrest warrants were sought, Mallon slipped away, supposedly farther down the rail line to Wells, Nevada.

PERRY MALLEN,

AN ALLEGED DETECTIVE, UNDER ARREST IN TOLEDO, O.

Perry Mallon (name misspelled above) from an article in the National Police Gazette, *September 2, 1882, page 12. Courtesy* National Police Gazette.

By the time Mallon showed up in Pueblo, Colorado, in May 1882, Virginia Shannon was old news and Doc Holliday was the new target. Mallon likely thought he could run another quick swindle, pretending to be a law officer to bring in Holliday and collect the $500 reward money for his apprehension, but he didn't count on the national notoriety Doc's arrest would bring. When the papers touted the name of the arresting officer as Perry Mallon, old debts came due, beginning with Hiram Rublee, the man from Omaha who'd lost $50 over the reaper patent con. Rublee traveled to Denver to confront Mallon publicly and demand his money back, exposing Mallon as a fraud. The papers that had first championed the California sheriff who'd caught Doc Holliday now turned on Mallon, who chose to skip town once again with another swindle to pay his way—this time conning a hotel clerk into joining him in a hunt for another escaped outlaw with a supposed $1,500 reward awaiting. The clerk put up $310 for travel expenses for himself and Mallon, who then left him in Kansas City with no outlaw apprehended and no reward money. The clerk wasn't the only one duped by Mallon. Another guest at the hotel had given him $130, and the former mayor of Alamosa, Colorado, had been taken for $50 and a pistol. None of the men would get their money back, though all were likely glad to hear that Perry Mallon had been arrested in Pittsburgh, Pennsylvania, and was awaiting a governor's requisition to return him to Colorado.

But Mallon didn't wait around for a requisition to arrive, and he wasn't done running confidence games or abusing women. His next conquest was twenty-year-old

Phoebe Hooper, the daughter of a prosperous Michigan farmer, whom he married that summer after a whirlwind romance. The honeymoon trip took them to Toledo, Ohio, where Mallon proceeded to beat his wife and demand that she sell her property and give him the money. When Phoebe ran home to her family, Mallon found another Toledo lady to woo, then used her name and property to try to arrange a $2,500 loan from a California bank. Then Phoebe's father went to the police and asked them to charge his new son-in-law with Assault and Battery and Assault to Kill, and the story hit the papers and brought other charges from other venues, including another lady in Indiana who had been deserted by her new husband under similar circumstances. But the only crime Mallon was sentenced with in Toledo was for being a Suspicious Person and Disturbing the Peace at the train station, for which he served 120 days in the county's stoneyard.

Mallon seemed to have stopped using his own name after doing his time in Toledo, as his legal record ended there, though even with a changed name it's not likely that the wife-beating, child-abusing con man changed his ways. If not for his daring arrest of Doc Holliday in Denver, his name wouldn't be remembered by history at all.

19

DENVER & RIO GRANDE

On the morning of May 31, the Denver & Rio Grande Express left Denver's Union Station with Doc Holliday on board, guarded by a trio of law officers: City Marshal Bat Masterson of Trinidad, Sheriff Charles Linton of Arapahoe County, and Sheriff Bob Paul of Tucson. The lawmen weren't worried about cowboys in Colorado trying to attack the prisoner, just making sure that Doc didn't try to escape. But Doc was content to be peaceable and make his court date in Pueblo, knowing that it would be the start of a very, very long case that would be dragged out as long as necessary to keep him safely away from Arizona.

The train pulled into Pueblo's Union Depot at 1:30 pm, and by mid-afternoon Doc was standing before the judge of the county court, facing charges of swindling one Charles White out of $400. Whether the unfortunate Mr. White really existed or was just an invention of Bat Masterson's creative legal mind didn't really matter, as long as the charges were filed. So, Doc waived examination and accepted the assigned bail of $300 and agreed to be back in court for trial on July 11. And until then, he was free to enjoy the sporting life once again and get accustomed to his new status in the community. He was a celebrity in Pueblo now, as the *Pueblo Chieftan* had carried front-page reports of his arrest in Denver and the legal tangle that followed.

The truth was, he was a celebrity almost everywhere now, as the Denver stories had gone by wire clear across the country, being added to by journalists who didn't know what was real and what wasn't, giving Doc Holliday adventures in print that he never had in real life. According to the press, he was a medical doctor from Los Angeles, a cattle rustler boss in the Calico Range of California, a railroad con artist in Chicago, a stage robber, a train robber, and a killer with dozens of dead men to his credit. Many of the false stories started with the scheming Perry Mallon, who snuck out of Denver after trying another con, and then promoted himself as the captor of the infamous Doc Holliday. In Ohio, where he briefly landed, Mallon gave an interview to the *Cincinnati Enquirer* that was carried by the wire service to other papers, and helped to create the legend of Doc Holliday:

> So called because of a peculiar dexterity he possessed in the care and cure of gunshot wounds, is a tall, dark looking man of about forty years of age, with a form herculean in its activity and strength. Coupled with a pleasing shape and a handsome face is a sort of dashing, independent air, which at once arouses in the mind of a beholder feelings of the deepest resentment. In fact, one cannot behold him and not feel that he is enjoying the society of a human tiger, only more fierce and relentless than the animal. . . . It is supposed that he originally came from Georgia; but be this as it may, he first turned up in Missouri some ten years ago as a cowboy, with very strict ideas of honor and the like, for one in such a position as his. His socialistic ideas concerning the ownership of various cattle in that section caused a slight misunderstanding with the presumed owner, which, as is usual in such cases, ended in blood. Whose blood it was that was spilled may be gleaned from the fact that Doc suddenly left the neighborhood, and with good reasons, too, since twenty men were on his track with the ostensible intention of fitting his throttle to a brand-new rope if they captured him.[1]

The real Doc Holliday must have had a good laugh at the story when it made its way from Cincinnati to the *Denver Republican* and down to Pueblo. The only truth in the tale was his birthplace of Georgia—and of course, his handsome face and dashing air, though that seemed an odd compliment coming from a man who'd tried to collect a bounty on him.

Mostly, he wanted to fade into the crowd and enjoy the amusements Pueblo had to offer. South of the depot was the sporting district, with the usual saloons and gambling halls, while the city proper had several good hotels and restaurants and a famous health resort, Clark's Magnetic Mineral Spring. He may even have taken in another show at Tom Kemp's Comique & Variety Theater, where he had first come across the peculiar Mr. Mallon. But after a week or so in Pueblo, he was ready to move on, taking the Denver & Rio Grande west to Cañon City and the entrance to the Royal Gorge of the Arkansas River. Although he'd worked for the Santa Fe Railroad in the battle over the right-of-way through the Gorge, he'd never seen it for himself, and the sight was awe-inspiring. The red granite walls rose to nearly two thousand feet above the canyon floor, the space between them so narrow at times that it seemed nothing but rock and river and rails. Then the Gorge narrowed again until there was only enough room for the river, and the rails were carried by a hanging bridge suspended over the turbulent water. The still famous Hanging Bridge was a marvel of modern engineering, having cost nearly $12,000 to complete, but worth the money for the railroad to reach the rich silver country beyond.

But Doc's travel plans didn't include the silver camps just yet, as the train steamed through mountain valleys and over nine-thousand-foot Marshall Pass into the remote Black Canyon Country. He was headed to Gunnison City, where Wyatt Earp and the rest of the posse had gone into hiding while he had been in Denver dodging an extradition order. And even there, the now-famous Doc Holliday couldn't hide from the press, as the *Gunnison Daily News-Democrat* trailed him for an interview:

There arrived in this city two days ago a gentleman who has gained a great deal of notoriety within the past few weeks, through the columns of the press. The News-Democrat's reporter's attention was first called to the gentleman, by a business man, who pointing across the street said; Do you see that man yonder? That's Doc Holladay, of Arizona.

The man pointed out, was dressed in a dark close fitting suit of black, and wore the latest style of round top hat. His hair was seen to be quite gray, his mustache sandy, and his eyes a piercing dark blue. A member of the sporting fraternity happened to come along, the reporter was introduced, and received a strong free and friendly grip of a hand, which said very plainly, "here is a man who, once a friend is always a friend; once an enemy, is always an enemy."

The gentleman from Arizona was quick to scent the purpose of the reporter, and half laughingly and half in seriousness said, "I'm glad to see you, Mr. Reporter, but I'm not traveling around the country in search of notoriety, and I think you newspaper fellows have already had a fair hack at me."

The reporter gently explained that he wouldn't, for seven true fissure veins, violate the privacy of any man, and then proceeded, as reporters best know how, to apply the pump, with the following results:

(Lest Mr. Holladay should recklessly attempt to annihilate the reporter upon sight for his breach of confidence, he is hereby informed that the reporter's pockets are filled full of little two ounce cans of nitro-glycerine which will certainly explode if they are subjected to any violence.)

"I shall probably be here until about the 30th, when I have some business in Pueblo which will take me away for awhile, but I shall come back again and most likely remain at Gunnison City during the summer."

"Is this your first visit here?"

"It is, and I think you have a fine country here. I like it very much."

"Did you ever live in Texas?"

"Yes. I lived in Dallas and Dennison for several years. I practiced dentistry there, having graduated at the Pennsylvania College of Dentistry in Philadelphia. That is how I got my title of Doc. I settled in Dallas and followed dentistry for about five years. I attended the Methodist Church regularly. I was a member of the Methodist Church there and also a prominent member of a temperance organization till I deviated from the path of rectitude."

"You are not a native of Texas?"

"No. I was born in Georgia, thirty-one years ago."

"When you left Texas where did you go?"

"I came north. I lived in Denver in 1875 and 1876."

"When did you go to Arizona last time?"

"I went there three years ago."

"You are acquainted with the Earps, I believe."

"Yes; we are friends."

"You had some trouble in Arizona with the cow-boys, didn't you?

"Well, yes," drawled the doctor. "You might call it trouble. Bill [Virgil] Earp was city marshal of Tombstone. Morg Earp was a special policeman. Wyatt Earp was a deputy U.S. marshal. One day six of the cow-boys came into town and proposed to run it. The Earps were informed of their doings, and they invited me to go over to where the cow-boys were. One of the Earps said, 'Throw up your hands; we have come to disarm you.' Instead of putting up their paws they put up their revolvers and began firing. Three of them were killed on the spot and two of the Earps wounded. I received a slight wound on the hip, which caused me some inconvenience for a few days."

"When was this affair?"

"It occurred on the twenty-sixth of last October. Morg Earp was killed about four months afterwards while playing pool in Bob Hatch's saloon in Tombstone. Berg [Virg] was waylaid one night and shot in the arm. He is now in California under medical treatment. Stillwell, the man who helped murder Morg Earp was killed in Tucson while awaiting trial for stage robbery."

"You say three cow-boys were killed on the twenty-sixth of October; are there any of that gang still living?"

"Two of them have since been laid out."

"Did you ever have any trouble in Fort Steele?"

"No; I do not know where it is."

"You have been in Fort Griffin, haven't you?"

"Yes; I lived there."

"Who is this Perry Mallen that arrested you in Denver?"

"He is some crank trying to gain notoriety."

"Were you acquainted with him?"

"I never saw him till one night in Pueblo a few weeks ago, when he called me out of a theater and said: 'You saved my life in Santa Fe once, and I want to do you a favor. A man came in on the train who says he is going to kill you.' I said to him, 'Mr. Mallen,' he had given me his name, 'I don't want to be killed, and I am much obliged to you.' He then said, 'If you give me away I'll kill you.' I went for my revolver and he went for his. He found me on my guard, and he invited me to drink. The next morning he took the train for Denver."

"Had you been long in Denver when he arrested you?"

"I got there that day. I was on my way to the Wood River country. That evening I was going down to the Windsor Hotel to meet the superintendent of the Little Pittsburg mine, a personal friend of mine, who had offered me what money I wanted to make the trip."

"Is this Mallen a man of sand?"

"Well, to show you what kind of man he is, after he had arrested me, and was taking me to jail, he sat in front of me with two revolvers pointing directly towards me, and I entirely unarmed and defenseless."

"When did Mallen leave Denver?"

"About four days before I got out. He knew I was going to get out," added Mr. Holladay with a smile.

"Shall you do anything at his trial?"

"No, that is not my way of doing. I avoid trouble. My father taught me when young to attend to my own business and let other people do the same. I shall let him alone if he does me."

"What do you think will be the result of his trial?"

"I think he will go to the pen for a few years. I have a letter from the house of Comfort & Harlan, in Denver, which says the fraternity will spend a thousand dollars if necessary to send him there."[2]

The story gave facts about Doc's life not previously known to the public: where he attended dental school, where and how he lived in Texas, when he had first come to Colorado, and where he had been heading when the Denver arrest derailed his plans. The story also revealed his intent to return to Gunnison for the rest of the summer after making his court date in Pueblo. As he said, he liked the locale, with the Gunnison River flowing to the west of town and the Tomichi River to the south, and views from scrubby mesa to the Crested Butte thirty miles to the north. In the three years since its founding, Gunnison City had quickly grown to five-thousand residents with two-hundred businesses, six church congregations, two daily newspapers, a string of saloons and an opera house, and a five-man police force to keep things orderly. Judd Riley, who served as a Gunnison policeman that summer, remembered Doc and Wyatt and the posse:

The bunch was well heeled and went armed. Earp was a fine looking man, tall with a drooping mustache that curled at the ends. He was quiet in manner and never created a bit of trouble here, in fact, he told us boys on the police force we should call on him if we needed help at any time. He was a dead shot, I guess, always wore two guns high up under his arms, but he never used them here. Doc Holliday was the only one of the gang that seemed to drink much, and the minute he got hilarious, the others promptly took him in charge and he just disappeared.[3]

"Hilarious" didn't mean funny, just drunk and having a good time. But after a few weeks in Gunnison, Doc took the train back to Pueblo for his July court date, stopping along the way in Salida, as reported in the *Salida Mail*: "Doc Holliday, late of Arizona, is in town [and] will remain several days. The Arizona authorities tried to get Holliday back to that territory on a charge of murder but Governor Pitkin refused to honor the requisition."[4]

Salida was Spanish for "departure," an appropriate name for a town born of the Denver & Rio Grande as a rail hub along the Arkansas River. The stone depot and the rail yards sat on the western bank of the Arkansas, the city proper sat on the eastern bank, and a foot bridge at F Street connected the two sides. Like Gunnison, the town was growing quickly, and even had the luxury of a "Salida Bath Room" with hot and cold baths right next door to the Hawkins Hotel, as well as several saloons and gambling houses—Jessie Brown's Place, Dell Crane's Gold Room, and the appropriately named Railroad Saloon. But according to local stories, Doc didn't stay exclusively in town while stopping in Salida—he also made a side trip to the nearby Poncha Springs to soak in the healing mineral waters.

Since leaving Las Vegas and the Montezuma Hot Springs, Doc had been remarkably healthy. None of the Tombstone papers mentioned his consumptive cough, nor did any of the daily Denver reports of his legal woes add illness to his list of troubles. He surely attributed his apparent recovery to the soaks and drinks at Montezuma, and he may have taken advantage of the same treatments at Glendy King's hot springs resort in the canyon above Henry Hooker's Sierra Bonita Ranch. Now, after all his travels and his jail time in Denver, he could use a few days of mineral water soaks, and Poncha Springs was an easy excursion, being just five miles west of Salida, and a short thirty-minute train ride away. He may have even stayed over a night or two at Poncha Springs' Jackson Hotel that catered to health seekers.

Then, rested and refreshed, he climbed aboard the eastbound Denver & Rio Grande for his day in the Pueblo courts, leaving Salida just after nine o'clock in the morning and arriving in South Pueblo at 1:35 in the afternoon after another breathtaking trip through the Royal Gorge. According to court records, the grand jury voted to indict J. H. Holliday on a charge of larceny and issued a capias and advised the sheriff to accept bail in the amount of $500. Then, "said defendant in his own proper person as well as his counsel, W. G. Hollings, Esq., also came and being ready to plead to the indictment said defendant says that he is not guilty in manner and form as charged in said indictment, and puts himself upon the county, and the said people, by their said attorney, say they do the like."[5] With the defendant's plea of not guilty, the case was continued until mid-November, and for a while, Doc was done with legal trouble.

But although Doc had said he planned to return after his court date to spend the rest of the summer in Gunnison, something changed his mind. On July 18, the same day that the *Pueblo Chieftan* reported that his larceny case had been continued, the *Leadville Daily Herald* announced that "Doc Holliday is visiting Leadville."

Why did Doc decide to forego a return to Gunnison, where Wyatt and the rest of the posse were reportedly still in residence? Why did he move on alone to Leadville, leaving his old friends behind? According to Kate Elder, it may have been another quarrel that changed his plans, when Doc accused Wyatt of having worn a "steel shirt" in the shootout with Curly Bill Brocious, accounting for his "miraculous" safety while the rest of the posse went unprotected into battle. Where Doc would have gotten such information is unknown and Wyatt always denied wearing any kind of body armor. But Kate places the argument in Gunnison, where as she remembered the story, Doc told Wyatt, "If you want me to go into anything with you, you have to take the same chances I take or else we quit right here."[6]

Was Doc talking about ending a friendship, or opting out of some scheme? Several sources say that Wyatt left Gunnison that summer and made a clandestine trip back to Arizona to wrap up some unfinished business: finding and killing the last of his brother Morgan's murderers. Wyatt could have made such a journey, riding the rails from Colorado to New Mexico and into the Arizona Territory, then going the rest of the way on horseback to find Johnny Ringo and put a bullet in his head. Or Ringo may have shot himself, committing suicide as was determined by a coroner's jury after the cowboy's body was found in mid-July, lodged in a tree in a canyon near Tombstone. Whoever did the deed, Ringo's death was not on Doc Holliday's conscience.

DAPPER DRESSER

While Doc was traveling between Pueblo and Gunnison after his Denver legal adventures, an old friend from Georgia was describing him in the June 21, 1882, edition of the *Atlanta Constitution*: "He weighs about a hundred and thirty pounds, is about five feet ten, has gray eyes and a bright red mustache. His movements are quick, and he will fight at the drop of your hat. . . . Before he left Georgia he was a quiet fellow. . . . He was small of stature, but he was pluck through and through."

Derby Hat. iStock by Getty Images.

In her later memoirs, Kate Elder said he was, "Close to six feet tall, weight one hundred and sixty pounds, fair complexion, very pretty mustache, a blonde, blue-grey eyes, and a fine set of teeth. . . . He was considered a handsome man. He was a gentleman in manners to the Ladies and everyone. Being quiet, he never hunted for trouble. If he was crowded, he knew how to take care of himself. . . . He was a neat dresser."[7]

The newspaper in his hometown of Valdosta, Georgia, recalling his schoolboy days, said he was always, "neat as a pin."[8] The *Gunnison Daily New-Democrat* that interviewed Doc Holliday the summer of 1882 agreed that he was dapper, being "dressed in a dark close fitting suit of black, and wore the latest style of round top hat."

The "round top hat" he wore in Gunnison was a derby, like the one his friend Bat Masterson was famous for wearing. The derby had been introduced in England in 1849 as an alternative to the more formal top hat—the derby with its low crown and sturdy construction made it a good choice for riders and other outdoorsmen, and it quickly became the most popular man's hat of the nineteenth century. Both cowboys and railroad workers preferred the derby to wide-brimmed hats because it would not blow off in a strong wind while riding or sitting by an open railcar window, prompting author and railroad historian Lucius Beebe to call it "the hat that won the West." In addition to Doc Holliday and Bat Masterson, other famous Western derby wearers included Black Bart, Butch Cassidy, and Billy the Kid.

Bat Masterson, 1879. Wikipedia Commons. In the public domain.

PONCHA SPRINGS

According to local stories, when Doc Holliday stopped off in Salida on his way between Gunnison and Pueblo, he also spent some time in the nearby town of Poncha Springs, known for its healing hot springs, with one hundred separate pools by some counts.

The Ute Indians were the first known visitors to the area, as they traveled between their summer camps in the high Rockies and their winter camps in the lower mountain valleys, but the name of the place came from a military expedition under Juan Batista de Anza in 1779: "Poncho," Spanish for a warm and comfortable covering, later Anglicized to Poncha. In the following years, French trappers and fur traders stopped in the area, and in 1806 Lt. Zebulon Pike spent Christmas Day nearby. In 1832, frontiersman Kit Carson passed through the area, and some credit him with spreading word of the hot springs. Prospectors came next, with Nat Rich and Bob Hendricks building the first cabin. The first homesteaders arrived in the 1860s, with John and Menerva Burnett building a log cabin and Indian trading post, where John served as an Indian agent and Menerva taught school. By the 1870s, Poncha

Jackson Hotel in Poncha Springs near Salida, Colorado. Sketch of c. 1880's photograph by A. V. Wilcox. Author's Collection.

was turning into a real town, with H. A. Jackson's Poncha Springs Hotel opening in 1878 and the railroad arriving in 1881.

By the time Doc Holliday visited in 1882, Poncha Springs had three hotels, seventeen saloons, and a newly dedicated church building. The next year, the first schoolhouse was opened and Poncha Springs was on its way to a population of two thousand. The railroad brought other notable visitors to the springs over the years, including President Ulysses S. Grant, Silver King Horace Tabor and Baby Doe, and even Jesse James. But the town famous for its hot springs was also troubled by fire, with a blaze in 1887 destroying many of its wood-frame buildings, including all seventeen saloons. The town is now a quaint reminder of its hot springs heyday, with a few original structures remaining: the first prospectors' cabin, the first schoolhouse, and the historic Jackson Hotel that Doc Holliday would have known, and which still serves guests passing through the mountain valleys.

Train in Black Canyon of the Gunnison by William Henry Jackson c. 1880. Courtesy Art Source International (P-0256–train).

WYATT'S HIDEOUT

I think you have a fine country here. I like it very much.

—DOC HOLLIDAY

When Doc Holliday gave his appraisal of Gunnison, Colorado, to a reporter from the *Gunnison News Daily-Democrat* in the summer of 1882, he was surely talking about more than just the town itself. It was the countryside around the town that was bringing sightseers on the newly laid rails of the Denver & Rio Grande Railroad, pushing westward from the Royal Gorge, over nine-thousand-foot Marshal Pass, and through the Black Canyon of the Gunnison River on toward Salt Lake City. And it was in the Black Canyon country that Wyatt Earp and his remaining posse members had made their camp while Doc Holliday had taken his chances on Denver.

For men who'd spent too much time being chased by the law, the Black Canyon of the Gunnison seemed like a good place to hide. Explorer John Gunnison, for whom the area was named, called it the "roughest, most hilly, and most cut-up" land he had ever seen. It was also dark, the two-thousand-foot-deep canyon being so narrow that only a few hours of daylight reached the bottom recesses, making the canyon walls look black and giving the place its foreboding name. But there was tremendous natural beauty in the wilderness of the canyon, with its towering cliffs and waterfalls cascading into the river below.

The Denver & Rio Grande Railroad faced a difficult decision as it laid rail in the Black Canyon Country: take an expensive route up and over the tops of several steep mesas, or go through the canyon itself, a cheaper but more dangerous job. The canyon walls were hard granite that had to be blasted with the new explosive called nitroglycerine, which resulted in the death and maiming of several railroad workers. Once the road was opened, engineers had to watch for avalanches that could sweep down from the cliffs and tumble a locomotive into the frigid waters of the Gunnison River. As the *Gunnison Review-Press* reported in August 1882, Black Canyon was "the largest and most rugged canon in the world traversed by the iron horse."

Wyatt Earp and his men, camping in the Black Canyon country that summer, were likely grateful for the rugged and difficult terrain where it was easy to hide—and hard to be found.

THE STRANGE DEATH OF JOHNNY RINGO

In the movie *Tombstone*, Doc Holliday saves the life of his friend Wyatt Earp three times: once when Johnny Tyler is gunning for him, once when Johnny Ringo is gunning for him, and once again in a final duel that was supposed to have been between Wyatt and Ringo before Doc stepped in to finish the job. It's good storytelling and dramatic movie making—but it didn't happen that way. In fact, Doc Holliday had nothing at all to do with the strange death of Johnny Ringo.

John Peters Ringo. Courtesy Arizona Historical Society/Tucson (AH#78486).

On July 14, 1882, the body of cowboy John Peters Ringo was found lodged in the crook of a tree in West Turkey Creek Canyon, near Chiricahua Peak overlooking Tombstone. He had a bullet hole in his head, a revolver with one round fired hanging from his finger, and pieces of his torn undershirt wrapped as rags around his feet. The man who found him, a teamster named John Yost who was hauling wood in the area, said one pistol shot had been heard the day before, but nothing more.

Yost's testimony at the coroner's inquest in Tombstone describes the unsettling scene:

> *He was dressed in light hat, blue shirt, vest, pants and drawers. On his feet were a pair of hose and an undershirt torn up so as to protect his feet. He had evidently traveled but a short distance in this foot gear. His revolver he grasped in his right hand, his rifle resting against the tree close to him. He had on two cartridge belts, the belt for revolver cartridges being buckled on upside down. The undernoted property was found with him and on his person: 1 Colt's revolver, calibre 45, No. 222, containing five cartridges; 1 Winchester rifle octagon barrel, calibre 45, model 1876, No. 21,896, containing a cartridge in the breech and ten in the magazine; 1 cartridge belt, containing 9 rifle cartridges; 1 cartridge belt, containing 2 revolver cartridges; 1 silver watch of American Watch company, No. 9339, with silver chain attached; two dollars and sixty cents ($2.60) in money; 6 pistol cartridges in pocket; 5 shirt studs; 1 small pocket knife; 1 tobacco pipe; 1 comb; 1 block matches; 1 small piece tobacco. There is also a portion of a letter from Messrs. Hereford & Zabriskie, attorneys at law, Tucson, to the deceased, John Ringo.[9]*

American Waltham Watch Co. Pocket Watch, 1880. Rachel K. Turner/Alamy Stock Photo (Image #E6XWMH).

The testimony reveals interesting things about Ringo: he smoked a pipe, wore shirt studs and a silver watch and chain, carried some cash, and had two loaded guns on him when he died. The fact that the silver watch and the cash weren't stolen indicates that the death wasn't part of a road robbery. The fact that only one bullet was spent and only one shot heard the night before suggests that the death wasn't the result of a gun battle. So, who killed Johnny Ringo? Given the physical evidence and lack of witnesses, the coroner's inquest ruled the death a suicide.

After the inquest, other information came forward. *Tombstone Epitaph* editor Sam Purdy had run into Ringo in the weeks before the shooting and said the cowboy "was as certain of being killed, as he was of being living then. He said he might run along for a couple of years more, and may not last two days."[10] At Tombstone's Fourth of July celebrations, Ringo was seen drinking heavily, as he was when Deputy Sherriff Billy Breckenridge ran into him:

It was shortly after noon. Ringo was very drunk, reeling in the saddle, and said he was going to Galeyville. It was in the summer and a very hot day. He offered me a drink out of a bottle half-full of whiskey, and he had another full bottle. I tasted it and it was too hot to drink. It burned my lips. Knowing that he would have to ride nearly all night before he could reach Galeyville, I tried to get him to go back with me to the Goodrich Ranch and wait until after sundown, but he was stubborn and went on his way.[11]

On July 9, Ringo was seen eating dinner at a ranch in the South Pass of the Dragoon Mountains, still drinking heavily. That was the last report of Ringo before his death. Eleven days after the shooting, Ringo's horse was found wandering about two miles from where the cowboy's body was discovered, his boots tied to the saddle. As the *Tombstone Independent* reported: "His saddle was still upon him, with Ringo's coat upon the back of it. In one of the pockets were three photographs and a card bearing the name of 'Mrs. Jackson.'"

The "Mrs. Jackson" whose name was on the card in Ringo's saddle pocket was Johnny's sister, Fanny Fern Ringo Jackson, and it's from the family that more of the story comes forth. After the O.K. Corral gunfight and the trouble that followed, Johnny traveled to California to pay a visit to his estranged sisters in hopes of reconciling and starting a new life. He even bought some new boots from a Tombstone boot maker to make a good showing at his sisters' home, and still owed money on them when his sisters refused to let him in. So, it seems that, turned away by his family, with his friends and business associates either dead or driven out by the work of the Earps and Doc Holliday, Johnny Ringo drank himself into a stupor and shot himself in the head. Ironically, his father had also died of a gunshot wound to the head when a shotgun misfired as the family traveled by wagon train across the plains. It's said that young Johnny was the one who found his dead father's body, and the image never left him.

So where were Doc Holliday and Wyatt Earp when Ringo died? Doc was eight hundred miles away, making his court appearances in Pueblo, Colorado. Wyatt Earp was even farther from Tombstone, in the Black Canyon country of the Gunnison, though in later years he sometimes took credit for Ringo's killing. But Wyatt's confessions to several authors do not match the time or circumstances of the shooting, so they may have been more wishful thinking than recollection—killing Johnny Ringo would have finally fulfilled his promise to his dying brother, Morgan.

20

HIGH LINE RAILROAD

Leadville was the reason the Denver & Rio Grande and the Atchison, Topeka & Santa Fe had fought over the right-of-way through the Royal Gorge. Called "Cloud City" because of its ten-thousand-foot elevation, Leadville was both the highest city in the country and the richest silver camp in the world, and the Royal Gorge had been the shortest route through the mountains to reach it. In 1880, when the rails finally reached the town, the Leadville mining district was producing $14 million worth of silver, and the hills were warrened with mine shafts, cluttered with stamp mills, and overhung with the haze of smelters that never stopped burning.

With all that money and a population of forty thousand and growing, Leadville seemed destined to take over Denver's place as the state capital. The city's main thoroughfare of Harrison Street was crowded day and night with coaches and carriages, ore wagons and delivery drays, foot traffic and fine horses and trains of burros bound for the mines. There were brick and stone sidewalks fronting tall business buildings, stores filled with every description of merchandise, a grand Opera House provided by Horace Tabor, and enough law offices to handle all the legal entanglements of claims and claim jumpers, mine deeds and multiple-owner partnerships. There were, in fact, nearly as many lawyers in Leadville as there were saloons—and there were nearly a hundred of those, making saloon-keeping the biggest business in town. And where there were saloons, there were all the lesser establishments that went along with them: gambling houses, dance halls, bordellos, and opium dens.

Leadville was a dizzying town, and not just because of the number of entertainments available. At nearly two-miles high, the altitude and the rarified air left visitors breathless for days after arriving, with restless sleep and morning nausea and a tiredness that was almost painful. Even the *Tourist's Guide to Leadville and the Carbonate*

Fields cautioned: "Persons troubled with weak lungs or heart disease should give the camp a wide berth. The rare atmosphere accelerates the action of both these organs and unless they are in perfect condition, serious results may follow." For someone with consumption, making a visit to Leadville could be a fatal mistake.[1]

But Doc Holliday disregarded the warnings. He had business to finish in Leadville, finally meeting with Mr. John Vimont, the man he'd been on his way to see when he was arrested by Perry Mallon in Denver. Vimont was superintendent of the Little Pittsburg Mine in Leadville, an acquaintance from Doc's mining speculation days in Tombstone, who had offered him money to pay for his Colorado travels—and money was Doc's biggest need. He hadn't practiced dentistry since leaving Las Vegas, and hadn't run a faro bank, his other paying profession, since leaving Tombstone. And now that he was no longer riding with Wyatt, there was no more money coming his way from Wells Fargo to cover expenses. So, he looked up Vimont in his offices on Harrison Street, and found a job doing what he'd done on his last visit to Colorado: working as a card dealer.

A local writer described Doc during his Leadville days as:

> *a thin, spare looking man; his iron gray hair is always well combed and oiled; his boots usually wear an immaculate polish; his beautiful scarf, with an elegant diamond pin in the center, looks well on his glossy shirt front, and he prides himself on always being scrupulously neat and clean. He usually talks in a very low tone. . . . In his pocket he always carries a beautiful, silver-mounted revolver, 45 caliber, and while talking to a stranger, his right arm restlessly wanders in that vicinity.*[2]

In addition to his work at the gambling tables, Doc also got involved in politics, joining the 123 men who founded the Lake County Independent Club that resolved to vote neither Democrat nor Republican in the upcoming state races. The group's first meeting was October 20 at Leadville's Turner Hall, and Doc Holliday, likely the best educated man in the room, presided over the proceedings. Interestingly, one of the members of the new club was a man Doc had known in less cordial circumstances back in Tombstone: Johnny Tyler, the California gambler who had started the card room quarrel that led to the Milt Joyce affair.

If Doc still had hard feelings against Tyler, they weren't made public, and soon he had other matters to deal with. He was due back in Pueblo in mid-November for the continuation of his court case, as the *Pueblo Chieftain* noted: "Doc Holliday, who among others has not been in Arizona this fall, is in town attending court."[3] On November 25, his case was heard and continued again until the April session of court "on application of the defendant by his attorney."[4]

The next day, the paper reported that he had left for Denver.[5]

He was back in Leadville by the beginning of December, just in time to make the news again. In the early morning hours of December 6, a gas lamp exploded in the Texas House Saloon on Harrison Street, and the place caught fire. The fire department worked the blaze for more than two hours, but by 8:30 am the fire had devoured most of the saloon. According to the *Leadville Evening Chronicle*: "What was a few hours before the elegantly equipped Texas house, was a mass of charred and blackened ruins, with nothing but the smoking walls left of what was once the finest gambling hall in the west. . . . The firemen acknowledge with thanks the services rendered by Sandy McCusick, Doc Holliday, Thomas Flood, Thomas Ransom, and George Fonda."

December may have begun in a blaze, but it went on as all Leadville winters did, with bone-chilling cold and covered in snow. Old timers said there were only three seasons in those mountain valleys, not four, counting early winter, full winter, and late winter and not much else. In the daytime, the temperature struggled to reach freezing; at night, it sank to near zero. The streets were sheets of ice, the mountain passes impassible, and the already thin air seemed almost immaterial. And then the sickness started, with pneumonia and smallpox stalking the city. The Denver & Rio Grande at Leadville responded by holding a mandatory vaccination day for all railroad workers, offering free drinks for everyone who complied. The liquor clinched the deal, the workers rolled up their sleeves, and the spread of smallpox slowed, with only sixtynine lives lost that year.

Though Doc was spared smallpox, he took sick with pneumonia during that long, hard winter. And it may have been the illness that kept him in Leadville in April when he should have been back in court in Pueblo. Although the judge called for him three times, he didn't appear, and the court ordered his bond forfeited. The case wasn't closed, however, and could still be recalled if needed to keep him safely away from Arizona.

In May, while Doc was still recovering from his illness, Wyatt Earp and Bat Masterson were joining in an expedition to Dodge City to aid a friend in the gambling community there. Luke Short, owner of the Long Branch Saloon, was battling competing interests trying to drive him out of business. When he asked for a show of force from his old customers, a gang of former Dodge City denizens answered the call. Although no real fighting happened, the gathering of gunfighters made Luke Short's opponents back down, and all was settled amicably. Legend says that Doc Holliday went along for what became known as the Dodge City War, taking the train from Leadville to Pueblo and east to Kansas, and the newspapers even named him as part of the gang. But as neither Wyatt nor Bat recalled his participation in their later memoirs, that part of his legend may be just more newspaper sensationalism. Reporters had learned that Doc Holliday was good copy, and they would continue to use his name in stories that often had nothing to do with him.

The truth was, he was safe in Colorado and settled in Leadville, even though the long winters and short summers were wreaking havoc with his health, and he likely did little traveling that year. Other than his name being mentioned in those stories about the Dodge City War, there are no reports of his being anywhere else besides Leadville in 1883. So, it would have been in Leadville that he received a letter from Georgia, telling him news from home: his cousin Mattie had entered a Catholic convent in Savannah, taking vows as Sister Mary Melanie Holliday of the Sisters of Mercy. Mattie had found a sanctuary in service to God, as her cousin had found his sanctuary in the safety of the Colorado Mountains. Or so he thought, until the ghosts of Tombstone came back to haunt him.

Doc's regular job in Leadville was dealing cards at the Monarch Saloon on Harrison Street, three doors down from the Tabor Opera House. The saloon's clientele was a mix of miners and mining investors, shopkeepers and sporting men, with the occasional visiting vaudeville star. Dealing wasn't a lucrative career, but it paid the basics and allowed Doc free time to do his own gambling at places like the Board of Trade, across Harrison Street, and Mannie Hyman's Saloon next to the opera house, and to keep his eyes open for mining opportunities. But sometime in the fall, the Monarch's owner let Doc go and replaced him at the faro tables with former Tombstone gambler Johnny Tyler.

Doc was certain the old Sloper gang was behind the firing, trying to force him out of town. But he'd stood up to Johnny Tyler and his friends before and reckoned he could do it again. What he didn't wager on was another winter of cold and pneumonia, leaving him too sick to find another job or even to support himself with poker winnings. Broke and broken in spirit, he borrowed $5 from bartender Bill Allen and accepted a kindness from saloon owner Mannie Hyman, who gave him a room above his saloon in exchange for helping out at the bar. And that was when Johnny Tyler took advantage of a bad situation, challenging Doc when he couldn't fight back. As the July 22, 1884, *Leadville Daily Democrat* told the story:

The well-known Doc Holliday claims to have been the victim of a put-up job to murder him in Hyman's saloon yesterday morning, and the place has been on the verge of a shooting match ever since. At an early hour Holliday and John Tyler, another sporting man, got into an altercation in which the latter used very abusive language. Holliday said he didn't want to have trouble, and Tyler called on him to draw. Friends interfered and there was no blood shed. There were some bad threats made during the day, and trouble is anticipated. Tyler killed a man in Frisco and is regarded as "bad." Doc Holliday states that the trouble arose over an old grudge in Arizona where Tyler tried to put up a job to kill him, but failed to make it work. Tyler's friends say he wants to fight a duel with Holliday.

Doc had cause to be wary of gunplay, as he told the *Democrat*'s reporter: "If I should kill someone here, no matter if I were acquitted, the governor would be sure to turn me over to the Arizona authorities, and I would stand no show for life there at all. I am afraid to defend myself and these cowards kick me because they know I am down. I haven't a cent, have few friends and they will murder me yet before they are done."[6]

So, Doc had plenty of trouble already without an unpaid debt on his ledger. But the $5 loan he'd taken from bartender Bill Allen was still accruing interest—and bringing more threats. When Doc stopped into the saloon where Allen worked, he was put on notice.

"Holliday, I'll give you til Tuesday to pay this money," Allen said, "and if you don't pay it, I'll lick you, you son of a bitch."

But Doc didn't have the cash available, or even anything to offer as collateral, having already hocked his valuables.

"My jewelry is in soak," he replied, "and as soon as I get the money, I'll give it to you."

Allen gave him until noon on August 19 to pay up and told one of Doc's friends that if the money wasn't paid by then he would, "knock him down and kick his damned brains out."[7]

It seemed a dramatic demand over such a small amount of money, and Doc was sure that Johnny Tyler was somehow behind the threats. Nor were Bill Allen's words just tough talk. He was a tough man physically, as well, having been a professional racer and fitness trainer, and more than a match for the frail Doc Holliday. So, Doc felt compelled to do something desperate: he called on the local police and asked for protection. It was an unusual play for a man of his reputation, but he had nowhere else to turn. At least the Leadville police weren't in league with outlaws, as Sheriff Behan had been in Tombstone. Officer Faucett and his force mostly handed out fines and broke up bar fights and didn't challenge a man for carrying a gun unless he put it to bad use.

But although Johnny Tyler's gang was against him, Doc had newspaper friends who took his side. As Leadville's *Carbonate Chronicle* of July 24, 1884, editorialized:

> *It looks very much as though a gang of would be bad men had put up a job to wipe Doc Holliday off the face of the earth. There is much to be said in favor of Holliday—he has never since his arrival here made any bad breaks or conducted himself in any other way than a quiet and peaceable manner. The other faction do not bear this sort of a reputation.*

When August 19 arrived and Doc still had not been able to pay back the money, Bill Allen decided to collect at pistol point. But Doc wasn't trusting his life just to the police and had armed himself in preparation. As the papers reported the story:

> *At noon to-day Allen started out to seek for Holliday, who was at the time in bed. Meantime his friends went to him, notified him of the fact, and a little before 5 he got up and went to Wyman's [Hyman's] saloon, a well-known sporting and gambling resort. His friends and those of Allen stood about the sidewalk armed and waiting for what was really a duel to decide which should go and which should stay. Holliday stood just behind the end of the bar, and, when Allen entered a few minutes later, drew a large frontier revolver and fired. The ball struck Allen in the muscles of the right arm, coming out near the shoulder and knocking him down. As he fell Holliday leaned over and fired again, missing the head by a fraction of an inch. Outsiders then rushed in and stopped the fracas. Holliday was taken to jail and Allen was conveyed to his house.*[8]

At the jail, Doc gave a short interview to another reporter:

> *"It was not about the $5. That was taken as a pretext. It is the old trouble, and Allen was picked out as the man to kill me."*
>
> *"Please describe the shooting to me."*
>
> *"Well, Allen had told me he intended to do me up this evening. I was standing behind the counter when he came in and I saw that he had both hands in his*

pockets and that the handle of a pistol protruded from one of them. Of course I wouldn't let him murder me so I fired."

"What has Allen got particularly against you?"

"He is the tool of the gang."

"How do you account for no pistol being found on him?"

"Was there none found?"

"No."

"His friends spirited it away—that's all."

"How about your trouble in Arizona?"

"I lived there for three years, was part of the time a peace officer, and all I ever did was forced on me and I was tried for and honorably acquitted of. There are people in town who desire to murder me for notoriety. They know I am helpless and have spread the report that I am a bad man, to protect themselves when they do the work. I defy anyone to say they ever saw me conduct myself in any other way than a gentleman should."[9]

Doc had meant to protect himself and he did so, wounding Bill Allen in his shooting arm. The wound was serious but not fatal, with a large artery cut that had to be stitched back together by the local doctor, and Allen would carry the arm in a sling for months afterward. But though Doc was not aiming to murder Bill Allen, that was the claim brought against him. He was charged with Assault with Intent to Kill, then released on a $5,000 bond.

The preliminary hearing was held the next week in the imposing new Lake County Courthouse, and Doc was at last able to make a legal court record of the situation in his own words: "I saw Allen come in with his hand in his pocket, and I thought my life was as good to me as his was to him; I fired the shot, and he fell on the floor, and I fired the second shot; I knew that I would be a child in his hands if he got hold of me; I weigh 122 pounds; I think Allen weighs 170 pounds; I have had the pneumonia three or four times; I don't think I was able to protect myself against him."[10]

With Doc's confession that he had indeed fired his pistol at Bill Allen, the judge had no choice but to bind the case over for the December session of court, with bond being raised to $8,000. But when the money wasn't forthcoming, the court took pity on Doc's physical state and allowed a release on the original bond amount. As the papers had commented: "Should Holliday be obliged to remain behind bars up to the day of his trial it would probably go very hard with him, as his constitution is badly broken and he has been really sick for a long time past."[11]

But even ailing, Doc had shown himself to be a man of sand, still willing to wager against the odds and stand up for himself against an enemy. And that may have been what kept him safe for the next few months—Leadville had learned that if Doc Holliday were cornered, he would come out shooting.

The terms of his reduced bond likely kept him from leaving the area but didn't stop him from joining in a bit of railroad adventure, riding along on a day trip from Leadville to Breckenridge and back again. Though the Denver & Rio Grande had been the first railroad to reach the Cloud City, it had competition from the Union Pacific that was bringing its High Line Railroad over the Rockies, promising to cut an hour off the travel time from Denver to Leadville. To advertise the new route, the High Line was running a special one-day excursion train for a fare of $2.00 that included a picnic lunch at the turn-around town of Breckenridge. The local papers noted the presence of Doc Holliday on the platform, until he was lost in the crowd of three hundred eager riders. Only the weather dampened the mood of the day, with chilling cold and a drizzling snow. But for Doc, the weather may have been more than just uncomfortable, bringing unhappy memories of another cold autumn day. The date of the excursion was October 26, three years to the day since the O.K. Corral shootings.

When his case came up for trial in mid-December, Doc was sick again. He showed up in court bundled in a heavy camel's hair overcoat and asked for a continuance. Although the prosecution protested, the judge once again took his health into consideration and put off the trial date until the spring court session, giving him time to recuperate from what was likely another bout of pneumonia. But by the end of February, he was well enough to attend a dance at the city hall sponsored by the Miner's Union, which was "an elegant supper, an excellent orchestra, and an evening of dancing."[12]

On March 21, 1885, the case of *The People of the State of Colorado v. John Holliday, alias Doc Holliday*, finally convened in the Lake County Courthouse in Leadville, with a full audience in attendance. And as the case progressed, it became eerily reminiscent of another legal action in another venue. The shooting of Bill Allen in Leadville raised the same questions that were considered in the hearing following the O.K. Corral shootings in Tombstone: Is a man allowed to defend himself with arms when his life is threatened? If he only believes the man making the threats to be armed, is he still allowed to take arms himself? Doc claimed that Bill Allen was hiding a pistol in his pocket and meant to use it, though no pistol was found on Allen after the shooting. In Tombstone, the defense claimed Tom McLaury had been hiding a pistol in his pocket, though no pistol was found on him after the killings. In both shootings, it seemed someone had spirited away the weapons to throw guilt on the defendants. But Doc had been exonerated in the Arizona case, and believed he could be exonerated again—if he could bring witnesses testifying that threats had been made against him and that Bill Allen had meant to carry them out. The trouble was, his court-assigned defense team wasn't interested in chasing down witnesses in the saloons and gambling halls of Leadville. So, Doc took a most unusual approach to his own defense: requesting appointment as an officer of the court to carry subpoenas to the sports on Harrison Avenue. In Colorado Case No. 258, John Henry Holliday, alias Doc Holliday, was both defendant and subpoena server.

He knew which men he needed to bring to court, and on March 27 a long line of gamblers appeared in the courtroom, ready to testify that Bill Allen had made death threats against Doc Holliday and appeared armed on the day of the altercation, and that Holliday was merely defending himself against a stronger man who meant to kill him. When the jury finally deliberated on March 28 on the charge of Assault with Intent to Kill, they found the defendant not guilty. Doc Holliday was, once again, acquitted of all charges.

The second-best news of the day was that he was finally free to leave Leadville.

Tabor Opera House Leadville. Courtesy Colorado Mountain History Collection (#00086PL 317).

TABOR OPERA HOUSE

When Silver King Horace Tabor built his opera house in the remote mining camp of Leadville in 1879, the railroads had not yet arrived, so building materials had to be transported by wagon over 13,200-foot Mosquito Pass, one of the highest mountain roads in the country. Despite the challenge, construction was completed in one hundred days and the opera house became the cultural centerpiece of the Cloud City. With walls sixteen inches thick and a façade of iron and Portland cement, the brick and stone building was one of the most substantial structures in Colorado and touted as "the most perfect place of amusement between Chicago or St. Louis and San Francisco."

Tabor Opera House interior. Courtesy Colorado Mountain History Collection (00087PL 318).

The three-story opera house had retail shops on the street level, theater and business offices on the second level away from the street noise, and a third-floor annex of the Clarendon Hotel across St. Louis Avenue connected by a sixty-foot-long elevated passageway. Rumor had it that Horace Tabor kept a room at the Clarendon for convenient visits with his lady friends—Baby Doe was his most famous affair, but not his only one.

While Tabor was entertaining his mistresses, the citizens of Leadville were enjoying some of the finest stage performers in the country in one of the West's most elegant theaters. The second-floor theater had plastered ceiling frescoes and walls painted in rich tones of red, gold and sky blue, with custom carpets, velvet upholstered seats, hand-painted stage curtains and backdrops, and seventy-two gaslights to illuminate the stage—the first gaslights in Leadville. But while the opera house bespoke culture and civility, the city was still rough around the edges.

In 1882, the year Doc arrived in town, the Tabor Opera House hosted flamboyant Irish poet and playwright Oscar Wilde on his world lecture tour. Wilde described Leadville as:

> *the richest city in the world. It has also got the reputation of being the roughest, and every man carries a revolver. I was told that if I went there they would be sure to shoot me or my travelling manager. I wrote and told them that nothing that they could do to my travelling manager would intimidate me. . . . They afterwards took me to a dancing saloon where I saw the only rational method of art criticism I have ever come across. Over the piano was printed a notice: "Please do not shoot the pianist. He is doing his best."*[13]

Hyman's Club Rooms at 316 Harrison Avenue in busy 1882 Leadville. History Colorado, William Henry Jackson Collection (#10025680).

HYMAN'S PLACE

Doc Holliday's only shooting in Colorado occurred while he was living above Mannie Hyman's saloon and gambling hall on Harrison Avenue in Leadville. And the fact that the saloon owner had given him a free room when he was on hard times says a lot about Hyman's generosity—and maybe something about Doc Holliday's changing attitudes.

Mannie Hyman was a Prussian Jew, born in Schwersenz (in what is now central Poland) in May 1851—making him just a few months older than Doc. As a teenager, Mannie sailed from Hamburg in the German Empire aboard the immigrant ship *Borussia*, entering the United States at Castle Garden, New York. Little is known of his first years in America before he joined the mining rush to Colorado, where he managed mines and owned a saloon in the now-ghost town of Kokomo. When an 1881 fire nearly destroyed the camp and caused $3,500 in losses to his saloon, Mannie decided to try his luck elsewhere, arriving in Leadville the same year Doc Holliday hit town.

In the early fall of 1882, Mannie opened "Hyman's Club Rooms" at 316 Harrison Avenue, next door to the Tabor Opera House, and requested of the city council that "certain policemen be appointed to keep order in this house."[14] Mannie Hyman's place would be a proper sporting establishment, with a cigar store and drinking saloon in the front and gambling rooms in the back, according to Colorado law. And with two porters, three bartenders, and some of the first electric lights in Leadville, Hyman's was soon one of the busiest saloons in town. When a reporter from the local paper asked Mannie the secret of his success, he attributed it to customer service: "My patrons are treated alike—without discrimination as to wealth, worldly position or the clothes they wear. As a caterer to the public, I depend upon the public for success, and do not extend any more favors to the mining prince than I give to his humble employee. In my opinion all men are alike so long as they conduct themselves as gentlemen."[15]

Not all saloon patrons behaved as gentlemen, however, so Hyman's place had its share of trouble, from fist fights and broken furniture, to an opium addict who came into the saloon demanding money, food, and $1,000 in cigars—Mannie gave him one cigar and didn't press charges for the disturbance.

While Mannie Hyman was happy to sell drinks (the Club Room's specialties were German lager beers and apricot cocktails—pronounced with a German accent as "abricot"), he had also seen how gambling could ruin a man. As he told a reporter from the *Carbonate Chronicle*:

> *Wie gewonnen, so zerronnen. . . . Won easy, lost easy. . . . I have seen tens of thousands, during a year, won and squandered, and I've come to the conclusion that the money realized over the [faro] layout is of very little benefit to the winner. It's the same old story, however, and every day we see the German maxim, "Wie gewonnen, so zerronnen."*[16]

With sympathy for gamblers down on their luck, Hyman was a contributor to the Leadville Sporting Men's Relief Fund and offered free dinners for his patrons. So, when Doc Holliday took sick in the hard Leadville winters and couldn't support himself with his usual work as a faro dealer, it was Mannie Hyman who took him in, giving him a free room until he got back on his feet. If Doc had indeed split up with Wyatt Earp over anti-Semitic sentiments, he surely rethought his words while living on the Jewish Mannie Hyman's liberal-minded charity.

As for the shooting of Bill Allen that happened downstairs in Mannie Hyman's saloon, one memento remains: the bullet from one of Doc's two shots, still lodged in the frame of the front door of the historic Harrison Avenue building.

BABY DOE AND THE MATCHLESS MINE

On March 1, 1883, Silver King Horace Tabor finally legalized his relationship with Baby Doe when the couple was married in a lavish ceremony in Washington, D.C., surrounded by the political people he hoped would help to make him governor of Colorado—although most of the men attended the wedding without their wives. The newlyweds moved to a mansion in a fashionable part of Denver, but were not accepted into polite society, and a few months later Tabor lost his bid to be elected governor.

A year after the marriage, Baby Doe gave birth to a daughter, Elizabeth Bonduel "Lily" Tabor, who was christened in a $15,000 baby gown. A baby boy, Horace Joseph, died at birth in 1888. Another daughter, Rose Mary Echo "Silver Dollar" Tabor was

Baby Doe Tabor. Denver Public Library, Western History Collection, X-21980.

born in 1889. Baby Doe was reportedly a devoted mother, and "defiantly nursed . . . as she rode through the streets in Denver in one of her carriages."[17]

By 1890, just seven years after their wedding, the fluctuating silver prices were impacting the Tabors' extravagant lifestyle. When his investments began to fail, Horace was forced to mortgage the Tabor Grand Opera House in Denver, as well as other properties. To raise money for the family, Baby Doe sold most of her jewelry, and when the power to their mansion was turned off, she made the hardship a game for her children. Finally, the mansion and its contents were sold, and the family moved to a boardinghouse while sixty-five-year-old Horace went back to the mountains to work as a mineworker, before sympathetic friends arranged to have him appointed postmaster of Denver. With a yearly income of $3,700 (half the cost of Baby Doe's wedding gown), the family moved into a plain room at the Windsor Hotel, where the couple had once stayed in the most luxurious suite. Fifteen months after his appointment as postmaster, Horace Tabor died at the Windsor, having gone from rags to riches and back to rags again.

On his deathbed, Horace reportedly told Baby Doe, "hold on to the Matchless mine . . . it will make millions again when silver comes back." She fulfilled his wishes, eventually moving back to Leadville and ending up in a shack on the mine property. Her daughter Lily went to live with relatives in Wisconsin; her daughter Silver Dollar became a dancer in Chicago. For years, Baby Doe endured poverty and loneliness, spending her time writing fragments of memoirs and waiting for the Matchless Mine to fulfill her husband's promise. In the winter of 1935 after a severe snowstorm, the eighty-one-year-old Elizabeth Bonduel McCort "Baby Doe" Tabor was found frozen to death in her shack at the still silent mine.

SISTER MARY MELANIE

John Henry "Doc" Holliday's long-time correspondent in his travels across the West was his first cousin, Martha Anne "Mattie" Holliday. Mattie's father was the younger brother of John Henry's father, Henry Burroughs Holliday, and the cousins grew up visiting with each other at family gatherings in the north Georgia towns of Fayetteville, Jonesboro, and Griffin. During the Civil War, Mattie's family lived for a time on Henry

Holliday's farm at Cat Creek, seven miles from Valdosta in South Georgia. After the War, John Henry traveled to Jonesboro to spend a summer with Mattie's family before finishing school in Valdosta and going on to dental school in Philadelphia. When John Henry returned from dental school, he practiced dentistry in Atlanta, where Mattie was living as well. Some stories say the cousins had hoped to marry if Mattie's Catholic faith had allowed a union between such close relations. Instead, they stayed close through letters when he left Georgia for a new life in Texas and the West.

Profession of Novices.

Yesterday morning, at daylight, a congregation assembled in the chapel of the convent of the Immaculate Conception to witness an impressive ceremony. It was the formal profession by Miss Mattie Holliday and Miss Mary Murphy, who have already served their two years novitiate of the life of a Sister of Mercy. Miss Holliday will be known in religion as Sister Mary Melanie, and Miss Murphy will be known as Sister Mary Remegius.

Sister Mary Melanie Holliday's Profession in The Atlanta Constitution, *Atlanta, Georgia, February 2, 1886, page 7. Author's Collection.*

In 1884, when Doc was living in Leadville, Mattie Holliday entered St. Vincent's Convent in Savannah to begin training to become a nun. She was thirty-five years old that year and may have had to wait until then to save a "dowry" before she entered religious orders—nuns gave up their worldly possessions but had to pay for their living expenses in the convent. After two years as a novice, if she still desired to become a nun, she would make a formal profession of intent, be given a ring signifying her "marriage" to Christ and the Church, and take a new name beginning with "Mary" in honor of the mother of Jesus. The ceremony of Mattie's formal profession was held at Atlanta's Church of the Immaculate Conception on February 1, 1886 at daybreak, signifying the start of a new life. With the ceremony, attended by family and friends, she became Sister Mary Melanie Holliday of the Sisters of Mercy, and would spend her life teaching at the convent school in Atlanta and serving in the business office at St. Joseph's Infirmary (now Atlanta's highly regarded St. Joseph's Hospital).

The name she chose for her new life was an unusual one for the time: Melanie, honoring an early Roman Saint named Melania, who had entered religious orders after discovering that her husband was actually her first cousin, a marital relation not allowed by the Church. If Mattie Holliday chose the name because of its history, she may have been announcing that she, too, was in love with a first cousin whom she could not marry. Whatever the personal meaning of her new name, her new vocation was considered an honor and a blessing by her faithful Catholic family. For John Henry, far away in Colorado, knowing that his beloved cousin Mattie was praying for him was surely a comfort, as well.

21

DENVER & NEW ORLEANS

Doc was down, but he wasn't out, and all he needed was some help to get on his feet again. In other times, he might have turned to Wyatt Earp for aid, but those times were done. He might have asked Bat Masterson for assistance, but he already owed Bat a debt he could never repay. And the last time he'd borrowed money from another gambler, he'd ended up in court fighting for his life. But there was one man with the means to help him, if he would—his father, Henry Burroughs Holliday.

Twelve years had passed since Doc had last seen his father, since he'd left Georgia on the run from a shooting on the Withlacoochee River. Henry Holliday had been a man of position then and became prominent soon after, being twice elected mayor of Valdosta, and his son's troubled years had surely been a disappointment to him. But when the *Valdosta Times* reprinted an article from the *Tombstone Epitaph* of December 1881, Henry took heart. As the article reported, at the end of a month-long court hearing following the O.K. Corral shootings, the judge had exonerated J. H. Holliday and the Earps of any criminality, and said of Marshal Virgil Earp: "he needed the assistance and support of staunch and true friends, upon whose courage, coolness and fidelity he could depend, in case of an emergency."[1] John Henry Holliday had been one of those friends, and reading about his "courage, coolness, and fidelity," must have made Major Henry Holliday proud.

So, father and son were both amenable to a meeting, that spring of 1885, when Doc left Leadville looking for a kinder climate and some financial support. And it seemed a serendipity that Henry Holliday had already planned a trip west, taking the train from Georgia to New Orleans to attend a reunion of Mexican War veterans.[2] Although Doc had stayed in Colorado for safety's sake the past several years, he'd ended up not being safe there, after all, and reckoned he might as well travel, with the journey taking him by train from Colorado, across Kansas and Missouri, then south to the Mississippi River delta.

New Orleans was like nothing Doc Holliday had ever seen before: a city of grand churches and gaudy mansions, curving seductively around a crescent of river and flirting from under filigreed balconies. The Crescent City had been entrancing visitors for nearly two centuries, from French settlers, to Spanish governors, to the Americans who paid $15 million for her and got the rest of the Louisiana Purchase as a bonus. With an accent that tasted of Creole, Cajun, Indian and plantation, the city smiled when she said her name: "'N'Awlins!" And in that spring of 1885, she was shamelessly showing herself off to the world at the Cotton Centennial Exposition that celebrated one hundred years of cotton commerce out of the city's river port.

The Exposition was laid out in a grove of Louisiana live oaks along a two-hundred-acre stretch of the Mississippi, with one entrance by water from the French Quarter and two by land from St. Charles Avenue and Magazine Street. Visitors arrived by steamboat or streetcar or carriage, paying one silver dollar for a day's admission to tour the exhibit buildings, watch the horse races, sail on the newly dredged lake, and walk along the grassy paths illuminated by hundreds of strings of electric lights. The centerpiece of the exposition was the Main Hall, covering thirty-three acres of former plantation land, with walls of glittering windows and turrets topped with flagpoles, and an auditorium that could seat an audience of thirteen thousand. With public telephones and public comfort stations and an electric railway that ran through the grounds, the Cotton Centennial Exposition was a breathtaking vision of life in the late nineteenth century: a modern world of electricity and power and progressive invention.

The National Association of Veterans of the Mexican War had chosen New Orleans for its annual convention to coincide with the exposition, giving the group a larger audience for its platform. Since its founding in 1874, the association had been lobbying Washington for pension benefits for Mexican War veterans and their wives, with little success thus far. The federal government's stand was that too many of the veterans had also served in the Confederate Army and rebels didn't deserve pensions—most notably Jefferson Davis, who had been colonel of the First Regiment of Mississippi Volunteers during the Mexican War before becoming president of the Confederate States of America. So, the reunion in New Orleans was more than just a social gathering for Mexican War veterans like Henry Holliday, who had served as 2nd Lieutenant under General Zachary Taylor. It was also a chance to bring national attention to their cause, filling the auditorium of the Main Hall with attendees and hosting patriotic talks that would be reported in the *New Orleans Picayune* and reprinted in other papers across the country.

The hotel hosting the veterans was the Gregg House on Canal Street, close to the French Quarter and convenient to the steamboat landing. But Henry Holliday wouldn't be rooming there alone. He'd brought a traveling companion along with him, a young man from Valdosta named William Alexander Griffith, whom Henry had hired as his valet to carry his bags and run errands. For "Zan," as he was called, the trip was a once-in-a-lifetime adventure, taking him far from his South Georgia home and introducing him to a real-life Western legend: John Henry "Doc" Holliday.

Zan Griffith would later recount how Doc met his father there in New Orleans, and how the two men stayed up most of the night talking.[3] Henry had hoped to persuade his son to return home to Georgia, but Doc declined the invitation—though he did agree to one of his father's offers. Zan Griffith would accompany Doc back to Colorado, being a valet and traveling companion for him as he had been for the major. Though Henry was the older man, at sixty-six years he was still healthier than his thirty-three-year-old son, whose two winters of pneumonia had further damaged his already ailing lungs. So Zan went along to help Doc on his journey back to Colorado and returned to Valdosta full of stories of the Cotton Centennial Exposition and traveling the West with Doc Holliday.

It may have been on Doc's return from New Orleans that he had an encounter with an old enemy from Tombstone: Milt Joyce, the Occidental Saloon bartender who had taken away his gun and assaulted him after the fight with Johnny Tyler. According to Milt's reminiscence, he ran into Doc on a Denver, Colorado, street one evening in 1885:

> *As I reached the sidewalk he came along the edge of the crowd and brushed against me. Restraining my first impulse, I ignored what I thought was a challenge, and kept on my way. When I got half way to my hotel a thought struck me that maybe he imagined I was afraid of him because I was in a strange city where he had all his friends and satellites about him. Turning on my heel, I walked back and looked for him till I found him in the saloon where he hung out. I deliberately*

brushed against him, the same as he had against me. I looked at him and he looked at me, but neither of us spoke a word. Some old Arizona men who knew us both were in the place, but they didn't have any remarks just then. I walked around him three times, just to give him a chance if he wanted it, and to remove any idea he might have that I wanted to run away. He didn't look at all scared, but he wasn't looking for any more trouble. I have thought of it lots of times since then, and have thought how foolish I was to go back, but the impulse struck me to do it, and I couldn't help it.[4]

Doc wasn't looking for trouble, but he had some unfinished business to take care of. So, by the middle of June, he was back in Leadville and hunting for Bill Allen. According to local stories, when he found Allen, he reached into his vest as if going for gun, but instead pulled out $5, paying back the money that had started all the trouble between them.[5] He had promised to make good on the debt, and he did. He was a gentleman, after all, and a man of his word, though Bill Allen likely thought the money small recompense for the injury to his arm. Then on June 13, the *Aspen Times* reported another Leadville story, as Doc collected on a fifty-dollar loan he'd made to another gambler:

Some nights ago, a well-known rounder named Curley Mack was seated at a faro bank with a big stack of "reds" before him. Luck was with him and he made a winning of a hundred and fifty dollars. Holliday was standing behind him deeply interested in the game. Just as Curley was about to "cash in" his creditor stepped to one side so that Curley could see him, and drawing a six-shooter from the waistband of his pants he cooly remarked, "I'd like that fifty tonight Curley." When the player looked up and saw the muzzle of the gun and the cold, hard face of "Doc" with its determined expression he shoved the whole pile of chips over and said, "take them all." "Doc" counted out his fifty dollars and pushed the others back to the winner and walked out, and that settled it.[6]

With his debt repaid and his money collected, Doc Holliday was done with Leadville. But there were other silver camps where he could still wager on the cards and win a profit off the mines. So, he bought a train ticket to the Montana Territory, where the silver city of Butte was waiting to welcome him.

TRAVELING COMPANION

Doc Holliday's trip to the Crescent City is a story told by an old-time Valdosta resident named William Alexander "Zan" Griffith. Zan was a young boy when Doc Holliday left Georgia, and a teenager when he accompanied Major Henry Holliday, Doc's father, to a reunion of Mexican War veterans. According to Zan, Major Holliday invited his infamous son to meet him in New Orleans, hoping to convince Doc to go home to Georgia—Doc was ailing from the consumption that had ravaged his lungs and could use the care of being home with his family. When Doc refused his father's advice, Zan was sent along to keep the doctor company on his return to Colorado. Zan recalled his journey with Doc Holliday west to the

William Alexander "Zan" Griffith, Valdosta, Georgia. Courtesy Susan McKey Thomas Collection.

Rocky Mountains and the prized saddle he said Doc bought him as a souvenir of their adventures together. It's the saddle that gives the most credence to Zan's story of his travels with Doc Holliday, for in the 1880s Colorado was famous as the home of the A. C. Gallup Company's "Pueblo Saddle," and there wouldn't have been a more appropriate parting gift for a young man. Zan kept that special saddle until the 1920s, when the old hotel where he lived was destroyed by fire—sadly, along with the saddle. But family and friends remembered Zan's story of accompanying Major Holliday to New Orleans and meeting there with the major's famous son, Doc Holliday. If he'd been making up the story, the local folks would surely have known and challenged his facts.

Antique S. C. Gallup Saddle, Pueblo, Colorado. Courtesy iCollector.com for Brian Lebel's Old West Events.

FAMILY HEIRLOOMS

When Major Henry Holliday returned home after his trip to New Orleans for the reunion of Mexican War veterans, he gave an interview to the local paper, sharing some souvenirs from his time in the war—and shedding light on the family heirlooms his son John Henry had known growing up.

Henry Holliday had been a young 2nd Lieutenant in the US Army when he found a large bronze medal in the room of a Mexican army officer and took it home as a souvenir. As the Valdosta reporter wrote, "the medal is supposed to be 308 years old, and presented to [Spanish explorer] De Soto for some of his services and exploits." That may have been what Henry thought he'd found based on the Spanish words on the medal, *Desato a un Orbe de el Otro*, and that may have been what John Henry grew up believing. But the medal described in the article was actually a military decoration minted in 1822 to commemorate Mexico's independence from Spain. On the obverse were two globes representing the unchained Western and Eastern hemispheres, with the Spanish mottoes, *Con la triple garantia* ("the three basic rights" of religion, independence, and union) and the *Desato a un Orbe de el Otro* ("I unleash an orb from the other"). On the reverse was a laurel wreath and the motto, *Segunda Epoca* ("second era").

Another coin in Henry's large collection was supposedly over 1,300 years old when he acquired it, made of silver and struck in the time of Mohammed. Considering Henry's mistaken identification of the Mexican medal, the ancient silver coin may not have been what he thought it was, either. He also had several Spanish coins said to be from 1766, more likely accurate if they carried that date. But the most important heirloom Henry showed to the reporter was the family Bible, printed in Glasgow, Scotland, in 1776. On one of the fly leaves was written: "Martha Holliday, her Bible, it was given to her in June, the 30th day in the year of our Lord 1799." On another leaf was written: "Nancy Holliday, her book, God give her grace to look and not to look but to understand, and that learning is better than house or land, when land is gone and money spent, then learning is most excellent."

Henry Holliday evidently took the sentiment to heart, paying for his son's fine education that gave him the honorable title of Dr. Holliday.

chanan.

Valdosta, Ga., News: Major Holliday showed us on yesterday some interesting relics, consisting of old and rare coins and an old family Bible. There were about forty coins, but out of those more particularly worthy of mention is one of silver, made in the time of Mohammed, covered with strange characters and known to be 1,303 years old, and several Spanish coins made in 1776. There was in the lot an elegantly executed medal about two inches in diameter, on the obverse side of which are the words: 'Con La Triple Garantia." "De Sato a un Orbe de el Ortao." On the reverse, "Segunda Epoca." This medal was secured by the major when he was in the Mexican army, and was found in the room of a Mexican officer. It is supposed to be 308 years old, and presented to De Soto for some of his services and exploits. The major showed us also a Bible, rudely covered with buckskin, on one of the fly leaves of which is written: "Martha Holliday, her Bible, it was given to her in June the 30th day in the year of our Lord 1799." On another leaf is written: "Nancy Holliday, her book, God give her grace thereunto to look and not to look but to understand, and that learning is better than house or land, when land is gone and money spent, then learning is most excellent." The Bible was printed in Glasgow in 1776, and has the psalms in meter, "appointed to be sung by congregations and families."

The Cartersville Courant, noting the Indian

"Valdosta News" in The Atlanta Constitution, *Atlanta, Georgia, May 6, 1885, page 2. Author's Collection.*

1823 Mexico Independence Medal. Treasure & World Coin Auction #9: Daniel F. Sedwick, LLC.

THE PELLA PORTRAIT

In the Doc Holliday Museum in Glenwood Springs, Colorado, hangs a sixty-by-twenty charcoal drawing mounted in a gold wood frame. The subject appears to be a man of early middle age, with a receding hairline, deep-set light-colored eyes, neatly trimmed mustache, square jaw and prominent ears, his thin face and narrow neck seeming out of proportion to his wide-collared jacket and large square-knot tie. According to antiques trader George Hettinga, the subject is thirty-four-year-old John Henry "Doc" Holliday as he appeared on a visit to Iowa in 1885.

As Hettinga wrote in a 1989 "attestation" when the century-old portrait was sold:

"Pella Portrait" on loan to the Doc Holliday Museum, Glenwood Springs, Colorado. Courtesy Glenwood Springs Historical Society, Schutte Collection.

Doc Holliday was in Pella, Iowa around 1885. A Dutch-American Colonial artist by the name of A. Van Martin found Doc Holliday a very interesting subject as well as a very famous western figure of the times. Doc Holliday commissioned A. Van Martin to do his charcoal portrait which was to be 16 x 20. Portrait was then mounted in a 26" x 33" gold pine back frame. Shortly after Doc left Pella, Iowa; having to travel light Doc left the portrait in Pella. From Pella, the portrait traveled westward around the late 1880s to early 1890s to Glenwood Springs, Co. Ended up in a miner's cabin near Glenwood Springs and stayed there until estate sold to Paul and Doyle Beard in 1957. They took the portrait back to Sheridan, Indiana.

The Beard brothers were long-time Western collectors who had a recreated saloon and an antique stagecoach in a treasure-filled warehouse behind their Indiana appliance store. When they both passed away, their collection was sold at auction, with one of the most exciting items being the Doc Holliday portrait, as reported in the August 4, 1979, *Indianapolis News*:

Some items sold quickly, while others, like a charcoal portrait of Doc Holliday, were the subject of fierce bidding wars. The auctioneers and their assistants

*watched the crowd of more than 300 furtively for bids made by discreet nods.
The rhythm of "Yo! Yo! Yo!" every time they espied a bid picked up speed until a
climactic "Sold for $240" broke the spell. John Jenkins, an antiques trader from
Flint, Mich., paid that for Doc. He said he was going to "keep him for awhile.
Look at him. Admire him. Clean him up. I know a good thing when I see him."*

Jenkins admired Doc for awhile before the portrait was sold again and ended up
with George Hettinga in Pella, Iowa—ironically taking it back to where it started.
Then after more sales, the portrait went on loan to the Doc Holliday Museum in Glenwood Springs. The trail of ownership, called "provenance," seems fairly clear, but one
mystery remains: Why was Doc Holliday in Iowa in 1885? The answer lies in his family reunion in New Orleans—and another kind of reunion in Pella.

When Doc Holliday left New Orleans in April 1885, headed back to Colorado, he
had several travel routes available to him. The most leisurely was a steamboat ride up
the Mississippi River to Baton Rouge and the battle site of Vicksburg, to Memphis and
New Madrid, past the beer-making caves and under the Eads' Bridge at St. Louis, and
beyond to Burlington, Iowa, where he could board the Chicago, Rock Island & Pacific
Railroad headed west with a stopover in the town of Pella, Iowa—the former home
of the Earp family and the birthplace of Doc's murdered friend, Morgan Earp. If Doc
Holliday did travel from New Orleans to Pella, as the portrait suggests he did, there
can be only one reason: He was making a pilgrimage to honor his fallen friend, and the
Pella portrait captures the way he looked on that sentimental journey.

WYATT EARP HOUSE

Wyatt Earp was two years old when his family moved from his birthplace of Mon-
mouth, Illinois, to a farm in Marion County, Iowa, seven miles north of the town of
Pella. The town had been founded just three earlier years by Dutch immigrants seeking religious freedom under their minister, Dominee Hendrick Scholte. The industri-
ous Dutch settlers, who spoke a little English but mostly communicated in a dialect
of South Guelderisch from the Rhine River Valley, quickly built a church, homes, and
businesses—and Dutch-style windmills to grind their wheat and corn.

By the time Wyatt's younger brother Morgan was born, the Earp family had moved
from the farm into Pella, taking an apartment on the bottom floor of the Van Spanckeren Row House. While living in Pella, Father Nicholas Earp continued to farm and

Wyatt Earp House, Pella, Iowa. Library of Congress.

added to the family's finances by working as a recruiter for the US Army during the Civil War. Wyatt's older brother Virgil enlisted and left from Pella for the battlefront, but Wyatt was too young for military service, though he remembered running away from home on several occasions, hoping to join up. His father, however, always found him and sent him home again.

In 1863, with the Civil War still raging, Nicholas Earp determined to take his family west to California, helping to organize a forty-family wagon train. For fifteen-year-old Wyatt, it was a taste of Western adventure that would never leave him.

In 1966, the Van Spanckeren Row House became the first official office of the Pella Historical Society and Museums and the starting point of the Historical Village Museum. In 1990, the Van Spanckeren Row House was named to the National Register of Historic Places, both for its unique Dutch-American architectural design and because of its famous former tenant, Wyatt Earp. The Historical Village Museum is now a twenty-two-building complex covering Pella history from its Dutch founding though the nineteenth century, and features windmills, a blacksmith, bakery, werkplaats (wooden shoemaker), log cabin, sod house, and the recreated first church of Pella, built by Dominee Scholte. Descendants of Scholte still occupy his 1850s Pella home, where Doc Holliday's portrait was once displayed as part of Dutch Pella's surprising Wild West history.

22

NORTHERN PACIFIC

The mining camp of Butte had been off the beaten path for most sporting men, until the Northern Pacific Railroad built east across Montana and the Utah & Northern Railway built north from Salt Lake City with its connection to the Denver & Rio Grande through the Rocky Mountains. By 1885, Butte had become an easy destination and a popular new spot on the sporting circuit.

Doc Holliday knew something of Butte besides its nickname, "The Richest Hill on Earth." His friend Morgan Earp had once lived there and served briefly on the police force before moving to Tombstone. So, Doc had heard about the placer gold miners and the silver lode claims that produced thirty ounces of silver per ton and were giving Tombstone and Leadville a run for their money. When a crosscut vein of copper was discovered in the Anaconda Silver Mine—copper being a necessary element in the production of electricity—Butte City, Montana Territory, became the mineral capital of the West.

By the time Doc arrived in the summer of 1885, the rough mining camp of Butte had already burned down once and been rebuilt in solid brick and stone as a modern city with a population of fourteen thousand. Its location in the Silver Bow Creek Valley, high in the Rockies and straddling the Continental Divide, gave it stunning mountain vistas, while its place as the junction of two railroads gave it easy access to the rest of the world, and the world was hurrying to get there. Butte was attracting mine and railroad workers from all over the country and around the world, with eager immigrants from England, Ireland, Cornwall, Wales, Germany, Italy, Finland, Norway, France, Greece, Serbia, Slovakia, Croatia, Turkey, and China—giving Butte its own ethnic neighborhoods and even a bustling Chinatown.

And where there were miners and railroaders, there were also saloons and gambling houses, with bets on poker and faro cards, foot races, boxing matches, billiard tournaments, and horses at the new horse racetrack. When the sports needed a break from the games, they could spend their winnings in the red-light district called "The Copper Block," with establishments that ranged from elegant brothels to tiny cribs in the dark alleys. For a sporting man, Butte was a wild and wide-open town.

Doc Holliday's arrival was noted in the local papers with flattering words: "J. H. Holliday, better known as 'Doc' is in the city and quartered at the Revere house. Doc is well known throughout the entire country and is a hale fellow well met."[1]

The Revere House, where Doc took up lodgings, was the best accommodation in Butte City, the first three-story brick hotel in the Territory, with free transportation to and from the train depot and the racetrack, and a restaurant that advertised the finest dinners in town. Having been newly remodeled just months before, the Revere boasted carpeted rooms with walnut furnishings, spring beds, and a parlor on each floor—the fine accommodations suggesting that Doc had received some financial help from his father at their meeting in New Orleans.

After getting himself settled in, there was plenty to keep Doc busy in Butte, as long as his health held out, at the Irish pubs and German beer halls, and the saloons and gambling houses like Gwin & Morehouse and the Capital on Main Street. As the *Semi-Weekly Miner* later reported, "Holladay [sic] made a great many warm friends among the sporting community."[2] And it may have been over a Butte gambling game that he heard the story of another band of vigilantes chasing cattle rustlers across a Western territory, led by another cultured gentleman and his lawman friend. But this time, the gentleman wasn't from Georgia, but from France.

The Marquis de Morés—whose official name was Antoine Amédée Marie Vincent Manca Amat de Vallombrosa, Marquis de Morès et de Montemaggiore—was a French nobleman who'd married an American heiress and set himself up on a forty-five-thousand-acre spread in the Dakota Territory, near the Montana border. His called his home, built on a high bluff surveilling his kingdom, the Chateau de Morés, and the town he built to service his ranch he named Medora, after his wife, Medora Hoffman. To ensure that his town and ranch would thrive, the Marquis built a brick-making plant, a hotel, a general store, houses, and a recreation hall for his employees. His biggest expenditures, besides the land, were a meat-packing plant and icehouse that could process 150 carcasses of slaughtered beef a day for shipment on his new Northern Pacific Refrigerator Cars east to market. His biggest blunders were fencing in his land with barbed wire, an unforgiveable sin on the open range, and bringing in fifteen thousand sheep, a curse to other cattle ranchers. The Marquis may have been handsome and dashing, famous for his dueling skills and fearless in his business dealings, but his new neighbors detested him.

Local rancher Gregor Lang called the Marquis a "land grabber" and a "grandiose foreigner," though he himself was foreign-born in Scotland, then gave encouragement to local hunters who wanted to cut through the Marquis' barbed wire and help themselves to his cattle. Death threats, shots fired from ambush, and vandalism encouraged de Morés to seek help from the local law—a territorial justice of the peace stationed an inconvenient 130 miles away. The judge's advice on dealing with the rustlers echoed the advice given to Wyatt Earp after the O.K. Corral hearing: "Why, shoot."[3] The Marquis took the advice, shot the raiders, and was arrested for murder and then released by the same judge who had given him the advice, calling the killings self-defense.

But the Marquis had one friend among his neighbors: a young widower from the East who'd bought up another vast tract of land and started into the cattle business, calling it the "romance of my life."[4] His name was Theodore Roosevelt, and he'd been a member of the New York Assembly before the tragic death of his wife sent him west for solace. He came to hunt buffalo, then stayed to establish two ranches, the Elkhorn and the Maltese Cross, seven miles south of the town of Medora. Though Roosevelt wasn't raised to the Western life, he quickly accommodated and even spent some time as a deputy sheriff hunting down outlaws. According to one story, when a drunk in a Badland's saloon insulted him, Roosevelt grabbed the man by the neck and pounded his head against the wooden bar, proclaiming, "Bar's closed!" But like his neighbor, the Marquis de Morés, Roosevelt also had trouble with cattle rustlers.

In the summer of 1885, when Doc Holliday arrived in Montana Territory, ranchers Theodore Roosevelt and the Marquis de Morés were attending the first meeting of the new Montana Stockgrowers Association, where the rustler problem was prominent on the agenda. One of the leaders of the Association was Granville Stuart, who owned the largest ranch in the territory, and, like Henry Hooker in Arizona, was willing to fund action against the rustlers for the good of all. Stuart had already taken some action himself, assembling "Stuart's Stranglers" the year before to chase down and kill cattle rustlers—purportedly leaving sixty-three cowboys hanging in the Badlands. Roosevelt and the Marquis lobbied the new association to do something similar and launch a military action against the rustlers, but Stuart advised caution, making a speech in support of law and order and against direct-acting ranchers. Though

Roosevelt accused Stuart of "backing water" and obstructing a solution to the rustler problem, others considered the speech, "A fine piece of deception . . . set up to cover plans for stern retribution which, in all probability, were taking form in private at the very time the ranchers went on record as being officially against vigorous action."[5] Young Roosevelt and his fiery French friend, the Marquis, were supporters of action, public or private, but were declined a part on account of their fame, being too well known to work undercover.

Did Granville Stuart and the Stockman's Association seek advice from another famous face, that summer and fall of 1885? Doc Holliday had also chased rustlers in a similar setting, with legendary results—his name had filled the newspapers ever since the shootout in Tombstone and his arrest the next year in Denver. Might he have been invited to take a ride on the Northern Pacific Railroad east to Miles City, where the Stockmen's Association met, or on to Medora, to meet with the Marquis and Roosevelt? As the son of a Georgia plantation owner's daughter himself, Roosevelt would have understood Doc Holliday's sense of honor and admired his grit. Such a trip would explain why Doc was notably absent in reports out of Butte during those months, until his name appeared in the paper again in November:

> Last night Jack Dowd, who appeared to be in rather an interesting frame of mind, entered the Capital saloon, where at the time there happened to be some old time Coloradoans, including Doc. Holliday, and Tracey. Jack proceeded to declaim against men who had been killers and stranglers in other States, and declared that he could whip them all. He was rather loud in his talk, but no notice was paid to him, and having spoken his piece he departed. The scene attracted considerable attention, and the chances are that the end is not yet.[6]

It's interesting that Jack mentioned "stranglers," a term used for men who chased down and hanged cattle rustlers. In another column the paper added, "Jack Dowd may be a very bad man and a shooter, but we want to whisper to him that if he was only 'bluffing' in the Capital, last evening, he was playing a very dangerous game."[7]

Jack Dowd was a noted troublemaker in town, having been accused and arrested for swindles and robberies on a routine basis. And Doc, having had more than his share of troublemakers, may have decided to try his luck elsewhere until Jack's temper cooled some, for he was missing from Butte again long enough for the *Semi-Weekly Minor* to list undelivered mail for him on December 30.

Wherever he'd gone, Doc was back in Butte by January 15, 1886, taking a meal in the Eureka Restaurant at the back of the Gwin & Morehouse Saloon, when another challenger inspired him to pull his pistol. As a witness to the event later recalled:

> [Doc] drew a gun on a man and made him dance a quickstep because he had befriended him and the latter failed to reciprocate. Dave Meiklejohn was then city marshal of Butte, and the job of arresting Holliday fell to him. A warrant for Holliday's arrest was sworn out and given to Meiklejohn for service. Meiklejohn found his man in the old Arcade on Main street. Holliday knew Meiklejohn was after him, and when the latter entered the room he backed up against the wall and stood watching the officer. He intended to fight, but Meiklejohn was too foxy for him. There were several other men in the room and Meiklejohn asked one of them to take a drink. The two walked up to the bar and called for a drink. Then Meiklejohn turned halfway in the direction of Holliday, who still stood with his back against the wall watching Meiklejohn, and invited Holliday to join them. Holliday at once came down a peg and joined the pair at the bar. After taking the drink, Meiklejohn quietly informed Holliday he had a warrant for his arrest. By that time Holliday had begun to think that Meiklejohn was a pretty good sort of fellow, and permitted the warrant to be served without trouble. Holliday was taken to the city jail and gave a bond for his appearance.[8]

Was Doc Holliday the aggressor in the altercation this time? Or was he, as he had been in so many previous saloon fights, just defending himself against a perceived threat? Until the law decided if there were cause to continue the case, he was obliged to remain in Butte under bond. And while he waited to learn his fate, he took sick again in the brutal Montana winter where temperatures could drop to forty below zero, and was still in bed when the Silver Bow County Grand Jury met on February 17. As the local paper reported:

> Among the indictments found was one for the notorious "Doc" Holladay for drawing and exhibiting a deadly weapon, and a warrant was placed in the hands of Deputy Sheriff Buzzo to arrest the accused. The officer found Holladay in his bed, and Dr. Johnson stated that it would be dangerous to remove him to the County Jail, as he was very weak after having been confined to bed for about two

days, and he was accordingly permitted to remain in his room. He will to-day furnish bonds for his appearance when he is wanted.[9]

But Doc had no desire to make Butte or the Silver Bow County Jail his permanent residence. So, before the deputy could arrange a return visit to his sickroom, he dragged himself out of bed and headed down to the train depot. As the newspaper noted:

Late last night there was a rumor on the streets that "Doc" Holladay, who was indicted by the Grand Jury on Wednesday for drawing a deadly weapon, had made himself scarce, and had taken his departure for St. Paul. A reporter for The Miner started out to ascertain the truth of the report and soon became convinced that there was more truth than poetry in it. When the Deputy Sheriff went to serve the warrant upon him he was sick in bed, and the attending physician gave it as his opinion that it would not be safe to place him in jail, so he was left in his room. An inquiry at his lodgings and among his friends demonstrated that those who knew of his whereabouts were very reticent and nervous, and one person stated that he had seen Holladay board a train at the depot yesterday morning. There is but little doubt that he has left town, and cleared his manner of departure quite cleverly.[10]

Doc was clever, all right, leaving a trail that headed the wrong way. While the sheriff searched for him on the eastbound Northern Pacific heading to St. Paul, Minnesota, he was headed south on the Utah & Northern Railroad and its connection with the Denver & Rio Grande, heading back to his sanctuary state of Colorado.

MINING A CASTLE

The Anaconda Copper Mine made Butte, Montana, the "richest hill on earth"—and helped to finance *La Cuesta Encantada,* "the enchanted hill," where millionaire William Randolph Hearst built a California castle.

Hearst's father was George Hearst, born in Franklin County, Missouri, in 1820 where he received little formal education but observed copper works and seemed to have an uncanny understanding of the mining process. Local tribes (the county was home to the Shawnee, Delaware, and Osage) called him, "the boy that earth talks to." It was a language that would make him a sought-after advisor to mining operations across the West and bring him a fortune.

In 1850, George followed the gold rush to California, panning near Sutter's Mill and dealing in quartz mines. Already making a good living as a prospector and store owner, George heard about a silver claim called the Comstock Lode in Nevada and hurried to find his own claim, buying an interest in the Ophir Mine in western Utah, near what would become Virginia City. Within months, George and his partners had mined thirty-eight tons of high-grade silver ore, packed it across the Sierra Nevada mountains on muleback, had it smelted in San Francisco, and made $91,000 profit (about $2.5 million today). George next invested in the Ontario silver mine in Park City, Utah, that produced $17 million in ten years and carried him through the Panic of 1873. George went on to invest in the Comstock Lode and the Homestake gold mine in South Dakota that started the rush to Deadwood. With his fortune, he financed his friend Marcus Daly of the Comstock Lode in operating the Anaconda silver mine in Butte, acquiring

George Hearst. California Faces: Selections from the Bancroft Library Portrait Collection, University of California, Berkeley, 10045184a.tif.

an interest in that mine, as well. When copper was found in the Anaconda, George Hearst's fortunes grew even larger. George invested his money in land as well as mines, buying the forty-eight-thousand-acre Piedra Blanca Rancho on a mountain top above the Pacific Ocean in California, then adding the adjoining Santa Rosa and San Simeon ranchos. George used the land for a camping retreat, but his only son and heir, William Randolph Hearst, would create a kingdom overlooking the sea. Built between 1919 and 1947, Hearst Castle now comprises an estate of 165 rooms and 127 acres of gardens, terraces, pools, and walkways—an American castle filled with European antiques and works of art. The site is now the Hearst San Simeon State Historical Monument operated by the California State Parks.

Hearst Castle, San Simeon, California. Shutterstock.

THE BEST LITTLE WHOREHOUSE IN MONTANA

Like all mining camps, Butte offered a variety of entertainment for sale, from saloons and dance halls to gambling houses and bordellos. In 1885 when Doc Holliday was in town, the center of Butte's entertainment district was the Comique Theatre on Main Street, halfway between Park and Galena Streets. Although the Comique advertised itself as an "Elegant New Temple of Amusement . . . a whirlwind of pure fun, without coarseness or vulgarity"[11] the theater also had a seamier side.

While miners and other working men came through the front door to sit at tables on the sawdust covered main floor, gentlemen could enter through a back door that led upstairs to private boxes with locking doors and fine mesh screens so patrons could view the stage but not be seen, while drinks were served to them through a slot in the door. No record remains of what the gentlemen and their guests did in those locked, screened rooms while the vaudeville stage was filled with "pure fun," but the activities of other establishments were more openly known.

Since the earliest days of Butte City, whole streets were devoted to prostitution, from the tents and shacks on Park Street, conveniently close to the mines, to the rows of cribs and brothels on Galena Street where almost every building housed soiled doves. As an old miner's song celebrated, "First came the miners to work in the mine,

Theatre Comique advertisement in Butte Daily Miner, *Butte, Montana, January 1, 1886, page 56. Author's Collection.*

then came the ladies who lived on the line." By the late 1880s, respectable Montana businessmen found a way to profit off the prostitution, financing parlor houses and "hotels" that rented rooms by the day or hour. The businesses were usually managed by madams who paid rent discretely through an agent to the owners, and who split the working girls' wages of fifty cents per job.

The most famous of the Butte parlor houses was the Dumas Hotel at 45 East Mercury Street, one block south of Galena Street, built by French Canadian brothers Joseph and Arthur Nadeau and named after Joseph's wife, Delia Dumas Nadeau. The two-story red brick Dumas Hotel featured a grand parlor and vaulted skylights with an open staircase that led to numbered rooms with widows facing inward toward a central hallway, keeping them private from outside observers. The basement of the building had more basic accommodations, with small cribs and a tunnel system connecting it to the business district. In later years, the Dumas was expanded with a single-story addition and direct access to the infamous "Venus Alley," lined with more cribs. Amazingly, the Dumas Hotel continued in operation until 1982, the oldest publicly operated whorehouse in the United States, and now a museum site on the National Register of Historic Places.

ROUGH RIDER

Like Doc Holliday, Teddy Roosevelt didn't seem destined for life on the frontier. And like Doc, he had Southern roots, the son of a Georgia plantation owner's daughter and New York businessman, Theodore Roosevelt Sr. His mother, Martha "Mittie" Bulloch, grew up in her family's white-columned plantation house at Bulloch Hall in Roswell, Georgia. The couple met while Roosevelt Sr. was visiting friends in Georgia and married in the front parlor of Bulloch Hall before establishing their own home in New York.

Bulloch Hall, Roswell, Fulton County, Georgia, by Frances Benjamin Johnston, 1864–1952. Library of Congress.

As a child, Teddy Roosevelt suffered from asthma and was considered sickly. Determined to make over his body, he started a regimen of gymnastics and weight lifting, developing a rugged physique. Educated at home, he toured Europe and the Middle East with his family, then entered Harvard University in 1876. During college, Teddy met Alice Hathaway Lee, daughter of a prominent New England banking family, and the couple were married in 1880. Teddy started on a career in public service, being elected to two terms in the New York Assembly, and made his first trip to the Badlands of North Dakota in 1883, intent on hunting buffalo. According to biographer Dale L. Walker: "He wore a Derby hat, a Brooks Brothers suit, and thick pince-nez eyeglasses, and soon the scattered denizens of the Badlands were calling him 'Four Eyes.' They snickered at his Harvard accent and raspy tenor voice and remarked that he spurned tobacco and hard liquor."

Returning home to New York and his seat in the Assembly, Roosevelt suffered a stunning double tragedy: first his beloved mother, Mittie Bulloch Roosevelt, died of typhoid fever, then just hours later in the same house, his wife Alice Lee died—she had given birth to their first child just two days before. Teddy's brother Elliott said the house was "cursed." The grieving Roosevelt left his newborn daughter in the care of his sister and fled to the Dakota Badlands, far away from his tragedies.

In the Dakota Territory, Roosevelt bought two ranches—the Elkhorn and Maltese Cross near to the Montana border—and became a new man. No longer the out-of-place New Yorker, he learned the skills of a Western cowboy. As he described his changed appearance in his 1885 book, *Hunting Trips of a Ranchman*:

> *A ranchman dresses precisely like the cowboys, except that the materials are finer, the saddle leather being handsomely carved, the spurs, bit, and revolver silver-mounted, the sharps of seal-skin, etc. The revolver was formerly a necessity, to protect the owner from Indians and other human foes; this is still the case in a few places, but, as a rule, it is now carried merely from habit, or to kill rattlesnakes, or on the chance of falling in with a wolf or coyote.*

But there were still plenty of human foes in the form of rustlers stealing cattle. To help put a stop to the rustling, Roosevelt organized the Little Missouri River

Theodore Roosevelt, McDonald and Sherry Photographers, Albany, New York. Theodore Roosevelt Collection, 520-13-005 (WW442472_1), Houghton Library, Harvard University.

Stockman's Association in the Marquis de Morés' town of Medora, South Dakota, and joined the newly organized Montana Stock Grower's Association, attending their meeting in Miles City—and offering to take care of the rustlers himself.

Roosevelt spent two years in the Badlands before returning to his daughter and former life in New York, where he rekindled a romance with a childhood sweetheart, Edith Carow. The two were married in England in 1886 and settled in Oyster Bay, New York, in a house known as Sagamore Hill where they raised his daughter Alice and the five children they had together. Roosevelt spent his time writing books about American history, including *The Naval War of 1812* and the four volumes of *The Winning of the West*, was appointed to the US Civil Service Commission, and became president of the New York City Police Board. In 1897, newly elected President William McKinley appointed Roosevelt Assistant Secretary of the Navy, where he was serving when the US Battleship *Maine* was bombed by the Spanish in Havana Harbor, leading to the Spanish-American War. It was Roosevelt who instructed Commodore George Dewey to bottle up the Spanish squadron in the Philippines, inspiring the motto *Remember the Maine* and making Commodore Dewey the most celebrated military man of his time. Wanting to personally join the fight, Roosevelt resigned his position with the Navy to become commander of the 1st US Volunteer Cavalry, better known as the Rough

T. R. on the Round-up in 1885, Medora, North Dakota, T. W. Ingersoll (photographer). Theodore Roosevelt Collection 520.14-006 (olvwork437051). Houghton Library, Harvard University.

Riders, recruiting some of his old cowboy friends to join him. After a legendary charge up San Juan Hill in Cuba, Roosevelt and the Rough Riders returned to the United States as war heroes. As he later wrote: "I would rather have led that charge and earned my colonelcy than served three terms in the United States Senate. It makes me feel as though I could now leave something to my children which will serve as an apology for my having existed." But there were other adventures awaiting.

Roosevelt was promoted by the Republican Party to run for governor of New York and served one year, then resigned to run as vice president for President William McKinley's second term. When McKinley was assassinated nine months after the inauguration, Theodore Roosevelt Jr. became America's youngest president and the first "cow-

Colonel Theodore Roosevelt in uniform c. 1898. Library of Congress.

boy" in office, as detractors called him—in 1905, he appointed former Kansas lawman Bat Masterson a US Marshal for the Southern District of New York. As president, Roosevelt's experiences in the West inspired him to make conservation a top priority, as he wrote:

We have become great because of the lavish use of our resources. But the time has come to inquire seriously what will happen when our forests are gone, when the coal, the iron, the oil, and the gas are exhausted, when the soils have still further impoverished and washed into the streams, polluting the rivers, denuding the fields and obstructing navigation.

Roosevelt used his authority to protect wildlife and public lands by creating the United States Forest Service and establishing 150 national forests, 51 federal bird reserves, 4 national game preserves, 5 national parks, and 18 national monuments—in all, protecting 230 million acres of public land. In foreign policy, he began construction of the Panama Canal, expanded the Navy, and brokered the end of the Russo-Japanese War, earning him the 1906 Nobel Peace Prize. When the monumental carvings at Mount Rushmore were designed, Roosevelt seemed a fitting companion to Washington, Jefferson, and Lincoln. In 1918, just months before his death, he returned to the Badlands, making a speech in Fargo, North Dakota, where he said, "I owe more to the times when I lived out here and worked with the men who have been my friends than to anything else."

Theodore Roosevelt and John Muir on Glacier Point, Yosemite Valley, California, c. 1906. Library of Congress.

TEDDY AND THE OUTLAWS

In 1964, the editor of the *Park County News* in Livingston, Montana, was handed an intriguing photograph: a grouping of fifteen men in late nineteenth-century dress, lounging on the steps of the old Hunter's Hot Springs Hotel close to the Yellowstone River and nearby to Livingston. The photo came from the collection of Maurice Britton of Brady, Montana, who'd inherited it from his father, Henry Britton. The old photo had no date but did have a handwritten legend on the back identifying a few of the men in the group as Theodore Roosevelt, Wyatt Earp, Bat Masterson, "Liver Eating" Johnson, Harry Britton, and Ben Greenough. Hoping for some leads, the newspaper printed the photo with a short description that asked, "Does anyone know what the reunion or meeting was about?"

Guesses poured in, and by the 1970s other identifications were added, including Butch Cassidy and the Sundance Kid and Judge Roy Bean—not surprisingly, around the time the movies *Butch Cassidy and the Sundance Kid* (1969) and *The Life and Times of Judge Roy Bean* (1972) hit the theaters. The dates of 1883 or 1886 were also suggested, and reprints of the photo were sold under the title, "The Gathering: Most Unique Photo Ever Taken, 1883" and "Teddy and the Outlaws." Some of the

Hunter's Hot Springs Gathering, c. 1880's. Courtesy Mike Mihaljevich.

new identifications were easily dismissed, like Butch and Sundance who were just teenagers in the 1880s, and Judge Roy Bean who was never known to be out of Texas in those years. But the Park County newspaper's question remained: What was the meeting about—and who were those mysterious men?

Finding answers starts with the Hot Springs Hotel itself, a mineral springs resort near the tracks of the Northern Pacific Railroad. The resort's founder, Dr. Andrew Jackson Hunter, was a Virginia physician who had taken his family west after the Civil War to make a new life in the wilds of Montana and settled near the Yellowstone River. Hunter's Hot Springs Hotel offered a bathhouse by the springs and carriage service from the depot at nearby Springdale, and soon became a popular stop on the rail line from Butte to Miles City. Health seekers from across the United States visited the hot springs over the years, and the resort added a second hotel built by Dr. Hunter's son-in-law, Frank Rich. By 1885, the town of Hunter's Hot Springs had two hotels, a post office, one-room schoolhouse, dry goods store, laundry, and several homes.

Hunters Hot Springs, from History of Montana 1739–1885, *Chicago, Warner, Beers & Co., 1885. Courtesy Lewis and Clark County Library, Helena, Montana.*

Hunter's Hot Springs often hosted gatherings like the one in the photo, and some of the men identified were in the area at that time—most notably, Theodore Roosevelt, who was ranching in North Dakota and made trips to Montana for meetings of the Montana Stock Growers Association. On at least one of those trips, he had the company of his ranching neighbor, the Marquis de Morés—who looked very much like the man in the photo seated on the steps with a rifle laid across his knees. Both men were looking for a solution to the rustling trouble in the cattle country and had offered their services to the association. And although Doc Holliday wasn't one of the men originally identified in the photo (his name was added later and misidentified), he was also in Montana at

The Marquis de Morés on Horseback. Courtesy North Dakota State University Archives, Institute for Regional Studies, Fargo, 2024.A-12.

the time, trying his luck at the card tables in Butte and being challenged as one of the men "who had been killers and stranglers in other States."[12] Strangling, of course, meaning hanging—the punishment for cattle rustling. So Doc had been interested in the same topic that brought Roosevelt and de Morés together in Montana, and it would have been an easy train ride for him to pay a visit to the comforting mineral waters at Hunter's Hot Springs—and the man at the far left of photo, wearing a heavy overcoat, bears a resemblance to other known photos of Doc Holliday. Might the ranchers have been meeting to discuss a solution to the rustling problem, and invited the advice of other men who had done it well before? As for Wyatt Earp (who bears a striking resemblance to the man standing second from the left, next to "Doc"), his whereabouts in the summer and fall of 1885, when Doc was in Montana, are not known. He could have been anywhere—including Hunter's Hot Springs, still trying to chase down cowboys.

23

DURANGO & SILVERTON

Doc may have pretended to be sicker than he really was to make his escape from Montana, but there was no question that he was ill. He'd struggled with consumption for years and had gone through two winters of pneumonia, and something as simple as a cold might be the end of him. As Bat Masterson later said of Doc during that winter of 1886, "He went up to Butte City and contracted a severe cold, which I am afraid is going to do him up."[1]

It may have been while he was recovering from his Montana cold that Doc ran into Wyatt Earp in Denver, giving him a chance to make a reconciliation with his old friend. As Josephine Sarah Marcus recalled, the meeting happened at the Windsor Hotel:

> There coming toward us was Doc Holliday, a thinner, more delicate appearing Doc Holliday than I had seen in Tombstone. I have never seen a man exhibit more pleasure at meeting a mere friend than did Doc. He had heard that Wyatt was in town, he said, and had immediately looked him up. They sat down a little distance from us and talked at some length, though Doc's almost continuous coughing made it difficult for him to talk. Wyatt repeated their conversation to me later. Doc told Wyatt how ill he had been, scarcely able to be out of bed much of the time.
>
> "When I heard you were in Denver, Wyatt, I wanted to see you once more," he said, "For I can't last much longer. You can see that."
>
> Wyatt was touched. He remembered how Doc had once saved his life. Wyatt was arresting one drunken cowboy, when another was about to shoot him from behind. Doc risked his own life to extricate Wyatt and for this he had always felt

grateful. My husband has been criticized even by his friends, for being associated with a man who had such a reputation as Doc Holliday's. But who, with a shred of appreciation, would have done otherwise? Besides my husband always maintained that the greater part of the crimes that were attributed to Doc were but fictions created by the woman with whom he lived at times when she was seeking solace in liquor for the wounds to her pride inflicted during one of their violent disputes....

Wyatt's sense of loyalty and gratitude was such that [if] the whole world had been all against Doc, he should have stood by him out of appreciation for saving his life.

"Isn't it strange," Wyatt remarked to him, "that if it were not for you, I wouldn't be alive today, yet you must go first?"

Doc came over and chatted with us for a few minutes then he and Wyatt walked away, Doc on visibly unsteady legs. My husband was deeply affected by this parting from the man who, like an ailing child, had clung to him as though to derive strength from him.

There were tears in Wyatt's eyes when at last they took leave of each other. Doc threw his arm across his shoulder.

"Good-bye, old friend," he said. "It will be a long time before we meet again."
He turned, and walked away as fast as his feeble legs would permit.[2]

Doc's home in Denver was the Metropolitan Hotel on 16th Street. At $1 a night, the Metropolitan wasn't elegant digs, but it wasn't shabby either—the finest hotel in town only charged $4 a night—and had the advantage of being on the same street as the German National Bank, the famous Charpiot's Restaurant, and the entertaining Academy of Music Theater. The sporting district, however, was a disappointment that spring. The Denver newspapers were calling for a clean-up of the gambling halls and bawdy houses, and the police were threatening arrests. So the sporting community was moving elsewhere until things calmed down, and Doc followed them, as noted in the Leadville papers: "Doc Holliday, who remained here until he reached 'the end of his string,' went to Butte and fled from the wrath of a Grand Jury, and finally returned to Colorado, since which time, he has been roaming."[3]

One of the places he visited in his roaming that summer was the mining camp of Silverton, in the San Juan Mountains of southwestern Colorado. Though Silverton was the richest silver camp in those mountains, getting there had meant a harrowing wagon road across treacherous passes, until the Denver and Rio Grande decided to build a railroad to the camp, founding the town of Durango as the starting point of an engineering marvel through the mountains. The forty-five-mile-long Animas Canyon between Durango and Silverton was beautiful but too narrow in places to lay rail. So, the Rio Grande used dynamite to blast the canyon walls, carving a narrow rock shelf to carry the tracks high above the Animas River. Passengers on one side of a railcar could reach out an open window and touch the rocky face of the cliff wall, while passengers on the other side of the car could look out an open window straight down four hundred feet to the river below. A rockslide could push the narrow car right off the tracks and send it careening down into the gorge, but the train was mostly free of accidents.

From its debut in July 1882, the Durango & Silverton road was promoted as a scenic route for passenger service in addition to servicing the mines. The views were spectacular, the five river crossings splendid, and at the end of the line was Silverton, nine thousand feet high and nestled in its own quiet mountain valley. But the town itself was anything but quiet. As soon as the snows began to melt in the high passes, the miners made their annual trek down from the Sunnyside, the Little Giant, and the Old Hundred mines, to be welcomed by the spring influx of sporting men ready to help them spend their new paychecks. With only a few short months until the snows closed the town up again, Silverton stayed open twenty-four hours a day. From the train depot on 12th Street, to the bordellos of Blair Street, to the hotels and saloons of Greene Street, Silverton was one unending celebration.

Doc arrived along with the other sports in late May, with his presence noted by the locals and covered by a roving reporter from the *New York Sun* newspaper in an article titled, "He Started Many Graveyards."[4] Though the story was likely a lot of creative writing and a little bit of actual interview, it showed how a life could become legend while the legend was still alive:

> *June 1, 1882, Silverton—A crowd following a rather good-looking man around, stopping when he stopped, listening as to an oracle when he had anything to say, and all the time gaping at him in open-mouthed wonder, proclaimed the fact that an important personage was in town.*
>
> *"Who is that duck?" an old miner asked.*
>
> *"Sh-h-h!" replied a companion. "That's Doc Holliday. He's killed thirty men in his day, and there's no telling when he'll turn himself loose again."*

Then all hands took another good look at him, and after he had passed on out of sight one of the early settlers said: "Some of you fellows who have come here lately have a very faint idea of what Doc Holliday and a few other like him used to do in this country. When Doc ran things down in Arizona nobody dared say his soul was his own. I remember one time in Tombstone he killed two men in one night, and the next day he called on the editor of the paper and said that, as he was opposed to sensational literature, he hoped there would be no undue prominence given to the occurrences of the evening before.

"When the paper came out in the afternoon it had a three-line item saying that it was understood that two men had been found dead on the streets, but that the reporter had not learned their names. The same issue had a long editorial article on the advantages of Arizona as a health resort.

"Not long after that the Doc was in Tucson for two weeks, and killed six men during that time. He would have stayed another week, but he learned that a movement was on foot to nab him, and he left suddenly. All along the Southwestern border for three or four years he was robbing and killing almost continually. When any particular crime threatened to make trouble for him he would ship over to southern California for awhile, and once or twice he went to the Indian Territory. He could be tried now in any one of a half dozen States or Territories and hanged for murder, but there is no disposition to press him, as it is remembered that the country was pretty wild in those days."

Another man who had been a close listener stepped forward at this point and said: "I had a brush with the Doc once in the Calico range, down back of Fort Yuma. He and twenty-five other horse and cattle thieves were down there, and they sent word to the Sheriff that they were spoiling for a fight. That made the officer mad, and so he got up a posse and set out, I being in the party. When we came on the gang we saw that they outnumbered us two to one, and we concluded not to fight. As soon as the Doc saw that we were sloping he got mad, and jumping out in front of his party, he yelled that he would whip us single handed.

"He hadn't any more than said the word when he began firing, and we ran like cowards. He killed three of our party, though, before we got to cover, and we didn't have any anxiety to interview him again. A little while after that he left that part of the country, greatly to the relief of the Sheriff, who used to say that he never could be chief when the Doc was around."

While this speaker was giving his experience the Doc himself had drawn nigh, and, after listening to the conclusion of the story, he observed, "When any of you fellows have been hunted from one end of the country to other, as I have been, you'll understand what a bad man's reputation is built on. I've had credit for more killings than I ever dreamt of. Now, I'll tell you of one little thing that happened down in Tombstone in the early days. There was a hard crowd there, of course, and I happened in. I thought I saw a chance to make a little money, and so I opened a gambling house. Things went along all right for a time, but at length some of the boys got an idea that they were not winning often enough, and they put up a job to kill me. I heard of it, and the next night, when they came in, I made them a speech and told them what I had heard, said that sort of thing couldn't go on in a well-regulated community, and then, just to restore order, I gave it to a couple of them. That settled the whole trouble. I was in Tombstone six months after that and never had another difficulty. It has been that way wherever I have been. I never shoot unless I have to.

"Down on the border I had two or three little scrapes, but they didn't amount to much. A party of drunken greasers came climbing over us one night, and I had to fix one or two, and at another time, I had a fight with a roomful of them, and started a graveyard there, but it had to be done in the interest of peace. I claim to have been a benefactor to the country. Every crime that occurs in a new settlement is always laid on some one or two men. I've found out time and again that I had been charged with murders and robberies when I hadn't been within five hundred miles of the place. Down in Arizona once the Coroner and most of the members of his jury had killed and robbed a man, and when they sat on the case they laid it to Doc Holliday. In Dodge City once I was charged with burglarizing a store when the owner did the job himself. I've known army officers who couldn't find vouchers for all their property to put in the plea that Doc Holliday had stolen it, when I was never inside their lines.

"If you take the trouble to examine a good many of the crimes that I am charged with, you will find that when I have been charged with murder I have always been a long way off—never at hand. That looks odd, don't it? But it is just because I didn't do it. I've been in nearly all these towns since, and nobody says anything about arresting me, simply because they have no case. The claim that I make is that some few of us pioneers are entitled to credit for what we

have done. We have been the forerunners of government. As soon as law and order were established anywhere we never had any trouble. If it hadn't been for me and few like me there never would have been any government in some of these towns. When I have done any shooting it has always been with this in view."

The Doc's auditors listened attentively, nodded assent, and gradually slipped away. He has been arrested but once, and nobody here will undertake the job.

By mid-summer, Doc was back in Denver again, arriving in time to watch the Academy of Music Theater, across the street from his hotel, burn down. According to the *Rocky Mountain News*, "The flames spread so rapidly and the heat became so intense that in less than 15 minutes . . . the wires of the Western Union Telegraph Company, whose office is on the block directly across the alley from the academy, were melted and all the services were destroyed. The fire was the quickest ever witnessed in Denver."[5]

As the blaze spread to the neighboring buildings and jumped the street, the Metropolitan Hotel was filled with smoke, and Doc suddenly found himself homeless and in violation of the new Denver vagrancy laws. According to the law, a man without proof of gainful employment could be charged with vagrancy and arrested. The law was designed to rid the city of sporting men, and Doc Holliday was just the kind of man it meant to catch. He had no form of regular employment these days, other than his gambling, nor even a permanent address, so when a police officer found him standing in the shadows on 16th Street, having an evening conversation with the night watchman for the horse track at Jewell Park, he was quickly arrested. Confidence men traded horse race information, trying to work the odds, and that seemed proof enough that Doc was nothing but a gambler. Although the newspapers had supported him in the extradition fight only a few years before, they now reported that "His only means of living was gambling in its worst form and confidence work."[6]

When Doc appeared in Police Court the next morning, he expected the usual sentence of a fine and a suggestion that he take his sport elsewhere. But for the now-legendary Doc Holliday, the judge had something special in mind: Doc was ordered to leave Denver permanently and given a police escort to the train at Union Depot.[7]

MR. AND MRS. EARP

When Doc Holliday met with Mrs. and Mrs. Wyatt Earp at the Windsor Hotel in Denver, he was actually meeting with the *fourth* woman to call herself Wyatt's wife. The first was Aurilla Sutherland of Lamar, Missouri, whom the twenty-two-year-old Wyatt married in January 1870. Wyatt's family had returned from California and settled again in the Midwest, and Wyatt had recently been appointed constable in the town of Lamar, where Aurilla's parents owned the Exchange Hotel. In the summer following his marriage, Wyatt bought a lot on the outskirts of Lamar and built a house for his new family. Tragically, Aurilla died soon after, perhaps of typhoid fever, and some accounts say she was also pregnant at the time of her death. With the loss of Aurilla, Wyatt's life took a detour, as he lost his job and was accused of embezzlement, horse theft, and working in prostitution.

Wyatt's second wife, according to an 1872 arrest record in the Illinois River town of Peoria, was sixteen-year-old Sarah "Sally" Haspel. Sally's mother was a Peoria madam, and it appears that Wyatt and his younger brother Morgan had a share in the

Celia Ann "Mattie" Blaylock, Glenn Boyer Collection. Courtesy Scott Dyke.

brothel, as they were both arrested for Keeping and Being Found in a House of Ill-Fame. A few months later they were arrested at another brothel and jailed when they could not pay the fine of $44.55 each. Four months after that, Wyatt was arrested again at another brothel. When Wyatt gave up on Peoria and moved west to Wichita, Kansas, he took Sally Haspel along with him, the girl the *Peoria Daily National Democrat* said, "calls herself the wife of Wyatt." In 1874, municipal records in Wichita listed Sally Earp working in the brothel of Bessie Earp, Wyatt's sister-in-law. Both Sally and Bessie were arrested and fined several times for prostitution and spent time in jail. Wyatt may have been trying to reform himself, for when he found a job as a police officer in Wichita, Sally Earp disappeared from his life.

In 1876 Wyatt arrived in Dodge City, Kansas, where he again found a job on the police force and found a third wife: Celia Anne "Mattie" Blaylock, originally from Monroe, Iowa. Although Mattie was often referred to as Wyatt's common-law wife because there was no civil or religious ceremony uniting them, she was still considered his legal wife in every sense but a change of name. In 1877, the US Supreme Court had ruled that certain unions lacking a marriage ceremony or official record were still considered valid and enforceable marriages unless prohibited by state law. Kansas, where Wyatt and Mattie set up housekeeping together, was a state that recognized common-law marriage. So, while Mattie Blaylock was not officially Mattie Earp, she was still Mrs. Wyatt Earp, and it was as Wyatt's wife that she traveled with him to New Mexico, where they added Doc Holliday to their wagon train bound for Arizona. Doc stayed in the friendly climate of Prescott while the Earps pushed on to Tombstone, where Wyatt and Mattie bought a house together on Fremont

Josephine Marcus, Tombstone 1881, by Camillus Fly. Tombstone Western Heritage Museum.

Street. When Doc joined them in Tombstone and he and Wyatt went into the mining business together, Wyatt named one of his claims the "Mattie Blaylock." Mattie was known to suffer from gum disease and headaches and took laudanum (powdered opium in alcohol tincture) to ease the pain, becoming addicted to the drug. After the O.K. Corral shootings, the maiming of Virgil Earp, and the murder of Morgan Earp, Mattie left Tombstone for Colton, California, where Wyatt's parents had resettled, along with Morgan's widow Louisa and Virgil Earp and his wife Allie. That summer, Mattie sent Wyatt a letter asking for a divorce—because a common-law marriage was legally recognized, it also had to be legally ended. Wyatt either refused or simply ignored the request, and Mattie left the Earp home and moved to the mining camp of Pinal, Arizona. Struggling with addictions, Mattie committed suicide in 1888 by "opium poisoning" as stated on her death certificate. Because Wyatt had not given Mattie a divorce, she was still his legal wife until her death made him a widower.

But Wyatt didn't wait until he was a free man again before taking his fourth, and most famous wife, Josephine Sarah Marcus. Born in 1861 to a Jewish family in New York that resettled in San Francisco, Josephine attended primary schools and took dancing lessons and seemed destined for life as a proper Jewish wife and mother. But Josephine Marcus had adventure in her blood, and by the time she was fourteen she'd run off with a local madam who was taking girls to work as prostitutes in the Arizona mining camps. The beginning of the journey was exciting, as the girls boarded a steamer bound for Santa Barbara and took a stagecoach trip across the desert to Prescott, Arizona, where Josephine took a new name for her new career: Sadie Mansfield. She also began a romance with an older (and married) man named Johnny Behan. She started working in a Prescott bordello; he made regular visits to her there, and soon his marriage ended in divorce. By 1879, Josephine was traveling with Behan and working in his saloon in the mining camp of Tip Top, Arizona. The next year they moved on to Tombstone, and by 1881 Josephine was calling herself Mrs. Behan—until she found her Johnny in bed with another woman. Her first love affair was over, but twenty-year-old Josephine soon found another married man to ease her broken heart: Wyatt Earp. The love triangle became one of the legendary stories of Tombstone, portrayed with a happy ending in the movie *Tombstone*, as Wyatt's inconvenient wife dies of a drug overdose. Wyatt finds the heartsick Josie starring in a Denver theater production and proposes a long but poor life together, and Josie tells him not to worry because, "My family is rich."

Her family wasn't rich and she wasn't an actress, but Wyatt did go to find her (back home in San Francisco) after the Tombstone troubles, and the two stayed together for the rest of their lives. According to Josephine's differing recollections, they were legally married in 1885, or 1892, or 1901. Whenever and wherever the ceremony took place, it could not have been before 1888, when Mattie Blaylock died, or Wyatt (who had not given Mattie a divorce) would have been a bigamist. For the same reason, he could not have made Josephine his common law wife while Mattie Blaylock was still alive. So, when Doc Holliday met Wyatt and Josephine at the Windsor Hotel in Denver in 1886, they were not yet married under any law and were not yet Mr. and Mrs. Wyatt Earp.

DURANGO & SILVERTON NARROW GAUGE RAILROAD

After nearly a year of blasting and grading and laying rails through the spectacular Animas River Valley, the Denver & Rio Grande Railroad finally reached the remote town of Silverton high in the San Juan Mountains on July 8, 1882, and hauled out the first load of silver ore five days later. The road had cost the company $10,000 per mile to build, but the investment would be more than recouped through freight charges and passenger tickets. With the coming of the railroad, the population of the town doubled in a year, and by 1886 when Doc Holliday took the train to Silverton, the local mines were producing more than $1 million annually, with an eventual production of more than $65 million. And where the money was, the sporting men weren't far behind.

"Durango & Silverton Narrow Gauge." maxpixel.net.

First-class fare from Denver to Silverton was $37.50 ($4 more for the sleeper car), and passengers only had to make one change of trains: at Alamosa where the standard gauge rails connected to the narrow gauge that wound through western Colorado. By using the narrow three-foot width between rails instead of the standard 4 foot 8½ inch width, the Denver & Rio Grande's trains could make the sharper curves necessary in the mountains. The narrow gauge rails were also lighter, making them easier to haul and faster to lay—a benefit when building in high altitude and at difficult grades, often in harsh winter weather conditions. The Denver & Rio Grande would later advertise itself as the railroad that went "Though the Rockies . . . Not Around Them."

For sixty years the Denver & Rio Grande's narrow gauge rails were the most dependable transportation in and through the Colorado mountains. But when the era of railroads gave way to the era of autos and interstates, much of the Denver & Rio Grande's narrow gauge routes were closed and the rails taken up. Only a few sections of the old roads remain, now operated as historic and scenic railroads, including the Georgetown Loop Railroad near Denver, the Cumbres & Toltec Scenic Railroad into New Mexico, and the Durango & Silverton Narrow Gauge Railroad that carries two hundred thousand sightseers a year from the original depot in Durango on a seven-hour roundtrip ride to Silverton. Both the Durango & Silverton Narrow Gauge Railroad and the town of Silverton have been designated National Historic Landmarks.

Now the road that was built to bring money out of Silverton brings it in again from tourist dollars—and from film companies using the Durango & Silverton Narrow Gauge Railroad as an authentic location for Westerns like *Ticket to Tomahawk*, *Across the Wide Missouri*, *How the West Was Won*, *Lone Star*, *Butch Cassidy and the Sundance Kid*, and *Denver & Rio Grande*.

THE BORDELLOS OF BLAIR STREET

Wherever the railroads ran, the ladies of the line were soon to follow. In those out-wardly proper Victorian times, the ladies went by many euphemistic nicknames: fallen angels, frail sirens, soiled doves, lewd women, Amazons, courtesans, strumpets, harlots, and whores. But by any name, they were all employed in the world's oldest profession.

Silverton had a special relationship with its prostitutes, most of whom were only part-time residents, coming into town with the spring thaw, like the gamblers did,

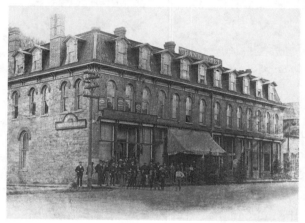

and leaving again when the winter settled down in earnest. The mines in the San Juan mountains were even more remote than the town, and the miners often lived through the winter in boardinghouses or shacks on the mine property, trapped in their snowy canyons. So, when the spring came, they collected their pay and hurried into town to spend it, lining up to see the ladies of the line before heading to the saloons and gambling halls. Although Silverton had strict laws regarding the sale of sex, the enforcement of those laws was

Silverton Grand Imperial Hotel, c. 1885, Silverton, Colorado. Courtesy San Juan County Historical Society.

generally lax, with the bordellos and cribs being regularly fined, but not shut down. The ladies were good for business, as long as they kept their business in its proper place—on Blair Street close to the railroad tracks and not in the more polite parts of town. Many of the old buildings remaining on modern Blair Street started as dance halls and whorehouses.

The better class of people took their amusement one block away on Greene Street, lined with variety houses, saloons, and gambling halls like the Alhambra, the Fashion, and the Arlington—where Wyatt Earp managed the gaming rooms in 1883. That was the year of the Dodge City War, when Bat Masterson recruited old friends to travel to Dodge in support of the owner of the Long Branch Saloon—which may account for local stories of Bat Masterson paying a visit to Silverton. Although Wyatt likely lived in a local boardinghouse during his stay in town, the traveling Bat Masterson and Doc Holliday may have stayed across Greene Street at the newly opened Grand Hotel. Built by a New York perfume importer and mill owner, the massive granite structure was the crown jewel of Silverton—the largest single structure south of Denver and the "pinnacle of luxury in the Southwest." Guest rooms occupied the third floor, away from the street noise; the second floor housed town and county offices, and the first floor was home to the local post office, town bank, general store, and newspaper.

Silverton Train Depot. Shutterstock.

The Grand, now known as the Grand Imperial Hotel, has been lovingly restored to its 1880s beauty as a popular tourist destination. But not everyone in town seems pleased about the renovation. According to the new owners, construction workers on the third floor inexplicably had nails and chunks of drywall chucked at them and guests sometimes hear whispered voices when no one is near. It's not the only building in town with ghostly happenings. At the old train depot, where Doc and Wyatt and Bat Masterson arrived in town, ghost hunters have recorded "voices"—perhaps echoes of Silverton's louder, lewder days.

DOC'S DENVER

As Horace Tabor's silver fortune made-over frontier Denver in the nineteenth century, so urban renewal and the inventions of the twentieth century have made over most of Doc Holliday's Denver. Union Station, where he came and went by train, was expanded, burned, and remodeled several times over a century before the decline in rail travel left the grand building with only

Denver Union Station by George L. Beam. Courtesy Denver Public Library, Western History Collection, #GB-8272.

two daily trains in service. Then in 2012, the landmark site underwent a major renovation, transforming it into a new multiuse complex, with the luxury Crawford Hotel on the upper levels and the ground level Great Hall serving as hotel lobby, public and retail space, and commuter train waiting room. Some of the old gray stone façade remains, and the old ticket counters are now part of the new Terminal Bar.

The corner of Sixteenth and Larimer, where Doc was twice arrested in stories that spread his fame and made him a national celebrity, is now part of the Larimer Street pedestrian mall, lined with restaurants and shops. At the time of his second arrest there, Doc had been having a conversation with the night watchman of the Jewell Park horse racing track, which looked and probably was suspicious. Jewell Park and its racing track had been built by the local Denver Circle Railroad to attract riders to the train and became such a popular spot that the park remained when the rails were taken up. In 1897 the horse-racing track became an auto-racing track, and in later years a golf course was added and the park was renamed the Overland Park Country Club—now the Overland Golf Course, the oldest running course west of the Mississippi, with views of Denver and the Rocky Mountains beyond.

But Denver's Windsor Hotel, where Horace and Baby Doe Tabor had lived in scandal and luxury and Doc Holliday had a last meeting with Wyatt Earp, is now a parking lot between Market and Larimer Streets—with nothing to memorialize its nineteenth-century history.

24

GLENWOOD SPRINGS STATION

There are plenty of stories about where Doc Holliday went when he was driven out of Denver, but there's not a lot of proof. Some say that he returned to Leadville to spend the autumn and winter working at Mannie Hyman's Saloon next to the Tabor Opera House.[1] But there's no documentary evidence to show him there, nor even a mention in the local papers that he had returned to his old haunts. And it seems unlikely that he'd have wanted to spend another winter in the coldest, highest city in Colorado, after what Leadville had done to his health in the past. Another story says that he traveled to the hot springs resort at Wagon Wheel Gap, where the Denver & Rio Grande Railroad had recently built a special spur right to the depot and the hotel.[2] Still another story has the credibility of being noted in the Leadville *Evening Chronicle*, which simply stated, "Doc Holliday is in New Orleans."[3] Though that may have been true, the newspapers had famously been wrong about him before and would be again. But one thing was certain: Wherever he went that winter of 1886–1887, he had a hard time staying warm.

It was the coldest December in a dozen years, the snowiest January, the bitterest February, the bleakest March. The newspapers blamed the long winter, the worst in memory, on the eruption of the mountain island called Krakatoa, three years before and half a world away. The explosion had blown two-hundred-million tons of rock and smoke and ash into the atmosphere, darkening skies and lowering temperatures all over the globe.

The "volcanic winter," as scientists called it, brought droughts to Europe and deadly floods to the Far East, hurricanes to South America and blizzards to North America. In San Francisco, three and half inches of snow fell on the beach. On the Kansas prairies, snowdrifts stopped Union Pacific locomotives, trains froze to the rails, and cattle froze to death where they stood. In Montana, ranchers lost over 350,000 head of cattle, more than half of the territory's herd, and in the Dakota Territory, Theodore Roosevelt wrote to a friend from his ranch near Medora, "Well, we have had a perfect smashup all through the cattle country of the northwest. The losses are crippling."[4] When the spring thaw finally melted the snow away, the American West was covered with the carcasses of the once massive cattle herds. Where there had been great round-ups, there was now the "Great Die-Up."

For Doc Holliday, sick with consumption and getting sicker, the cold and snows of that historically hard winter were more than uncomfortable. They also kept him away from the one place that might yet give him hope: the Indian vapor caves called *Yampah*, Big Medicine. The caves lay at the confluence of two rivers in the narrow-necked Roaring Fork Valley of Colorado, and the Ute Indians had considered them sacred for generations, gathering there for the annual Sun Dance and offering prayers to the great Manitou for healing in the steamy underground chambers. Then the white men came, carving new caves and channeling steamy sulfur water from the nearby hot springs into porcelain bathtubs along the river, the beginnings of what they hoped would be a popular and money-making health resort in the town they had newly named Glenwood Springs. But in that early winter of 1887, the elegant resort was still in the planning stages and Glenwood Springs was hidden in its mountain valley on the western slope of the Continental Divide, on the far side of Independence Pass, twelve thousand feet at the summit and snowed in from October until May.

Doc could have made the trip by horse-drawn sleigh during that long winter, as some travelers did, but the eighteen-hour journey in the freezing cold could have been deadly for a man in his condition. So, he waited until May, when the temperatures warmed and the snows melted, then took one last train ride to Leadville, the closest rail stop, and bought a ticket on the Carson Stage bound for Glenwood Springs—though even in pleasant weather, the ride was challenging. The stage crowded nine passengers together on three narrow benches, stopping six times for a change of horses and once for a meal, while tumbling along the twisting road over Independence Pass where a wrong step by the horses could send a coach careening over the cliffs. But after the bruising, bone-jarring journey, the stage finally pulled to a stop on Grand Avenue in Glenwood Springs.

The town was five years old that spring, having quickly grown from a settlement of tents along the river to a city of 1,200 residents, with two churches, six liveries, six blacksmiths, seven lawyers, four physicians—and more than twenty saloons. There were also eight restaurants, several boardinghouses, and two good hotels in town: the Kendrick House and the Hotel Glenwood, which was second only to Denver's Windsor Hotel for luxury accommodations. The Hotel Glenwood had seventy-five sleeping rooms, a well-appointed dining room, parlors for smoking and for billiards, a gentleman's barber shop and a guest laundry, and something not even the Windsor could match: electric lights in every room, courtesy of the country's first hydroelectric plant, with power coming from the two rivers that coursed between the narrow canyon walls, the same rivers that supplied cold running water pumped into every private bath while hot water was pumped from the nearby hot springs. A guest could walk into his hotel room, pull on a light, and draw a warm bath without needing to call on the staff for help. But with all its finery, the Hotel Glenwood was also the most expensive establishment in town.

Doc likely chose the less pricey Kendrick House when he first arrived in Glenwood Springs, with its convenient location on Seventh Street across from the river and close to the hot springs and the vapor caves. Although the Kendrick House didn't have a dining room or smoking parlor, a barbershop or a ballroom, the rest of the accommodations were comfortable, according to an advertisement in the *Aspen Daily News*, with "Good rooms with spring beds, feather pillows; everything new. Large reading room with the daily and weekly papers. Take meals where you please. Rate 50 cents per day, $2.50 per week."[5] The owner of the Kendrick House was Thomas Kendrick, who also owned the Grand Avenue Restaurant, and whose fifteen-year-old son Art worked as a bellboy at the hotel. Art Kendrick would later recall serving Doc Holliday, who tipped, "pretty good," giving him two dollars for a wake-up call and a bottle of whiskey.[6]

To help pay for his hotel bill and his liquor, Doc took a short-term job that suited his shooting skills: working as a guard on a nearby coal claim for $10 a day. It was good pay and easy work, sitting at the claim with his pistol loaded up and handy, and his boss was someone he'd known before: Gunnison policeman Judd Riley, who was also living in Glenwood Springs that year. Riley remembered that when Doc arrived in town:

> the Rio Grande was building thru Eagle River Canon. I was over there myself, for a year, part of the time as a deputy sheriff. One day a man came to me and wanted to give me ten dollars a day each for several men to guard a coal claim near Glenwood that he was trying to sell, and some other parties were ready to

jump. I got Holliday and we held down the claim until the fellow sold out. Got the ten dollars a day, all right, too.[7]

The claim Riley mentioned was a rich seam of coal south of Glenwood Springs called the Wheeler Vein. Two corporations were fighting over rights to the coal, and the Colorado Fuel & Iron Company hired armed men to defend their claim until an acceptable financial deal could be struck.[8] The high pay the company offered for guarding the Wheeler Vein—three times the amount the Santa Fe had paid for guarding the rails through the Royal Gorge—reflected the value of a coal claim. Coal heated homes, coal fired smelters that processed silver ore, coal fueled trains that carried silver bullion to eastern banks and turned mining men into millionaires. If silver were king in those Colorado Mountains, coal was his consort and queen, and one day of guarding a claim could pay for a whole month of hotel bills.

According to Dr. W. W. Crook, a surgeon for the Denver & Rio Grande who settled in Glenwood Springs, Doc also worked as a bartender for a few months. And while Doc kept an eye on the Wheeler Vein and poured the drinks, the local law was keeping an eye on him. Glenwood Springs pioneer Perry Malaby had been appointed a town policeman that year, and as he told his family, "the sheriff's office knew of warrants out for Doc Holliday, but the sheriff decided not to bother him unless Doc caused trouble."[9] The warrants were likely from Doc's arrest and skipped court date in Butte, Montana, which had been reported in the Leadville papers that were also read in Glenwood Springs. But the sheriff's office found Doc to be a peaceable citizen, and as Marshal J. W. Scott remembered him, Doc was a "well-dressed, soft-spoken Southern gentleman who was politely cordial to the ladies."[10]

Perry Malaby's wife, Eleanora, who'd come to Glenwood Springs as a bride by sleigh over snowy Independence Pass, remembered Doc practicing dentistry in the city. According to a Glenwood Springs historian: "Mrs. Malaby told me that once when she had gone to Holliday for dental work, he began to cough violently and asked to be excused. He went outside and she heard him hacking like he would tear out his lungs and when he returned he asked her to leave and come back later."[11]

It is possible that Doc tried to do some dentistry during his time in Glenwood Springs, a service the community needed as the closest dentists were doctors Todd and Green, both a forty-mile stagecoach ride away in Aspen. But bending over a patient while doing exacting dental work was hard for a man with troubled lungs, as the story shows.

Gambling as a profession took less physical strength and could bring in big profits when his luck was running. So, Doc made the rounds of the saloons along Seventh Street and Grand Avenue, where the new electric streetlights—powered by the hydroelectric plant by the river— made the days seem longer than natural. But he was mostly wagering on the vapor caves and the hot water, hoping to lengthen out his own days. He was only thirty-six years old that summer, with a whole lifetime yet to live.

The local papers described a visit to the vapor caves:

> *Twenty steps down lands us in an underground passageway that is well lighted by incandescent lamps of the Electric Light Company. When you enter this passage the heat is not sufficient to cause any inconvenience whatsoever, though the thermometer registers from 85 to 90 degrees F.*
>
> *An attendant opens the door at the end of this passage and you step inside. To attempt to describe the grandeur, the brilliancy, the awe and the heat that presses down on your vision and your breathing facilities as you enter the hot caverns is a task that will take time and study.*
>
> *Standing in front of you is a large cave with marble seats and walls of lime. To the left is another cave with seats, still larger, while to the right the great cavern, with its high ceiling and rigid walls, invites you in. The heat is so great that your first expression naturally is, "This is---!" But before you have finished the sentence you cry out, "How beautiful!"*
>
> *You step back into the cave after cooling off and you will notice that it is just a little hotter than when you came out. Having left all your clothing in one of the dressing rooms above, you cannot look at your watch to see just how long you have stood the great heat, but the attendants will tell you that 20 minutes is as long as you should stay in. You are sure by the way the sweat runs from the pores of your skin that a few minutes is as much as you can stand at one time at least. You will find that by lying down on one of the marble slabs that it is possible to remain in the cave longer than when standing.*[12]

Because of the strange beauty of the sweltering caverns, the vapor caves had gained a nickname: A Palace in Hell. Doc Holliday must have found it ironic to be going down to hell and back every day, hoping to live—he'd been raised on hellfire, after all, being taught by his mother to fear God and forsake the devil, though he hadn't always lived what he'd been taught. But if he still carried the testimony she'd had written for him, he likely spent time pondering on her words. She had believed that a repentant sinner could find salvation, and had wanted him to believe, as well. He certainly reflected on the words his cousin Mattie, now Sister Melanie, sent to him in their continued correspondence, reminding him of the paths of righteousness and encouraging him to set himself straight on that road. It may have been Sister Melanie who suggested that he strike up a friendship with the local Catholic priest, Father Edward Downey. Though Doc wasn't Catholic himself, Father Downey, as the shepherd of a congregation that ranged from St. Stephen's Church in Glenwood Springs to Rifle, Red Cliff, and Aspen, was accustomed to dealing with men of all faiths and situations and was glad to counsel with a troubled soul. And Doc had cause to be considering his eternal welfare: Despite the hot springs and the vapor caves and Mattie's prayers, he wasn't getting any better. As one resident of the town recalled, he was a man "breaking to pieces."[13]

The consumption that was slowly stealing his life away had a scientific name now: tuberculosis, named for the tubercle bacilli that had been discovered to cause the disease. German scientist Robert Koch had stunned the medical world in 1882 by revealing that microscopic organisms could infect a host, causing the "white death" of consumption: chest pain, bloody cough, fever, night sweats, chills, weight loss, exhaustion. As the disease progressed, it could affect the kidneys, spine, or brain; open wounds could appear anywhere as the bacteria consumed the body. But what the brilliant Dr. Koch hadn't discovered was a cure.

In September, Doc's health took a turn for the worse. Dr. Crook recalled that he had another bout of pneumonia, and that may have been when he moved to the pricey Hotel Glenwood with a doctor on staff for the care of invalids in addition to its other amenities—there was no hospital or sanitarium in town. He was still at the hotel a month later, sick in bed and struggling to breathe, when the railroad finally came to Glenwood Springs. It had taken the Denver & Rio Grande six years to get there, building from Leadville and over ten-thousand-foot Tennessee Pass to Red Cliff before running into money trouble and putting the project on hiatus. But when the rival Colorado Midland Railroad started building toward Glenwood Springs, the Rio Grande got back to work. On the evening of October 5, the inaugural train of the Denver & Rio Grande's new Glenwood Springs route rolled into town, and the city celebrated the end of its stagecoach days.

The first engine to pass through the Denver & Rio Grande tunnel passed last night at 11 o'clock. The trackmen were laying rails all night. The river front was *crowded with people all day today watching the tracklayers at work. . . . The merchants were decorating their stores all day with streamers, evergreens, and mottoes. A stand has been erected on the north side of the Grand river for a display of fireworks. At the foot of Grand avenue an arch has been erected covered with evergreens and bearing the word, "Welcome." From the Hotel Glenwood across the street to Kamm's store, a mottoe is suspended, "Denver and Rio Grande, pioneer railroad of Colorado." The committee raised $800 to celebrate the event and a grand banquet is given in honor of the occasion this evening at the Hotel Glenwood. A great gathering of people at the foot of Grand avenue at 7 o'clock. The band was on hand in full force with torchbearers and transperancies. One transperancy displayed the motto, "Glenwood Welcomes the Railroad and Remembers the Stage Coach with Kindness;" another, "We Welcome You to the Gateway of the Pacific Slope." About 7:20 a train was heard coming through the tunnel above. A signal was made to Chan Woodruff, master of fireworks, and to those having charge of bonfires, the electric light works whistle was sounded and the earth was shaken by the reports of gunpowder. The train drew near and the band began to play. . . . The train drew up and passed, and the immense crowd ceased their cheering, as it proved only a false entry, the train being a simple construction. The crowd took the disappointment in good part and waited patiently another half hour, when a loud whistle was heard which continued long and loud. There could be no mistake this time and the demonstration was renewed with vigor, and as the train passed slowly by the landing, the reports of giant powder, the whistling of engines and the shouts of the people were deafening. As the train drew up and stopped Mayor Thomas proposed three cheers for the Denver & Rio Grande road, which was responded to with a will. The distinguished visitors then landed and were conducted to the triumphant arch where Mayor Thomas welcomed them and the rest to the gateway of the Pacific slope. He reminded them that three years ago the place on which they were standing was covered with sage brush. He spoke very condolingly of Kit Carson and his stage line and said Kit had bidden good bye to the back bone of the continent. . . . A procession was then formed, led by the town council and band up the avenue to the Hotel Glenwood, where great preparations were underway for the banquet. . . . The display of fireworks was grand and by far the best ever seen in Glenwood. . . . The banquet commences at 10 o'clock, and a large number will partake, including all of the guests.*[14]

But one hotel guest would not be attending the festivities: Dr. John Henry Holliday, dentist and sporting man, outlaw and champion of law and order, was dying of consumption in his room upstairs while Glenwood Springs celebrated the start of its new life as a railroad town. And it seemed a fitting ending, after his life on the rails, that the last loud sound he heard before slipping into unconsciousness was the roar of a steam engine.

VOLCANIC WINTER

When the volcanic island of Krakatoa in Indonesia blew its top in 1883, the explosion was heard three thousand miles away, with recorded shockwaves reaching around the globe five times. The plumes of ash and sulfuric acid shot fifty miles into the atmosphere, obscuring the sun, and the sudden darkness dropped temperatures worldwide, causing a "volcanic winter" that lasted for five years—the rest of Doc Holliday's life. The volcanic eruption also caused fiery sunsets and sunrises as the cloud of ash and acid spread worldwide in the following months. Newspapers published hundreds of accounts of the phenomena, as found in the *New York Times* of November 28, 1883: "Soon after 5 o'clock the western horizon suddenly flamed into a brilliant scarlet, which crimsoned sky and clouds. Many thought that a real fire was in progress. . . . The clouds gradually deepened to a bloody red hue, and a sanguinary flush was on the sea."

English journals called the sunsets "Blood Afterglows" and Poet Laureate Alfred Lord Tennyson described the volcanic sky in his poem, "St. Telemachus":

> *Had the fierce ashes of some fiery peak*
> *Been hurl'd so high they ranged about the globe?*
> *For day by day, thro' many a blood-red eve,*
> *The wrathful sunset glared . . .*

When the fiery skies reached Norway, astronomers at the Christiana Observatory recorded "the very intense red glow that amazed the observers" and became "a red band." It was likely the sky phenomenon that Norwegian artist Edvard Munch witnessed, as he described an eerie sunset walk with friends:

all at once the sky became blood red—and I felt overcome with melancholy. I stood still and leaned against the railing, dead tired—clouds like blood and tongues of fire hung above the blue-black fjord and the city. My friends went on, and I stood alone, trembling with anxiety. I felt a great, unending scream piercing through nature.[15]

Many other artists tried to capture the look and sound of that "blood afterglow" and the reverberation of shockwaves circling the world, but none did it with the intensity of Munch in his 1894 painting *The Scream*, which he later described as "the earth groaning."

This lithograph of the 1883 eruption of Krakatoa was published in The Eruption of Krakatoa, and Subsequent Phenomena. Report of the Krakatoa Committee of the Royal Society *(London: Trubner & Co., 1888).*

The Scream *by Edvard Munch (1863–1944). commons.wikimedia.org.*

COLORADO'S SANITARIUM

In the movie world of Doc Holliday, his last days are usually portrayed in a "sanitarium," a sterile hospital-like facility for the care of consumptives. But Glenwood Springs, where Doc went for his health in the spring of 1887, never had such a facility. Instead,

the whole town was considered a health resort as consumptives from across the state came to the place known as "Colorado's Sanitarium" for the bracing mountain air and the miracle cure of the Yampah vapor caves and springs.

The vapor caves had been part of the native Ute ancestral lands—a sacred place they called "Yampah," Big Medicine, used during the annual Sun Dance Ceremony. When white settlers took over the Ute land, the Yampah caves were developed as a health resort, with patrons paying for sessions in the steamy sulfur-filled underground

Old Cave #1, Glenwood Springs, Colorado. Courtesy Glenwood Springs Historical Society, Schutte Collection.

chambers. The resort also had porcelain bathtubs set near mineral springs along the bank of the Grand River, where bathers could soak after breathing in the hot sulfur steam of the vapor caves.

Several hotels grew up around the Yampah caves, with the nicest in Doc's day being the Kendrick Hotel and the newly opened Hotel Glenwood that was advertised as being the finest hotel between Denver and San Francisco. In addition to rooms with balconies bringing in fresh air, a dining room, billiard hall, parlor, and elevator, the Hotel Glenwood had bathing accommodations attached and even a doctor and nurse on staff. According to a story about the hotel in the *Aspen Daily*

Times of January 1, 1887, "there is nothing in surroundings that can do an invalid more good than that constant watchfulness over his comfort which causes him to feel that he is at home and among friends." Doc Holliday didn't die in a hospital bed attended by orderlies, but in a comfortable room in a good hotel—and with his passing mourned by his new friends in Glenwood Springs.

Hotel Glenwood, c. 1885. Denver Public Library, Western History Collection (X-17509).

PHOTO PROOF

In the "volcanic winter" of 1884–1885, photographer Augustus W. Dennis was traveling with a Denver & Rio Grande construction crew, documenting the road building toward Glenwood Springs. But somewhere past Red Cliff, the construction train ran into a snowstorm that covered the tracks and trapped the men in their railcar. By the time the rails thawed and the train moved on, the photographer had decided he'd had enough of taking photographs of railroad building and was ready to settle down. He left the employ of the Denver & Rio Grande and went on by stagecoach to Glenwood Springs, where he opened a photographic studio in the newly settled resort town.

When Doc Holliday arrived in town in the spring of 1887, Augustus Dennis had established himself as a popular photographer of local landscapes. According to an article in the *Aspen Daily Times* of January 1, 1887:

> *Mr. Dennis finishes his views in the best possible style and the lighting of many of them is very artistic and beautiful. The Glenwood post office can testify to the appreciation of his work by the number of views continually being sent to friends by the people of Glenwood. Mr. Dennis does a general photograph business, using only the dry instantaneous process, and those patronizing him are guaranteed first class work in every respect.*

One Glenwood Springs resident who may have patronized the studio was Doc Holliday, if an image attributed to Augustus Dennis is actually him: a rumpled-looking man who seems a bit thin, but not mere months away from death. Supposedly, the photograph ended up with Dr. William W. Crook, a Denver & Rio Grande Railroad surgeon who settled in Glenwood Springs, and son of Leadville physician Dr. Joel Crook. The younger Dr. Crook claimed to have been in Mannie Hyman's Leadville saloon when Doc

A. W. Dennis Photographer mark on reverse of portrait of Doc Holliday in Glenwood Springs. Courtesy William I. Koch Collection.

shot Bill Allen, although his recollection was that Allen died from his wounds, which he did not. As the story goes, Dr. Crook sent the photograph to Wyatt Earp, who then gave it to Hiram Sutterfield, a Deputy US Marshal in Arkansas at the turn of the century—and possible distant relative of the Earps.

Doc Holliday in Glenwood Springs;
photograph given by Wyatt Earp to lawman
Hiram Satterfield. Courtesy William I. Koch
Collection.

Hiram Sutterfield also claimed that Earp gave him a photograph of a girl with the penciled note, "Kate Fisher" on the back—the name the eighty-two-year-old Wyatt had called Kate Elder when sharing his reminiscences with biographer Stuart Lake. But did Wyatt write that name on the back of the photograph, or did Hiram Sutterfield himself make the notation after reading *Wyatt Earp: Frontier Marshal* with its mention of Kate Fisher instead of Kate Elder? It's not likely that Doc made the notation, since he knew both Kate's real birth name of Mary Katherine Harony and her pseudonym out west. Or was Kate Fisher someone else entirely than Kate Elder and Wyatt happened to have her picture? The girl's eyes look something like Kate's, but her nose does not.

Lacking better provenance, all we know for sure is that these are real photographs—but not necessarily the real Doc and Kate. Not every nineteenth-century man who sports a mustache is Doc Holliday, and visual evidence alone cannot prove the identification of a photographic subject. Which is why provenance—the verifiable trail of ownership—is so important.

NOBEL PRIZE, 1905

Doc Holliday's disease was called consumption because of the way it seemed to consume the body from the inside out: first the lungs or other organs, then spreading to the bones and skin. It was a long, slow illness—a sufferer might be diagnosed in the teenage years and still live to marry and have children, all the while knowing that an early, painful death was coming. Rarely did a consumptive live past middle age. The illness was thought to be hereditary, passed down in families with a tendency to a "weak constitution." Because consumptives grew thin and pale, they were often considered to be more spiritual and refined than their more robust friends. There was no social stigma attached to the "White Death," as it was called, because no one thought it was catching, and other than the annoying cough, no one was afraid to visit a consumptive dentist. Even the word "lunger" wasn't at first considered derogatory, just a descriptive nickname for those with lung disease.

Then German physician and microbiologist Robert Koch created a laboratory technology to grow and isolate bacteria, becoming the first to link a specific organism with a specific disease and supporting germ theory over heredity or spontaneous generation. Koch, who was at the time advisor to the Imperial Department of Health in Berlin, was convinced that the illness called consumption was caused by a bacterium and was infectious. In 1882, using his laboratory technology, he identified the cause of consumption:

Nobel Prize in Medicine, 1905, sculpted by Erik Lindberg. gkdigest.com.

the slow-growing *Mycobacterium tuberculosis*. But until a cure was found, the treatment remained the same: fresh dry air, cold temperatures, healthy food, mineral baths.

As reports of Dr. Koch's discovery were reprinted around the world, society's perception of the disease—and the diseased—slowly changed. Because tuberculosis was now known to be infectious, "lungers" were to be avoided like lepers, and health resorts turned from the comforting hotels of Doc Holliday's time to institutions with isolated rooms and cottages where patients could breathe healthy mountain air without breathing on anyone else. Communities responded to the threat by outlawing spitting, and women were encouraged to shorten their skirts to avoid contamination from city streets. The Colorado legislature debated a law requiring tuberculosis patients to wear bells around their necks, warning others of their presence.

In 1905, Dr. Robert Koch was awarded the Nobel Prize in Medicine "for his investigations and discoveries in relation to tuberculosis"—research that eventually led the way to finding a cure. When antibiotics were developed in the 1940s and 1950s, the disease that killed Doc Holliday—and helped to make him a legend—was no longer considered a death sentence, just a diagnosis.

25

RETURN TICKET

A notice of Doc Holliday's passing and burial appeared in the local newspaper, the *Ute Chief*, on November 12, 1887:

> *Death of J. A. Holliday, in Glenwood Springs, Colorado, Tuesday, November 8, 1887, about 10 o'clock a.m., of consumption.*
>
> *J. A. Holliday, or "Doc" Holliday as he was better known, came to Glenwood Springs from Leadville last May, and by his quiet and gentlemanly demeanor during his short stay and the fortitude and patience he displayed in his last two months of life, made many friends. Although a young man he had been in the west for twenty five years, and from a life of exposure and hardship had contracted consumption, from which he had been a constant sufferer for many years. Since he took up his residence at the Springs, the evil effects of the sulfur vapors arising from the hot springs on his weak lungs could be readily detected, and for the last few months it was seen that a dissolution was only the question of a little time, hence his death was not entirely unexpected. From the effects of the disease, from which he had suffered probably half his life, Holliday, at the time of his death looked like a man well advanced in years, for his hair was silvered and his form emaciated and bent, but he was only thirty-six years of age.*
>
> *Holliday was born in Georgia, where relatives of his still reside. Twenty-five years ago, when but eleven years of age, he started for the west, and since that time he has probably been in every state and territory west of the Mississippi river. He served as sheriff in one of the counties in Arizona during the troublous times in that section, and served in other official capacities in different parts of the west. Of him it can be said that he represented law and order at all times and places.*

Either from a roving nature or while seeking a climate congenial to his disease, "Doc" kept moving about from place to place and finally in the early days of Leadville came to Colorado. After remaining there for several years he came to this section last spring. For the last two months his death was expected at any time; during the past fifty-seven days he had only been out of bed twice; the past two weeks he was delirious, and for twenty-four hours preceding his death he did not speak.

He was baptized in the Catholic church, but Father Ed. Downey being absent, Rev. W. S. Rudolph delivered the funeral address, and the remains were consigned to their final resting place in Linwood Cemetery at 4 o'clock on the afternoon of November 8th, in the presence of many friends. That "Doc" Holliday had his faults none will attempt to deny; but who among us has not, and who shall be the judge of these things?

He had only one correspondent among his relatives—a cousin, a Sister of Charity, in Atlanta, Georgia. She will be notified of his death, and will in turn advise any other relatives he may have living. Should there be an aged father or mother they will be pleased to learn that kind and sympathetic hands were about their son in his last hours, and that his remains were accorded Christian burial.[1]

There were a few inaccuracies in the newspaper report of Doc Holliday's death. His initials were not J. A., but J. H., though that could have been a typesetter's error. He wasn't eleven when he left Georgia and traveled west, but twenty-three years old, after graduating dental school and practicing dentistry for a year. He wasn't baptized a Catholic, though he may have been planning to receive that rite. And he certainly did not represent law and order "at all times and places," though he had mostly stood on the side of the law. But beyond those points, his obituary written by Glenwood Springs reporter James Riland was thorough, detailed, and surprisingly sympathetic to a man who'd only lived in the town for six months, two of them bedridden.

The *Denver Republican*, which had sometimes supported Doc and sometimes not, also wrote kind words in honor of his passing:

Doc Holladay is dead. Few men have been better known in a certain class of sporting people, and few men of his character had more friends or stronger champions. He represented a class of man who are fast disappearing in the New West. He had the reputation of being a bunco man, desperado and bad man generally, yet he was a very mild mannered man; was genial and companionable, and had many excellent qualities. In Arizona he was associated with the Wyatt Earp gang. These men were officers of the law and were opposed to the "rustlers" or cattle thieves. Holladay killed several men during his life in Arizona and his body was full of wounds received in bloody encounters. His history was an interesting one. He was sometimes in the right, but quite often in the wrong, probably, in his various escapades.

The Doctor had only one deadly encounter in Colorado. This was in Leadville. He was well known in Denver and had lived here a good deal in the past few years. He had strong friends in some old-time detective officers and in certain representatives of the sporting element. He was a rather good looking man and his coolness and courage, his affable ways and fund of interesting experiences, won him many admirers. He was a strong friend a cool and determined enemy and a man of quite strong character. He has been well known to all the States and Territories west of Kentucky, which was his old home. His death took place at Glenwood Springs Tuesday morning.[2]

The Denver paper, too, got some points wrong—Doc wasn't around to correct his early history, after all, nor did he have family close by to state the facts—but anyone who'd heard him speak knew that he came from somewhere in the South. What both obituaries agreed on was that Doc Holliday had made many friends in Colorado—among them, Glenwood Springs policeman Perry Malaby, who claimed that he "passed the hat around town to raise money to defray Doc's funeral expenses."[3]

The money collected for Doc's final expenses went to Jacob Schwarz, who had an undertaker and embalmer shop in the back of his furniture and home decorating store on Grand Avenue, across Eighth Street from the Hotel Glenwood.[4] Schwarz may have paid a house call to the hotel to prepare Doc's body for burial, bringing along a satchel fitted out with jars filled with milky fluid, a small knife, a lancet and a syringe with various sized nozzles, or he may have had Doc's body carried to his shop to do the embalming. As another undertaker of the time explained the process: "The art of embalming as practiced today is simply to preserve the body in a natural condition for a limited time."[5] But as Doc's time until burial was to be very limited—just a few hours—there may have been nothing more done than washing and dressing his corpse before placing it in a casket for a short trip to the cemetery.

The cemetery property had been donated by the undertaker himself earlier that year, to replace the original and inadequate cemetery in the center of town. The new site, on a high bluff with a panoramic view of the Valley of the Grand and a tortuous trail leading up from the edge of town, was originally called Jasper Mountain in honor of Glenwood Springs pioneer Jasper Ward, who'd been killed in a skirmish with Ute Indians that summer and buried on the bluff. But by the time Doc's casket was hauled up the trail by wagon, with a line of friends following along as processional, the burial ground had been officially named Linwood Cemetery.

Although Doc had many friends in attendance at his graveside service, the funeral address delivered by the local Presbyterian minister would have been less than comforting. The Presbyterian belief that some men were destined for heaven and some for hell, with their earthly works showing which way they were headed after death, was one of the reasons his mother had broken with that denomination and left her written testimony for her son. But the Reverend Rudolf's sermon celebrating the resurrection of the just was likely also a reminder of the wages of sin, of ashes to ashes and dust to dust, and a warning to other sporting men. And then Doc Holliday's remains were consigned to the care of God.

But that wasn't the end of his story, nor of his travels on the railroad. For according to a tradition out of his old hometown, Doc took one more ride on the rails—as freight loaded on a train back to Georgia. As the story goes, when Henry Holliday learned of his son's death in the cold mountains of Colorado, he had the grave opened and the casket brought up and sent back home for a second burial in a private and unmarked grave in Griffin.[6]

That story began to be retold in the early twentieth century, when a group of ladies working to beautify Griffin's Oak Hill Cemetery were given a tour of some of the prominent burials by the cemetery's sexton—including the grave of the famous Doc Holliday. The old gentleman told the ladies that caring for Doc's grave had been the duty of the sextons for years, along with the care of other special burial sites. So, based on the tradition, the city of Griffin placed a small marker at the site, stating simply, "Some historians believe that Doc Holliday is buried here."

In 2014, a series of brass plaques was planned to mark sites relating to Doc's childhood in Griffin: the Tinsley Street home where he was born in 1851, the Presbyterian Church where he was christened in 1852, the Solomon Street building that was his inheritance from his mother and where he practiced dentistry before going west, and the possible plot in Oak Hill Cemetery. But when the local paper published a story about the placement of the plaques, a Griffin lawyer contacted the city commissioner in charge of the project.

"I hear you're going to put a Doc Holliday marker in my family's plot," the man said.

The commissioner was surprised by the call and disappointed to hear that Doc Holliday wasn't back in Griffin, after all.

"Oh, he's there, all right," the lawyer said. "My great-grandfather was friends with Doc when they were young, so when his father needed a place to put him, he contacted the family and made the arrangements. That story has been in our family for a hundred years."

It's not proof, of course, but it's the next best thing: a family story that's been kept quiet to protect the privacy of a man whose life had been far too public. Now a beautiful brass plaque marks the spot where some say—and many believe—John Henry Holliday is finally home from his journeys and resting in peace.

MORE FAMOUS LAST WORDS

While Morgan Earp's shooting and death were witnessed by many people, with various recollections of his last words debated over the years, his friend Doc Holliday died a quiet, private death. None of the people who may have attended Doc's passing recorded any last words, and his obituary in the local paper noted, "during the past fifty-seven days he had only been out of bed twice; the past two weeks he was delirious, and for twenty-four hours preceding his death he did not speak." What Doc may have said in his delirium is anyone's guess.

But every legend deserves some famous last words, so Doc Holliday was given some by author Walter Noble Burns in his 1927 historical novel *Tombstone*:

> *"I used to offer odds of eight to five," he said, "that in spite of consumption, I'd cash out some day at the end of a six-shooter when I happened to run afoul of a man an eighth of a second quicker on the draw. It seems almost like tough luck to lose that bet." Holliday's last words were, "This is funny." The friends watching at his bedside thought his mind wandering. But, with his sense of humour strong to the last, the doctor doubtless considered it a choice joke that, after all his desperate adventures and narrow escapes, he should be dying in bed with his boots off.*

But no one who actually knew Doc echoed those dying words. In Stuart Lake's 1931 *Wyatt Earp: Frontier Marshal*, based partly on interviews with Wyatt, Doc's death is only mentioned in passing with no details of the circumstances. Likewise, Bat Masterson, who gave many interviews about Doc over the years, only said that he "died at Glenwood Springs." Kate Elder gave Doc a little more to say in her unpublished and sometimes conflicted memoirs, but she also missed the "This is funny" comment: "Well, I am going just as I told them—the bugs would get me before the worms did." And with that, the story fell silent as the grave.

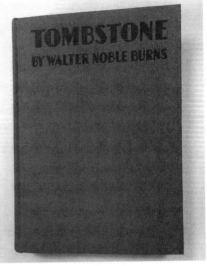

Tombstone: An Iliad of the Southwest *by Walter Noble Burns, hardcover 1927 edition.*

Then in 1955, a television series called *The Life and Legend of Wyatt Earp* debuted, and shortly after that two biographies of Doc Holliday were published: *Doc Holliday* by John Myers and *The Frontier World of Doc Holliday* by Pat Jahns. The Jahns book stuck to the newspaper version of Doc's death with no last words, but Myers chose to retell the story from Walter Noble Burns's 1927 novel:

> *witnesses said that one step short of eternity, Holliday emerged from coma to perform three conscious acts and to speak twice. Toward ten o'clock on the morning of November 8, he astonished those gathered at his bedside by opening clear eyes and asking for a tumbler of whiskey. An attendant officiating, he drank the liquor with deliberate satisfaction. Leaving no heel-taps, he gave the man an appreciative smile before he spoke once more. "This is funny," he said, and closed his eyes for ever.*

With two authors now sharing those same words, "This is funny," became the accepted version of what Doc Holliday said as he lay dying. So, when screenwriter Kevin Jarre needed some last words for Doc Holliday to say at the end of the 1993 movie *Tombstone*, he used the same quote and created a classic Doc moment. In *Tombstone*, the dying Doc is receiving his last rights from a Catholic priest named Father Feeney when his old friend Wyatt comes to see him, bringing a little pamphlet he's penned called, "My Friend Doc." The two men trade witty and sentimental comments, then Doc begs Wyatt to leave. The final rights go on and Doc looks down to see his feet poking through the bedsheets. His last words, as they were in Burns and Myers's books, are, "This is funny."

Of course, a patient dying of tuberculosis is very near to suffocating and not likely to be engaging in witty conversation, even if not unconscious as Doc was. And Doc's friendly Catholic priest in Glenwood Springs was Father Downey, not Father Feeney, and he was out of town when Doc died—which was all right, from a religious standpoint, because Doc wasn't actually Catholic and would not have been receiving the final rites of Holy Church, anyway. Nor had Wyatt just stepped out of the room when Doc breathed his last—Wyatt Earp was in California and didn't learn about Doc's death for some time after. But all that aside, like another classic Doc line penned by Walter Noble Burns, "I'm your huckleberry," if the dying Doc Holliday didn't really say, "This is funny," he should have.

TO DOC FROM KATE

Doc Holliday owned several fine firearms during his Western career, including an 1851 Navy Colt revolver that was a gift from his uncle, Dr. John Stiles Holliday, a nickel-plated Colt 1877 Lightning noted in testimony at the O.K. Corral Hearing, and a Colt Thunderer mentioned in a Tombstone newspaper story. He also used a shotgun traded from Virgil Earp for his walking cane shortly before the gunfight in Tombstone, and a rifle loaned by a helpful banker as the Earp posse left Tombstone on the Vendetta Trail. There may have been other firearms in his collection, as well. But there was one piece that was not his: a pearl-handled 1866 Remington Derringer engraved on the silver backstrap *To Doc from Kate*, a fraud that cost the Glenwood Springs Historical Society $84,000.

According to a March 9, 2017, article in the Glenwood Springs *Post Independent*:

> *The derringer is believed to have been one of few possessions in the hotel room when he [Doc] died. . . . The hotel burned down in 1945. Hotel bartender William G. Wells received the gun as partial payment for Holliday's funeral, and it remained in the family until gun dealer E. Dixon Larson purchased it in 1968. Larson wrote about the derringer and other Holliday guns in a 1972 article in Guns magazine. The early '80s saw another individual purchase the gun, and the current owner bought it in July.*

The engraving suggested that the derringer was a gift from Doc's mistress Kate Elder, perhaps purchased in Tombstone, making it a most historic piece. So, trusting in a 1968 affidavit that told the story of the gun's history from the family of William Wells to the gun dealer who bought it and first introduced it to the public, the Historical Society authorized a purchase (made with loans and donations) that would return the little derringer back to Glenwood Springs where Doc last saw it. The latest owner said he needed a quick sale as he was moving and didn't want to store the gun, which meant that the Historical Society had to move on the purchase before doing a thorough check on the provenance. But what an exciting addition it would be to the society's collections!

Derringer engraved, "To Doc from Kate" on display at the Doc Holliday Museum, Glenwood Springs, Colorado. Courtesy Glenwood Springs Historical Society, Schutte Collection.

As the mayor of Glenwood Springs said at the time, "Doc Holliday is a very important character in the history of Glenwood Springs, and we are extremely excited that this piece of history will return to the city where he spent his final days. Along with visiting the cemetery where he is buried, we have no doubt that this will be yet one more attraction that will draw visitors to Glenwood Springs."

But soon after the purchase was completed, the provenance of the derringer came into question. The name of William G. Wells, the bartender who supposedly got the gun in partial payment for Doc's funeral expenses, could not be found on any legal record in Colorado, and the street where the Wells family supposedly lived in Colorado Springs does not exist. The signature of the notary attesting the document is missing. And the dealer who supposedly bought the gun from the Wells family and announced it to the world was known for fabricating histories and adding engravings to firearms. In other words, the "To Doc from Kate" gun was a fraud—an authentic 1866 Remington Derringer with an engraving added to make it seem connected to Doc Holliday, multiplying its value many times. But having gone into debt for $84,000 to purchase the gun, the Glenwood Springs Historical Society has opted to keep it on display for interested tourists. It is, at the least, an example of the kinds of hoaxes that happen in the world of Western collecting, and yet another lesson in the important of provenance.

DOC HOLLIDAY, LOST AND FOUND

Doc Holliday was one of the most famous former residents of Glenwood Springs, but somehow, they lost him. Although the local paper reported, "the remains were consigned to their final resting place in Linwood Cemetery at 4 o'clock on the afternoon

of November 8th, in the presence of many friends," as the years went by and the friends moved on or passed away, there was no one left to remember which grave was his. There had likely been no permanent marker placed at the site for the man who came to Glenwood Springs trying to live, but who died anyway. And interestingly, there were stories early on that he'd been moved, and no one knew where.

Several "Doc got moved" scenarios were put forth for the lost legend: He was actually first buried down in the old cemetery in the middle of town, then moved up the hill when Linwood was created; he was first buried down in the old cemetery because the road to Linwood was too snowy for a wagon carrying a coffin; he was first buried in the old cemetery because the ground at Linwood was frozen too hard to open a grave. And there is some reason for those scenarios. Glenwood Springs did have an old cemetery in the middle of town that was closed when the new Linwood Cemetery was opened in 1887, and

Doc Holliday Memorial, Linwood Cemetery, Glenwood Springs, Colorado. Findlay/Alamy Stock Photo (#DFCM9J).

the old burials were moved up the hill. But the old cemetery was already closed when Doc died, so he could not have been buried there. The road to Linwood is quite steep and could have been difficult for a heavy-laden wagon in the snow. But it wasn't yet snowing when Doc died in early November, and other burials in Linwood took place on the day before and the day after his death, so the road couldn't have been an obstacle. The ground could potentially freeze too hard for a grave to be dug. But Doc died in the fall, not the winter, and the ground was far from frozen. So, the story of Doc being lost because he was moved could not mean that he was moved from somewhere else to Linwood—but it could mean that he was moved from Linwood to somewhere else.

And that's where an old story from Griffin, Georgia, adds another scenario: Doc was first buried in Linwood Cemetery, as the paper reported, and then was dug up and moved back home. It wasn't an unusual thing to do. All those old burials from down in the city had been dug up and moved up the hill to Linwood, after all—Doc was just another grave that needed moving. There was nothing illegal about it at the time. Until the Colorado Health Act was passed in 1899, the state had no regulation regarding the disinterring or transporting of remains. And it would explain, better than any other scenario, why one of Glenwood Springs' most famous graves is missing—it isn't there anymore.

Doc Holliday Memorial, Oak Hill Cemetery, Griffin, Georgia. Author's Collection.

But Doc's grave was there originally, so he now has a very appropriate gravestone in Linwood Cemetery honoring his death in Glenwood Springs—and another in Griffin's Oak Hill Cemetery honoring what might be his final resting place. Doc Holliday, who liked playing the odds, would probably approve.

TEDDY AND THE VAPOR CAVES

Doc Holliday and Theodore Roosevelt had crossed paths before, when they were both in Montana in the fall of 1885—and may have even met there. In 1901 their paths crossed again, when Vice President-elect Theodore Roosevelt took a much-needed vacation to his beloved Western states following a strenuous political campaign. Making camp near Meeker, Colorado, Roosevelt and his party killed twelve mountain lions before boarding the Colorado Midland train to Glenwood Springs. Along the way, an excited Roosevelt asked the engineer if he might ride in the engine, and the engineer happily obliged. On his arrival in Glenwood Springs, Roosevelt was escorted from the train to the Yampah vapor caves for a session in the sulfur steam

President Theodore Roosevelt. Library of Congress.

Hotel Glenwood, c. 1901. Courtesy Glenwood Springs Historical Society, Schutte Collection.

before changing into formal wear for a dinner at the Hotel Glenwood—where Doc Holliday had spent his last days.

In September of the same year, Theodore Roosevelt became the twenty-sixth president of the United States after the assassination death of President William McKinley. In 1905, President Roosevelt returned to Glenwood Springs, making the elegant new Hotel Colorado his "Little White House" while he set out on another hunting expedition to Colorado's western slope. The President's hunting party spent a week on the Muddy and Upper Divide Creeks, returning to Glenwood Springs with a bear pelt that was much admired by Roosevelt's teenage daughter, Alice, who said she would name the piece, "Teddy" after her father. When a toymaker heard the story, he began producing a line of "Teddy Bears" in honor of the outdoorsman president. Although old-timers in the Glenwood Springs area often told the story, the Smithsonian Institute claims the Teddy Bear craze began after the president made a hunting trip to Mississippi and refused to shoot a baby bear. But considering Roosevelt's love of hunting and the West, the Glenwood Springs story seems more likely. One thing is certain: Teddy Roosevelt visited Doc Holliday's vapor caves and dined in Doc Holliday's last hotel—two icons of the Wild West separated by time but sharing a storied place in American history.

ACKNOWLEDGMENTS

A work of history, especially one filled with vintage images, is dependent on more than just a writer with a vision. I am grateful for the help of the many historians, archivists, librarians, and photographers mentioned throughout this book. As always, my gratitude to my dear friend and Doc Holliday's most eminent historian, Dr. Gary L. Roberts, for his generous support of my *Saga of Doc Holliday* novels and now this illustrated travelogue—neither would have happened without him. And the finished book would not have happened without the terrific team at TwoDot Books: Editorial Director Erin Turner, who championed this new way of looking at Doc Holliday's life, Assistant Editor Courtney Oppel who managed the many details of text, images, and permissions with dogged determination, and Senior Production Editor Elaine McGarraugh for getting us all to our final destination. Thanks, y'all. It's been an adventure!

ENDNOTES

Chapter 1: Macon & Western

1. Quimby Melton, *History of Griffin, GA, 1840–1940* (Griffin, GA: Hometown Press, 1996), 85.
2. Alice Copeland Kilgore, Edith Hanes Smith, Joseph Henry Hightower Moore, and Frances Partridge Tuck, *A History of Clayton County, Georgia, 1821–1983* (Clayton County, GA: Ancestors Unlimited, 1983), 607–11.

Chapter 2: Atlantic & Gulf Line

1. "Where Doc Holliday Lived: Valdosta, Ga. Was His Home Before He Became Famous," Valdosta, Georgia, January 22 (Special), *Atlanta Constitution*, January 23, 1896, 3.
2. Martha Ann Holliday, "Memoirs of the Holliday Family in Georgia," in *In Search of the Hollidays*, edited by Albert S. Pendleton Jr. and Susan McKey Thomas, 1973/2008, appendix, p. 9.
3. Obituary written by Reverend N. B. Ousley in the *Valdosta Watchman*, clipping in the scrapbook of Annabelle Myddleton, in possession of Helen Hightower, Valdosta.

Chapter 4: Eads' Folly

1. Anne Collier, "Big Nose Kate and Mary Catherine Cummings: Same Person, Different Lives," *Journal of the Wild West History Association* 5, no. 5 (October 2012): 5.

Chapter 5: Terminus

1. *Atlanta-Post Appeal*, July 8, 1882.
2. Spalding County, Georgia Deed Book E, January 14, 1873.

Chapter 6: Houston & Texas Central

1. Alfred H. Benners, "My Life in Dallas, Texas–1875 to 1885," Birmingham, Alabama, June 3, 1929.
2. *Dallas City Directory and Reference Book for 1873–74*, 64, 96.
3. *State of Texas v. Dr. Holliday*, Cause No. 2236, Gaming, Minutes of the Fourteenth District Court, Dallas County, Texas, 1874–75, May 12, 1874, vol. 1, p. 209.

Chapter 7: The Katy

1. *State of Texas v. J. H. Holliday*, Cause No. 2643, Assault to Murder, Minutes of the Fourteenth District Court, Dallas County, Texas, 1874–1875, January 18, 1875, vol. 1, p. 486, 516.
2. *State of Texas v. Lynch*, Curly, Hurricane Bill, and Dock Holliday, Case 13-4, June 9, 1875, and *State of Texas v. Mike Lynch and Doc Holliday*, Case 34-14, June 12, 1875.

3. W. B. (Bat) Masterson, "Doc Holliday," *Famous Gunfighters of the Western Frontier* (Dover Publications, 2009), 39, first published in *Human Life Magazine*, 1907.

4. Gary L. Roberts, *Doc Holliday: The Life and Legend* (John Wiley, 2006), 434 fn. 82.

Chapter 8: Denver & Kansas Pacific

1. Thomas J. Noel, Duane A. Smith, *Colorado: The Highest State*, 2nd ed. (University Press of Colorado, 2011), 109.

2. *Denver Republican*, June 22, 1887.

3. Masterson, *Famous Gunfighters of the Western Frontier*, 39.

4. Masterson, *Famous Gunfighters of the Western Frontier*, 36.

5. *Rocky Mountain News*, December 1, 1876.

6. Karen Tanner, *Doc Holliday: A Family Portrait* (University of Oklahoma Press, 1998), 104.

7. *Cheyenne News*, quoted in the *Denver Rocky Mountain News Weekly*, December 8, 1875.

8. Ted P. Yeatman, *Frank and Jesse James: The Story behind the Legend* (Cumberland House Publishing, 2003), 119.

Chapter 9: Texas & Pacific

1. *State of Texas v. Dr. Holliday*, Minutes, Fourteenth District Court, Dallas County, Texas, January 3, 5, 7, 8, 1877, vol. J. 80.

2. *State of Texas v. McCune [and] J. Holliday*, Cause No. 3764, Minutes, Fourteenth District Court, Dallas County, Texas, September 14, 1877, vol. J. 466-467.

3. J. Marvin Hunter, *The Story of Lottie Deno, Her Life and Times* (Kessinger Publishing, 2007), 58.

4. Letter from Mary Catherine Cummings to Anton Mazzanovich, 2.

5. Lawrence Vivian to Gary L. Roberts, August 13, 1998.

6. Sam Baldwin in Roberts, *Doc Holliday: The Life and Legend*, 85.

7. Cummings to Mazzanovich, 4.

8. "How Wyatt Earp Routed a Gang of Arizona Outlaws," *San Francisco Examiner*, August 2, 1896.

9. Stuart Lake, *Wyatt Earp: Frontier Marshal* (Pocket Books, 1931), 193–94.

10. Charles Robinson III, *The Frontier World of Fort Griffin* (Arthur C. Clark Company, 1992), 85.

11. Robinson, *The Frontier World of Fort Griffin*, 86, quoting from the Ledger of Judge A. A. Clark, 165.

12. Maggie Van Ostrand, "Lottie Deno: Queen of the Paste Board Flappers," *Legends of America*, August, 2007, legendsofamerica.com.

13. Glenn G. Boyer quoting Mrs. W. J. Martin to A. W. Bork, circa 1941, "The O.K. Corral Fight at Tombstone: A Footnote by Kate Elder," *Arizona and the West*, Spring 1977, 76.

14. *Denver Republican*, May 22, 1882.

Chapter 10: Atchison, Topeka & Santa Fe

1. Masterson, *Famous Gunfighters of the Western Frontier*, 39.

2. Eddie Foy and Alvin Fay Harlow, *Clowning Through Life* (E.P. Dutton, 1928), 113.

3. Statement of Wyatt Earp at the OK Corral Hearing, 1881.

4. Craig Miner, *West of Wichita: Settling the High Plains of Kansas, 1865–1890* (University Press of Kansas, 1986), 112.

5. Miner, *West of Wichita*, 112.

6. Roberts, *Doc Holliday*, John Flood, Interview with Wyatt Earp, John D. Gilchreise Collection, undated but likely 1927.

7. A. W. Bork and Glenn G. Boyer, "The O.K. Corral Fight at Tombstone: A Footnote by Kate Elder," *Arizona and the West*, Spring 1977, 76.

8. Roberts, *Doc Holliday*, 102.

9. Cummings to Mazzanovich, 6.

10. Milton W. Callon, *Las Vegas, New Mexico . . . The Town That Wouldn't Gamble* (Las Vegas, NM: Las Vegas Publishing, 1962), 128.

11. Louise Harris Ivers, "The Montezuma Hotel at Las Vegas Hot Springs, New Mexico," *Journal of the Society of Architectural Historians* 33, no. 3 (October 1974): 206–13.

Chapter 11: Railroad Wars

1. *New Mexico v. John H. Holliday*, Case No. 931, Keeping Gaming Table, March 8, 1879, SMCDCR, Las Vegas, New Mexico, NMSRCA.

2. *Otero Optic*, June 5, 1879, 4.

3. Foy and Harlow, *Clowning through Life*, 103.

4. *Dodge City Times*, June 14, 1879, 8: "Sheriff Masterson left Monday on a special train with fifty men, for Canon City, where warlike demonstrations were pending between the railroad corporations."

5. Deputy Sheriff John Joshua Webb was also in charge of payroll for the Dodge City expedition. Santa Fe vouchers list him as J. J. Webb receiving $3,348.00 to pay the men—$3 a day for ten days for one hundred men. Larry Green, *Royal Gorge War Timeline* (unpublished manuscript), 29.

6. Roberts, *Doc Holliday*, 107.

7. Lela Barnes, ed., *Letters of Cyrus Kurtz Holliday, 1854–1859*, vol. 6, no. 3 (August 1937): 241–94, kshs.org.

8. "Amtrak Brings the Trains Back," *Emporia Gazette*, August 4, 1976.

9. Paula Mitchell Marks, *And Die in the West* (University of Oklahoma Press, 1996), 85, and Robert K. DeArment, *Bat Masterson: The Man and the Legend* (University of Oklahoma Press, 1979), 103.

10. *The Ford County Globe*, March 9, 1880.

11. *Colorado Springs Gazette*, May 12, 1877, 10.

Chapter 12: End of Track

1. Roberts, *Doc Holliday*, quoting Miguel Otero Jr., *My Life on the Frontier*.

2. *Las Vegas Daily Optic*, August 4, 1886.

3. San Miguel County Deed Record Book 11, 449–50, W. G. Ward Claim, October 7, 1879.

4. San Miguel County Deed Record Book 12, 182–83.

5. *Territory vs J. H. Holliday*, Case No. 990, Keeping a Gaming Table and Case No. 982, Carrying a Deadly Weapon.

6. *Territory vs J. H. Holliday*, Case No. 990, Keeping a Gaming Table and Case No. 982, Carrying a Deadly Weapon.

7. San Miguel County Deed Record Book 11.

8. Cummings to Mazzanovich, 10.

9. U.S. Census, June 1880, Prescott, Yavapai, Arizona, 4.

10. Mike Parks, *Nebraska in the Making* (World Publishing Company, 1966), 39.

Chapter 13: Southern Pacific

1. Marks, *And Die in the West*, 24.

2. *Great Register of Pima County, District 17* (Tombstone), No. 1483, September 27, 1880.

3. *San Francisco Examiner*, May 28, 1882.

4. *Tombstone Daily Nugget*, October 12, 1880.

5. *Tombstone Daily Nugget*, October 12, 1880.

6. *Denver Republican*, May 22, 1882.

7. Casey Tefertiller, *Wyatt Earp: The Life behind the Legend* (John Wiley & Sons, 1997).

8. *Denver Republican*, May 22, 1882.

9. Roberts, *Doc Holliday*, 148.

10. Roberts, *Doc Holliday*, 148.

11. *Tombstone Daily Nugget*, July 9, 1881.

12. Roberts, *Doc Holliday*, 155, quoting Joe Chisholm, "Tombstone's Tale (The Truth about Helldorado)."

13. Roberts, *Doc Holliday*, quoting Wyatt Earp to Walter Noble Burns, March 15, 1927.

14. Alford Turner, ed., *The O.K. Corral Inquest* (Creative Publishing Company, 1981), 196.

15. *Denver Republican*, May 22, 1882.

16. Turner, *The O.K. Corral Inquest*.

Chapter 14: Benson Freight

1. Bork and Boyer, "The O.K. Corral Fight at Tombstone," 79.

2. Turner, *The O.K. Corral Inquest*, 160.

3. Testimony of Virgil Earp, *Tombstone Daily Nugget* and *Tombstone Daily Epitaph*, November 20, 1881.

4. Cummings to Mazzanovich, 12.

5. Turner, *The O.K. Corral Inquest*, 192.

6. Roberts, *Doc Holliday*, 190.

7. Roberts, *Doc Holliday*, 189.

8. Roberts, *Doc Holliday*, 193–94, quoting John H. Flood. Jr., "Wyatt Earp: A Police-Officer of Tombstone," unpublished manuscript.

9. Turner, *The O.K. Corral Inquest*, 164.

10. Bork and Boyer, "The O.K. Corral Fight at Tombstone," 80.

11. Turner, *The O.K. Corral Inquest*, 48.

12. Roberts, *Doc Holliday*, 396, quoting Joseph Chisholm.

13. Turner, *O.K. Corral Inquest*, 219–20.

14. Johanna Eubank, reprinted in "Tales from the Morgue: The Railroad Comes to Tucson," *Arizona Daily Star*, March 20, 2016.

Chapter 15: Contention City

1. George W. Parsons and Lynn R. Bailey, eds., *A Tenderfoot in Tombstone: The Private Journal of George Whitwell Parsons: The Turbulent Years 1880–1882* (Westernlore Printing, 1996, Entry for December 28, 1881).

2. *Weekly Arizona Miner*, December 30, 1881.

3. Parsons, *Journal*, Entry for January 17, 1882.

4. Parsons, *Journal*, January 31, 1882.

5. Roberts, *Doc Holliday*, 241.

6. Parsons, *Journal*, Entry for February 15, 1882.

7. Roberts, *Doc Holliday*, 244.

8. Tefertiller, *Wyatt Earp*, 21.

9. *Gunnison News-Democrat*, Gunnison, Colorado, June 4, 1882.

Chapter 16: Tucson Train Yard

1. *Denver Republican*, May 14, 1893.

2. Tefertiller, *Wyatt Earp*, 227.

3. *Denver Republican*, May 22, 1882.

4. George Hand, *Whiskey, Six-Guns, and Red-Light Ladies*, 1994, 228.

5. Roberts, *Doc Holliday*, 249.

6. Parsons, *Journal*, March 23, 1882.

7. Parsons, *Journal*, March 23, 1882.

8. *Denver Republican*, May 22, 1882.

9. Tefertiller, *Wyatt Earp*, 239.

10. Bork and Boyer, "The O.K. Corral Fight at Tombstone," 81.

11. *Arizona Daily Star*, March 19, 1882, 2.

Chapter 17: Summit Station

1. Robert J. Chandler, "Smoking Gun: Did Wells Fargo Pay Wyatt Earp to Kill Curly Bill and Frank Stilwell? New Evidence Seems to Indicate—Yes," *True West Magazine*, July 1, 2001.

2. *Tombstone Epitaph*, April 5, 1882, and *Tombstone Nugget*, April 6, 1882.

3. Roberts, *Doc Holliday*, 260, quoting Forrestine C. Hooker, "An Arizona Vendetta (the Truth about Wyatt Earp—and Some Others)," unpublished manuscript, circa 1929, 72.

4. Roberts, *Doc Holliday*, 261.

5. *Tombstone Daily Epitaph*, April 14, 1882.

6. Tefertiller, *Wyatt Earp*, 246.

7. Chuck Hornung and Gary L. Roberts, "The Split: Did Doc and Wyatt Split Because of a Racial Slur?" *True West Magazine*, November 1, 2001.

8. Hornung and Roberts, "The Split."

Chapter 18: Union Depot

1. Masterson, *Famous Gunfighters of the Western Frontier*, 41.

2. *Denver Republican*, May 22, 1882.

3. *Denver Republican*, May 26, 1882.

4. *Denver Rocky Mountain News*, October 23, 1898.

5. *Provo Daily Enquirer*, Provo, Utah, October 1, 1881. Much of our understanding of Perry Mallen comes from the excellent work of historian Peter Brand, *The Life and Crimes of Perry Mallon*, Meadowbank, NSW 2114, Australia, 2006.

Chapter 19: Denver & Rio Grande

1. *Cincinnati Enquirer*, quoted in the *Denver Republican*, May 29, 1882.

2. *Gunnison Daily News-Democrat*, June 18, 1882.

3. Judd Riley interview, Stuart N. Lake Collection, Box 11, Folder 41, Huntington Library, San Marino, California.

4. *Salida Mail*, July 8, 1882.

5. *The People v. J. H. Holliday*, Case No. 1851, Larceny, July 11, 1882, District Court Records of Pueblo County, Colorado, vol. 5, 354–55.

6. Cummings to Mazzonovich, 16.

7. Bork and Boyer, "The O.K. Corral Fight at Tombstone," 83.

8. "Where Doc Holliday Lived," 3.

9. *Tombstone Weekly Epitaph*, July 22, 1882.

10. *Tombstone Weekly Epitaph*, July 22, 1882.

11. William M. Breckenridge, *Helldorado: Bringing the Law to the Mesquite* (Houghton Mifflin Company, 1928), 187–88.

Chapter 20: High Line Railroad

1. Patricia Jahns, *The Frontier World of Doc Holliday: Faro Dealer from Dallas to Deadwood* (Indian Head Books, 1957), 261.

2. *Leadville Sketches*, 1883.

3. *Pueblo Chieftan*, November 22, 1882.

4. *The People v. J. H. Holliday*, G. D. No. 1851, Larceny, November 25, 1882, Pueblo County District Court Records, Pueblo, Colorado, vol. 6, 38.

5. *Colorado Daily Chieftan*, November 26, 1882.
6. *Leadville Daily Democrat*, August 20, 1884.
7. *Leadville Daily Herald*, August 26, 1884.
8. *The Raton Comet*, August 29, 1884.
9. *Leadville Daily Democrat*, August 26, 1884.
10. *Leadville Daily Democrat*, August 26, 1884.
11. *Carbonate Chronicle*, August 27, 1884 in *History of Leadville and Lake County*, fn 450.
12. Roberts, *Doc Holliday*, 357, quoting the *Carbonate Chronicle*.
13. Oscar Wilde, "Impressions of America," 1882.
14. "The Wise Men," *Leadville Daily Herald*, December 27, 1882, 1.
15. "Secrets of Success," *Leadville Daily Herald*, December 16, 1883, 4.
16. "Secrets of Success," 4.
17. Glenda Riley and Richard Etulain, *Wild Women of the Old West* (Golden, CO: Fulcrum Publishing, 2003).

Chapter 21: Denver & New Orleans

1. *The Valdosta Times*, June 1, 1882, quoting the Tombstone *Epitaph* of December 1, 1881, and *The Daily Picayune*, New Orleans, April 16, 1885.
2. *The Valdosta Times*, April 18, 1885: "Major Holliday, who was in the Mexican war [War], attended the reunion of the Mexican veterans in New Orleans on the 15th inst."
3. Roberts, *Doc Holliday*, 361 and 492 fn 124.
4. *San Francisco Examiner*, November 10, December 1, 1899.
5. Mary Billings McVicar, Leadville, Colorado, to the author.
6. "How Doc Holliday Collected a Debt," *Aspen Times*, June 12, 1885.

Chapter 22: Northern Pacific

1. *Butte Daily Town Talk*, July 13, 1885.
2. "Doc. Holladay Dead," *Butte Semi-Weekly Miner*, November 23, 1887, 3; and Peter Brand, "Holliday in Montana," *Wild West Magazine*, October 2016, 30.
3. "French Nobleman Founded Medora," *Deadwood Magazine*, Spring 2003.
4. Theodore Roosevelt, *Hunting Trips of a Ranchman*, Modern Library 1998, first private printing 1885.
5. Mark Brown and W. R. Felton, *Before Barbed Wire: L.A. Huffman, Photographer on Horseback* (Bramhall House, 1956).
6. *Butte Daily Miner*, November 6, 1885.
7. *Butte Daily Miner*, November 6, 1885.
8. *Anaconda Standard*, November 8, 1905, 8.
9. *Butte Semi-Weekly Miner*, February 19, 1886.
10. *Butte Semi-Weekly Miner*, February 20, 1886, 1.
11. *Butte Miner*, September 27, 1885, 1.

12. *Butte Daily Miner*, November 6, 1885.

Chapter 23: Durango & Silverton

1. "Doc Holliday's Career," *Boston Daily Globe*, August 4, 1886, and in Gary L. Roberts, "Doc Holliday's Lost Colorado Years," *True West Magazine*, May 13, 2013.
2. Roberts, *Doc Holliday*, 365, quoting Josephine Sarah Marcus Earp, Mabel Earp Cason, and Vinnolia Earp Ackerman, "She Married Wyatt Earp: The Recollections of Josephine Earp," unpublished manuscript, circa 1938.
3. Leadville *Daily/Evening Chronicle*, July 1, 1886, also in the Leadville *Carbonate Chronicle* July 6, 1886.
4. "He Started Many Graveyards: Pulling the Shooting Iron Often in Behalf of Law and Order," *The Sun*, New York, June 7, 1886, 2, col. 5.
5. *Rocky Mountain News*, July 6, 1886.
6. *Denver Tribune-Republican*, August 4, 1886.
7. Roberts, *Doc Holliday*, 369.

Chapter 24: Glenwood Springs Station

1. Jahns, *The Frontier World of Doc Holliday*, 281. Jahns gives no source for this information. She may have misinterpreted a line from his obituary in Glenwood Springs about his coming to Glenwood Springs from Leadville as meaning he had been living in Leadville before going to Glenwood Springs. But the paper was more correctly giving the origin of his travel, as at the time Leadville was the closest railroad and the rest of the journey came from that city by stagecoach over Independence Pass.
2. Carl Briehan and Wayne Montgomery, *Forty Years on the Wild Frontier* (Devin-Adair Publishers, 1985), 91. The story mentions Doc living at Creede, Colorado, the modern name for the town of Wagon Wheel Gap, a popular hot springs resort on the Denver & Rio Grande Railroad line.
3. Leadville *Evening Chronicle*, September 9, 1887.
4. Chester L. Brooks and Ray H. Mattison, *Theodore Roosevelt and the Dakota Badlands*, 1958.
5. *Aspen Daily News*, September 12, 1886.
6. Centennial—Past Section, *Glenwood Post*, August 23, 1887, 13; Roberts, *Doc Holliday*, 371 fn 153: Letter from Eugene Parsons to Stuart N. Lake, June 30, 1930.
7. *Gunnison News-Champion*, July 17, 1930.
8. H. Lee Scamehorn, *Pioneer Steelmaker in the West: The Colorado Fuel and Iron Company, 1872–1903*, 1976, 89.
9. Angela K. Parkison, *Hope and Hot Water; Glenwood Springs from 1878 to 1891* (Glenwood Springs Legacy, 2000), 93.
10. Parkison, *Hope and Hot Water*.
11. Nellie Duffy, "Glenwood Cemetery: Doc Buried Here?" *Glenwood Post*, 1977.
12. Harlan Feder, *Yampah Spa: Centuries of Cleansing Vapors*, 1995, 11.

13. Roberts, *Doc Holliday*, 370, quoting Eugene Parsons to Stuart N. Lake, June 30, 1930.

14. *Aspen Daily Times*, October 6, 1887.

15. Donald W. Olson, Russell L. Doecher, and Marilynn S. Olson, "The Blood-Red Sky of the Scream," *APS News* 13, no. 5 (May 2004), aps.org.

Chapter 25: Return Ticket

1. Glenwood Springs *Ute Chief*, November 12, 1887. No remaining copies of the paper exist, but the obituary is found in the scrapbook of reporter James L. Riland, in the collection of the Colorado Historical Society MSS #520, Scrapbook #3, p. 53.

2. *Denver Republican*, November 10, 1887.

3. Duffy, "Doc Buried Here?" It seems appropriate that when historian Nellie Duffy, who wrote about Doc Holliday's burial, died on August 4, 1997, she became the last person to be buried in the old Linwood Cemetery where Doc was laid to rest.

4. Willa Kane, "Undertaking a New Life in Glenwood," *Post Independent/Citizen Telegram*, November 9, 2014.

5. "The Art of Embalming," *Aspen Daily Times*, July 20, 1887.

6. Della A. Jones, "Where's Doc?," tombstonetimes.com. The story of the Griffin grave was also told to the author by the grandson of Laura Mae Clark and by Oak Hill superintendent Osgood Miller, who both heard it from the former sexton of the cemetery. The story of the lawyer's family plot was told to the author by Griffin City Commissioner Dick Morrow.

INDEX

ABOUT THE AUTHOR

Victoria Wilcox is Founding Director of Georgia's Holliday-Dorsey-Fife House Museum (the antebellum home of the family of Doc Holliday, now a site on the National Register of Historic Places), where she learned the family's untold stories of their legendary cousin. Her work with the museum led to two decades of original research, making her a nationally recognized authority on the life of Doc Holliday. She is author of the documentary film *In Search of Doc Holliday* and the historical novel trilogy *The Saga of Doc Holliday*, for which she twice received Georgia Author of the Year honors and was named Best Historical Western Novelist by *True West Magazine*. She has lectured across the country, appeared in local and regional media, guested on NPR affiliates, and was featured in the Fox Network series *Legends and Lies: The Real West*. She is a member of the Wild West History Association, Western Writers of America, Women Writing the West, and the Writer's Guild of the Booth Museum of Western Art, and has been a featured contributor to *True West Magazine*. In the summer of 2017, Wilcox joined actor Val Kilmer (*Tombstone*) as guest historian at the inaugural *Doc HolliDays* in Tombstone, Arizona, site of the legendary O.K. Corral gunfight. In October 2019 she returned to Tombstone as guest of the annual *Helldorado Days* celebration with a special appearance at the Old Tombstone Courthouse State Historic Park. Her website is www.victoriawilcoxbooks.com.